Sons of the Mexican Revolution

Diálogos Series

Kris Lane, Series Editor

Understanding Latin America demands dialogue, deep exploration, and frank discussion of key topics. Founded by Lyman L. Johnson in 1992 and edited since 2013 by Kris Lane, the Diálogos Series focuses on innovative scholarship in Latin American history and related fields. The series, the most successful of its type, includes specialist works accessible to a wide readership and a variety of thematic titles, all ideally suited for classroom adoption by university and college teachers.

Also available in the Diálogos Series:

The Pursuit of Ruins: Archaeology, History, and the Making of Modern Mexico by Christina Bueno

Gendered Crossings: Women and Migration in the Spanish Empire by Allyson M. Poska

From Shipmates to Soldiers: Emerging Black Identities in the Río de la Plata by Alex Borucki

Women Drug Traffickers: Mules, Bosses, and Organized Crime by Elaine Carey

Searching for Madre Matiana: Prophecy and Popular Culture in Modern Mexico by Edward Wright-Rios

Africans into Creoles: Slavery, Ethnicity, and Identity in Colonial Costa Rica by Russell Lohse

Native Brazil: Beyond the Convert and the Cannibal, 1500–1900 edited by Hal Langfur

Emotions and Daily Life in Colonial Mexico edited by Javier Villa-Flores and Sonya Lipsett-Rivera

The Course of Andean History by Peter V. N. Henderson

Masculinity and Sexuality in Modern Mexico edited by Anne Rubenstein and Víctor M. Macías-González

For additional titles in the Diálogos Series, please visit unmpress.com.

Sons of the Mexican Revolution

Miguel Alemán and His Generation

Ryan M. Alexander

University of New Mexico Press • Albuquerque

Printed in the United States of America
21 20 19 18 17 16 1 2 3 4 5 6

Library of Congress Cataloging-in-Publication Data
Names: Alexander, Ryan M., 1982– author.
Title: Sons of the Mexican Revolution : Miguel Alemán and his generation / Ryan M. Alexander.
Description: Albuquerque : University of New Mexico Press, 2016. | Series: Diálogos Series | Includes bibliographical references and index.
Identifiers: LCCN 2015049832 | ISBN 9780826357380 (cloth : alk. paper) | ISBN 9780826357397 (pbk. : alk. paper) | ISBN 9780826357403 (electronic)
Subjects: LCSH: Alemán, Miguel, 1905–1983. | Presidents—Mexico—Biography. | Mexico—Politics and government—1946–1970. | Mexico—Politics and government—1910–1946.
Classification: LCC F1235.5.A44 A79 2016 | DDC 972.08/27092—dc23
LC record available at http://lccn.loc.gov/2015049832

Composed in Minion Pro

Cover photograph courtesy of
Biblioteca Mexicana de la Fundación Miguel Alemåan, AC

Contents

Preface and Acknowledgments

At its broadest extent, this is a book about what happened to Mexico's explosive 1910 revolution, the first in a series of major revolutionary upheavals to occur in the twentieth century. The movement brought a welter of social reforms in the 1920s and 1930s, but ultimately its most conservative elements prevailed, leaving the nation with an authoritarian political system and an economy defined by severe inequality. By the 1940s official commitment to the revolution's most radical initiatives—among them the redistribution of rural land and the renovation of national culture—had withered away, terminating the movement before its greatest promises could be realized. Why was this the case?

This seemingly straightforward question invites a series of related questions relevant to all revolutionary processes. Were the individuals charged with converting the goals of revolutionaries into concrete policies inferior to the task? Did they become corrupted in their pursuit of power? Did the circumstances of context change too drastically, draining the movement of relevance and energy? Was the revolution, since it was rooted in the realities of one moment, simply unable to survive the passage of time? Were the old patterns of oligarchic rule more resilient than the revolutionaries had anticipated? Did the shift from one generation to another bring with it such new ideas that the movement became obsolete?

There is no single answer to all these questions. As with any movement this large and complex, there were multiple reasons that the Mexican revolution ended in incomplete form. Nevertheless, part of the explanation can be found in the generational shift that took place at the highest levels of government in the second half of the 1940s. Taking this change in ruling generation as its subject, this study examines a transformative moment at both the national and global scale, as Mexico simultaneously retreated from its revolutionary orientation and adjusted to the new geopolitical and economic realities of the early Cold War years. The responsibility for leading the nation through this watershed period fell to a generation of cosmopolitan civilians led by the son of a fallen revolutionary general. In my effort to understand the motives of the individuals who made up this generation, I have incurred many personal debts, and I would like to acknowledge as many of them as possible here.

Like many scholars, I consider the publication of my first book manuscript to be a major career milestone. On the long road to reaching that milestone, I have had the good fortune of sharing countless memorable experiences with wonderful people. This book represents that formative journey distilled into a relatively compact product. At the University of Arizona, I thrived under the guidance of Bill Beezley, who taught me how to operate in this profession. A number of other professors—Kevin Gosner, Martha Few, Jadwiga Pieper-Mooney, Katherine Morrissey, Richard Eaton, and above all Bert Barickman—influenced how I think as a historian. What made Arizona a truly great program was the community of fellow graduate students who shared in both the triumphs and the frustrations of academic life. Although there are too many to list here, Amanda López, Karin Friederic, Tracy Goode, Cory Schott, Tyler Ralston, Amie Kiddle, Steve Neufeld, Rob Scott, Michael Matthews, Erika Korowin, Kathryn Gallien, Adam Schwartz, and Lisa Munro stand out. Not only were they stimulating colleagues, but they were, and remain, lifelong friends.

Beyond Tucson, the list of people to whom I owe a debt of gratitude is long. Rod Camp was generous in sharing research materials, and Steve Lewis was kind to read prior drafts and offer his critiques of them. At the Truman Presidential Library, Randy Sowell was helpful and knowledgeable, making my short time there enormously productive. I appreciate the funding the library provided as well. In Mexico, Alejandro de Antuñano Maurer, along with Pati Rojas and Susi Gallegos, made archival research a pleasant daily occurrence, often for months on end. I offer my sincere thanks to Miguel Alemán Velasco, along with Lorenzo Lazo and Antonio Carrillo Castro, for lending me their time and support of the project.

At the Colegio de México, Luis Aboites, Romana Falcón, and Paul Garner offered stimulating courses, while Guillermo Palacios and Ariel Rodríguez Kuri provided valuable institutional support. I also thank Soledad Loaeza for her time and insights. My fellow classmates there, especially Diego Pulido, Regina Tapia, and Pavel Navarro, remain good friends and colleagues. I have developed true affection for Mexico as a result of spending a great amount of time there, and that would not have been possible without financial support. The Fulbright-Hays program, along with various institutions at the University of Arizona, deserve credit for that. The history department and dean's office at SUNY Plattsburgh have been similarly generous in funding travel for research and conferences.

My fascination with history extends back to my undergraduate days at Willamette University. Through no design of my own, I came under the sway of great professors while there. Ellen Eisenberg, Seth Cotlar, Paul Howard, John Uggen, and especially Bill Smaldone, who first put the history bug in my ear, served as models of the possibilities that a life in academia could offer. In my home department at SUNY Plattsburgh, I count myself as lucky to work with eleven other dedicated and talented historians. Each has contributed something valuable to my growth as a young scholar, and in particular I thank Jeff Hornibrook, Vincent Carey, Sylvie Beaudreau, Jim Rice, and Jessamyn Neuhaus for their efforts to ease me into life here in Plattsburgh. It has been a pleasure.

I owe a special thanks to everyone at the University of New Mexico Press involved in the preparation of the manuscript. I appreciate Lyman Johnson's initial interest in the project and his guidance in the early stages of publication. I was equally impressed with Kris Lane once he took over the Diálogos Series. He made the transition as smooth as could possibly be imagined, and continued to lend valuable guidance through the rest of the process. Clark Whitehorn has been a responsive, friendly, and knowledgeable executive editor, and the anonymous peer-review process was speedy and useful. In the latter case, I only wish I could thank you in person.

Finally, I would be nothing without the support of family. I thank my parents, George and Shelly, for their love and support. Above all, I want to thank Anna for sharing this road with me. Through all of the journey's inevitable bumps and detours, we reached this milestone together.

INTRODUCTION

From College Boys to Cadillac Revolutionaries

MIGUEL ALEMÁN, A MAGNETIC YOUNG POLITICIAN KNOWN FOR HIS decadent lifestyle, became the chief protagonist and the most potent symbol of Mexico's political transformation after World War II. His presidential inauguration in 1946 signaled the first full generational shift within the nation's ruling elite since 1911, when bands of revolutionaries overthrew the oligarchic dictatorship of Porfirio Díaz.[1] The self-made generals who had controlled national politics since the earliest days of the revolution had seen their influence fading for some time,[2] but 1946 marked the first year they failed to put up a real electoral fight. In their place stood a new cadre of national leaders headed by Alemán. He and the other university-trained men who came to power with him had been children during the decade of revolutionary violence from 1910 to 1920, and thus shared little in terms of personal background with the military leaders they replaced.

Longtime union leader Vicente Lombardo Toledano famously nicknamed Alemán and his cohort the "Puppies of the Revolution," conveying the impression that they were heirs to a movement not of their own making. Their opponents, critical of their lack of revolutionary credentials, dismissed them as college boys. Yet despite the objections of those who questioned their experience or suspected their convictions, this new generation of civilian leaders became the dominant force in Mexican politics during the crucial early years of the Cold War. Alemán and his colleagues set their nation on the path toward rapid industrialization and urbanization that it would follow for four decades, and they established the political protocols that kept the authoritarian Institutional Revolutionary Party (usually called the PRI) in power over the second half of the twentieth century without the threat of military or popular backlash.

Most of the men in Alemán's inner circle, despite having diverse class backgrounds and regional origins, shared common educational experiences that prepared them for lives in politics, unified them as a generation, and distinguished them from their military predecessors. The majority of these future leaders first met at the National Preparatory School and then trained in law during the 1920s at the National University. Prep school and university, probably without them even knowing it, provided a forum for political networking and recruitment that would prove decisive in their careers.[3] The combination of social activism, political participation, intellectual stimulation, and material comfort that defined their lives as students in Mexico City instilled in them a fundamentally different set of values than those possessed by the revolutionaries, who had earned their political stripes in combat.

In the following decade, as national politics consolidated into a single-party controlled system, they applied those values to their professional pursuits. Alemán and the majority of his closest colleagues entered politics early in their careers, often right after graduation. On their gradual climb upward, they slowly pushed the military establishment to the margins of national politics. Their experience in the newly consolidated political system, especially in the 1930s, allowed them to refine their political approach and stake their claim to the nation's revolutionary heritage, which had taken the form of institutions organized under the leadership of a semi-official ruling party beginning in 1929. Along the way, they became exemplars of the kind of men who would occupy national office during the second half of the century. As a result of the multiple and sometimes contradictory traits of these leaders—as shrewd politicians who were bold and visionary, but also greedy and occasionally cruel—scholars have found remarkably little consensus regarding their long-term impact.

A Legacy of Extremes

The legacy of the Alemán administration has generated no shortage of debate or controversy. Optimistic scholarly assessments of the political system tended to prevail in the half century after the revolution began, and this celebratory attitude toward the revolution extended to Alemán. Admirers praised him and his colleagues as the first to envision their country as a middle class–oriented, urbanized society with impressive industrial capacity. In the estimation of his supporters, Alemán was the first president to pursue a modernizing path that placed supreme priority on growth, something that began with moving bilateral relations with the United States toward permanent and mutually beneficial cooperation. Several observers regarded the country's post–World War II development as the next stage in a progression from revolution to evolution.[4] According to this perspective, the decade of upheaval from 1910 to 1920, followed by the uneven implementation of reforms from 1920 to 1940, paved the way for a new crop of ambitious, modernizing leaders. With Alemán as their chief spokesperson, this new generation ushered in the period of sustained economic growth from the 1940s through the 1970s acclaimed as the Mexican Miracle.

Scholarly consensus would not turn decisively against Alemán until after 1968, the year in which a government-ordered massacre left an estimated three hundred peaceful student protesters dead just days before the Mexico City Summer Olympics. The tragedy marred the reputation of the PRI, especially in the minds of middle-class citizens, initiating a gradual slide into widespread disillusionment and a crisis of political legitimacy. It also prompted scholars to rethink the successes of the revolution, which did little to burnish Alemán's reputation. Even those most eager to defend Alemán had no choice but to acknowledge what his critics had said all along: that his administration introduced an unprecedented level of corruption at the highest levels of government. Despite spending the majority of their professional lives in public office, Alemán and many of his associates accumulated substantial wealth as a result of their political connections.[5] While prominent politicians lined their pockets, the nation's poorest citizens, supposedly the beneficiaries of its hard-fought revolution, sunk further into poverty and misery. Some critics have been even less charitable, labeling them counterrevolutionaries who betrayed the movement they inherited.[6]

Alemán's image, in both popular culture and scholarship, has tended to reflect this sour assessment. In 1947 historian and economist Daniel Cosío Villegas targeted the Alemán administration in a scathing appraisal of the PRI, which he called "Mexico's Crisis." In his essay, he accused the revolutionaries of falling short of fulfilling their own mandate, suggesting that better leadership might breathe some life into Mexico's dying body politic. His work clearly struck a dissonant chord. Shortly after he published the essay, Cosío Villegas received a stern warning from Alemán's private secretary, Rogerio de la Selva, that he should exercise more caution if he wished to maintain his standing in the nation's academic establishment.[7] In marked contrast to Cosío Villegas's academic venom, one of the most astute critiques of Alemán came in the form of a pithy comment from journalist Carlos Denegri. "The Revolution," he lamented, "has gotten off its horse and into a Cadillac."[8]

Decades later the nation's popular political culture still associated Alemán with corruption. Luis Estrada's 1999 satirical film *Herod's Law*, a clear condemnation of the single-party system as it lay on its political deathbed, used the Alemán years as its historical backdrop. In hilarious fashion the film equated the corruption of the 1990s with Alemanismo. The movie's protagonist, a bumbling bureaucrat named Juan Vargas, failed in his initial attempt to bring Alemán's goal of "Modernity and Social Justice" to the remote hamlet of San Pedro de los Saguaros. Along the way, he got swept up in a cycle of corruption that rewarded his political ambitions but left him personally ruined and morally bankrupt.[9]

Scholars have not limited their criticism of Alemán to the issue of corruption. Instead, they have attacked him on multiple fronts, excoriating him for moving the nation's government in a regressive direction and for pursuing an overly aggressive policy of industrial development that compromised the interests of the nation's most vulnerable citizens.[10] The extremes of opinion that have characterized scholarly appraisal of Alemán, from initial enthusiasm to ultimate denunciation, have obscured the central importance of his administration to the nation's development in the twentieth century. To date, Lázaro Cárdenas stands as the twentieth century's most studied president. Cárdenas, who nationalized Mexico's vast petroleum assets and distributed nearly fifty million acres of land to poor rural citizens, inspired deep popular affection in his time, and among scholars his legacy remains a topic of intense scrutiny to this day.[11] Nevertheless, more recent analysis, benefiting from new sources and a less polemical tilt, has acknowledged that the Alemán years represented a defining moment in Mexico's modern history.[12]

This study takes that basic premise as its initial point of departure. But whereas most prior analysis has either offered polemical judgment of Alemán and his colleagues or dry appraisals of his administration's policies, this book places the individuals who made up the Alemán generation at the center of its analysis. In doing so, it makes two overarching claims. The first is that previous analyses, particularly those emphasizing the negative aspects of the Alemán years, have missed a crucial point: that Alemán and his colleagues possessed and acted on a coherent, sincere vision of national development. The concrete expression of that vision was Alemanismo—the constellation of policies, attitudes, and priorities that defined the governing approach of Alemán and his colleagues. Unlike the familiar "isms" most commonly seen in English-language usage (for example, communism, libertarianism, or anarchism, among many others), Alemanismo was not bound to any particular set of ideological precepts. Rather, in keeping with the Mexican precedent of applying an "ismo" more loosely, it represented a far more practical plan to adapt Mexico to the post–World War II world.

Alemanismo represented the driving vision behind an administration that swapped revolutionary zeal for efficiency and pragmatism, and gave favor to industry, commerce, and foreign investment at the expense of ongoing social reform aimed at ameliorating the conditions of the nation's poor. Alemán summarized his own interpretation of the era in a 1947 interview with *Time* magazine with a succinct but telling statement: "Mexico has had its revolution."[13] For good reason, there is consensus that Alemanismo produced its share of undesirable results. This study is not intended to challenge that assessment, nor to apologize for the misdeeds or shortcomings of the Alemán administration. Nevertheless, one of the central contentions of this book is that such a one-sided view fails to capture the complex motives of these leaders and sidesteps altogether the far more difficult task of carefully placing them in context.

The book's second major argument is that the Alemán years saw not only a change in policy priorities, but also (and more importantly) a deeper shift in the basic values that underpinned government policy. A compelling explanation of where those values originated, and what effect they had on the nation's political development, has heretofore eluded scholars. Newly unearthed sources provide fresh insights into the collective mindset of Alemán and his colleagues. Among the most fruitful are the transcripts of a series of interviews with former associates of Alemán, including administration officials, politicians, fellow university students, business colleagues, family members, and personal friends. These sources, conducted by the philanthropic foundation in Mexico City bearing Alemán's name, provide a perspective that cannot be gleaned from official documents housed at public archives. But when coupled with official documents from the years of his administration, including numerous recently declassified government intelligence files, they provide considerable insight into not only how but also why they governed in the manner in which they did.

Part of the answer can be found in the biography of Alemán, who came from a revolutionary family and who in earlier decades championed the central causes of the revolution. His life story, like that of any compelling biographical figure, unlocks a number of larger historical lessons.[14] It is doubly useful in this case, since it tells us a great deal about the gradual process of elite socialization and generational formation experienced by various figures within his administration.[15] In using Alemán as a point of entry into the experience of an entire generation, I have taken a cue from the Spanish historian José Ortega y Gasset, who called generations "a dynamic compromise between the masses and the individual," regarding them as "the most important concept of history and, consequently, the hinge on which history moves."[16]

Interweaving biographical and generational approaches has allowed me to escape some of the limitations of a strictly biographical method, which, if insufficiently tempered by historical analysis, can overstate the power of its subject without regard for the constraints he faced. It is an important limitation in this case, since Alemán and his colleagues governed amid a political sea change that forced them to react out of necessity. How they reacted had a lot to do with their collective experiences coming of age and rising through the political ranks together. Thus, the explanation for why Alemán and his colleagues made the choices they did lies in the interplay between their motivations as individuals and the contextual circumstances in which they operated.

The Price of a Perfect Dictatorship

Alemán and his colleagues played a significant role in shaping the unique political system that Peruvian novelist Mario Vargas Llosa, in a 1990 debate with Mexican author Octavio Paz, would famously call the "perfect dictatorship." The single-party dominant system has also been described as a "dictablanda," or "soft authoritarian" model, as well as a "Pax PRIísta."[17] Each of these terms emphasizes the same general point: that while the nation's leaders were capable of repression, they preferred using gentler forms of coercion. The result was a hybrid—and sometimes contradictory—system that balanced top-down control with a willingness to negotiate. While this arrangement had its origins in the process of political consolidation in the 1920s and 1930s, it came together in its most enduring and recognizable form under Alemán. Just months prior to his inauguration, the nation's leaders gave the ruling party its third and final name, the Institutional Revolutionary Party, or PRI (pronounced "pree"), signaling that destructive upheaval was a thing of the past.

Beginning with Alemán, national politics under the leadership of the PRI became an exercise in contrast. In many ways, the system had appealing qualities. It proved far more durable, and far more stable, than its counterparts elsewhere in Latin America, and it was particularly impervious to the kind of military intervention that plagued the rest of the region. It owed its success in neutralizing the threat of military overthrow to a deliberate effort by government officials to minimize the political tendencies of the armed forces.[18] The possibility of military uprising was further kept at bay by the government's ability to satisfy the middle classes, which served as the primary domestic champions of military intervention in the Cold War elsewhere in the region. Not coincidentally, when the middle classes began to feel their sense of material security falter later in the century, talk of military interventionism bubbled to the surface.[19] Nevertheless, such cases proved to be exceptional. To avoid such an outcome, leaders used the corporatist structure of the party to distribute benefits in exchange for compliance and loyalty.

The single-party dominant system in its first decade combined elements of corporatism (formal political incorporation of class-based groups through institutions) and populism (a strategic combination of policy and rhetoric aimed at securing the support of the masses). Thus, it provided a forum through which all citizens—from urban workers to the rural poor to the middle classes—could express their grievances.[20] At the same time, it gave officials a means of creating mass-level and highly bureaucratized patron-client linkages with the population. Government and party leaders also maintained an absolute commitment to the revolutionary precept of non-reelection. Because the presidency changed hands every six years, the tendency for power to concentrate in one individual proved to be far less common in Mexico than elsewhere in Latin America. On paper, this system was close to perfect, and far from a dictatorship.

Yet, as is so often the case, the reality was far removed from the ideal. By the 1940s powerful antithetical forces had overtaken the system's positive qualities. While the system did not face a significant military threat, its leaders were not beyond repression. The crackdowns on organized labor in 1948–1950 and 1958–1959, the student massacres of 1968 and 1971, and the "dirty war" of the 1960s and 1970s attest to that.[21] Moreover, even if the military did not have its shot at controlling national politics, it maintained a level of participation and complicity in such acts of repression. Mexico's authoritarianism was also nurtured by intelligence services that underwent a process of expansion after World War II. Beginning with Alemán and continuing through the Cold War, government intelligence agencies worked on behalf of the PRI and aided the party in thwarting the political ambitions of numerous groups, especially those on the left.[22]

In theory, the party's corporatist institutions were designed to empower the masses by functioning as a kind of bureaucratic capillary system that would draw popular demands upward. Yet by 1946 the institutional structure of the party was more often used for domination rather than empowerment: the president issued directives that were then carried out by the leaders of the party's sectors, whose loyalties were assured by perquisites that proved irresistible. Thus, the party, rather than becoming a vehicle for grassroots political mobilization, instead served as an instrument of control for the president.[23] Beyond the executive branch, the legislative and judicial branches of government were models of ineptitude, and alternative parties on the left and the right either failed outright or existed as a kind of "loyal opposition."[24] In an effort to maintain a veneer of democratic legitimacy, the PRI even encouraged weak parties to put up straw-man candidacies in highly orchestrated and expensive electoral rituals.[25]

The PRI developed a peculiar relationship with the media, one that both symbolized and reinforced Mexico's hybrid political system. Unlike most single-party regimes in the twentieth century, which almost invariably relied on state-run media, Mexico's media outlets were privately owned and ostensibly free in their programming choices. Yet despite the lack of direct state control, pro-regime broadcast and print outlets enjoyed generous subsidies, while those with opposing views faced censorship and occasional repression. Alemán's personal investments in what would become the dominant television network Televisa, aided by his strong connections to media magnates Emilio Azcárraga Vidaurreta (and later his son, Emilio "El Tigre" Azcárraga Milmo) and Rómulo O'Farrill, only deepened the connection between the PRI and the media[26] and further blurred the line between the private and public sectors.[27] As one historian recently put it, the PRI and certain segments of the business community existed in a relationship of symbiosis.[28]

The tendency of the PRI to choose peaceful means of coercion rather than to exercise terror, while laudable, often required that untold sums of money flow across informal channels. The upside was that leaders pulled any number of levers to coax people into consent, meaning that informal, ad hoc measures actually played a role in stabilizing the system.[29] Put more simply, corruption got things done. Nevertheless, the ugly side of the PRI's patronage-based system was a pattern of blatant graft, bribery, and cronyism that was financially wasteful and corrosive to public confidence. The greatest rewards were reserved for those at the top, leaving fewer of the nation's finite resources for those at the bottom of the pyramid. For many, this uneven distribution of political benefits did not square with the ever more predictable promises made in official revolutionary rhetoric.

The Miracle and the Myth

The administration established the contours of national economic development that would remain in place over the next three decades. Alemán pursued a multi-pronged strategy of capitalist development that balanced state protection and foreign investment. His administration's agenda fit within the framework of import substitution industrialization (ISI), a region-wide economic program aimed at using government protection to increase domestic production for a growing consumer market while reducing dependency on export earnings.[30] The administration imposed import limits and high tariffs to promote domestic consumption, invested government funds in industry-supporting infrastructure, and devoted direct subsidies and tax incentives to domestic industrial firms. It also borrowed heavily to finance industrial and infrastructural development, especially from the US Treasury. The opportunity to secure credit from the United States, as it assumed its dominant position in the post–World War II global economy, motivated Alemán to retune US-Mexican relations through diplomacy.

In one sense, Alemán was continuing the work of those who had come before him. From 1920 onward, the national leaders who had emerged victorious during the armed phase of the revolution, especially the Sonoran generals Álvaro Obregón and Plutarco Elías Calles, had carried out what one historian has called a developmentalist strategy that equated the rebuilding of the nation with the pursuit of state-led capitalist development.[31] Thus, in the quarter century preceding the Alemán administration, Mexico's government laid the groundwork for much of what would later be associated with Alemanismo—the reinforcement of a strong national bourgeoisie, a concerted effort to attract foreign investment, and a tendency to encourage entrepreneurial values in the populace.[32] But even if some of the structural foundation had been laid in the decades leading up to 1946, Alemán took the nation's economic policy in a new direction from that point forward as he adapted Mexico to a new development paradigm centered on an inward-looking process of statist industrialization.

The adoption of ISI policies reflected prevailing trends in economic thinking at the time, particularly the proposition by Argentine economist Raúl Prebisch that Latin America's pathway out of dependency on raw exports would be through state-led industrialization. To that end, Alemán sought to make his country more economically potent by expanding the role of the government in economic affairs. At the same time, he used his personal influence to entice foreign businesses to pour money into the country, which had finally moved past the reputation for internal instability and hostility to influence from abroad that the revolution had left in its wake. Alemán also embraced a model of large-scale commercial agriculture, going so far as to revise the constitution to allow for increased mechanization, investment, and commercialization, even if this meant deviating from the revolutionary land-reform program. The administration coupled these efforts with policies aimed at expanding agricultural production through the introduction of hybridized seeds, chemical fertilizers, pesticides, and new machinery as part of a global experiment known as the green revolution.

This ambitious economic agenda produced mixed results. On the positive side, it created the structural basis for the impressive growth that characterized the next three decades. Alemán demonstrated a robust commitment to public works, claiming an especially noteworthy record in petroleum exploitation, irrigation, hydroelectricity, highway building, tourism development, and urban construction. Numerous domestic industries, especially those producing inexpensive, non-durable goods for the increasingly consumerist urban middle classes, flourished as a result of ISI. Such aggressive efforts at industry protection, coupled with public investment in infrastructure, helped to spur thirty years of sustained economic growth at the unprecedented average annual rate of 6 percent. Not surprisingly, the administration made showpieces out of projects that could provide symbolic reinforcement to this new era of breakneck growth.

The administration's biggest projects left an undeniable record of accomplishment. The list is impressive: the massive University City (Ciudad Universitaria, or CU) of the National Autonomous University of Mexico

(UNAM), the power-generating dams in the Papaloapan River Valley, the enormous urban *multifamiliares* (middle-class housing and commercial complexes) in the capital, the beachfront high-rise hotels of Acapulco, and the factories built in the Federal District and adjoining states, to name a handful. Collectively, these initiatives form a significant part of the administration's legacy. In pursuing them, Alemán became the first twentieth-century president to fuse the interests of government and big business into a common purpose.[33]

These gains notwithstanding, the ultimate price of these economic policies was high. The cost of creating new industry proved to be enormous and led to a pattern of troubling economic developments. From the 1940s to the 1980s, even as economic growth soared, structural crisis set in: the trade deficit widened to an alarming degree and periodic balance-of-payments crises led officials to devalue the peso in order to bring imports and exports into alignment and restore foreign-currency reserves. Successive governments fell back on foreign debt to support such rapid industrialization. The prevailing logic was that the debt was justified so long as the growth continued. While such dry and abstract economic indicators often fail to convey the severity of the problem, people certainly felt them in their everyday lives, since devaluation created inflationary pressures that made buying basic goods like tortillas and milk difficult for many.[34] By the 1980s the logic of debt-driven development, which accelerated dramatically in the 1970s, had led Mexico—indeed all of Latin America—into a crippling debt crisis.[35] Critics of state-led economic development seized on the crisis to implement free-market, or "neoliberal," reforms, thus drawing to a close the economic model first established under Alemán.

This economic program also set off a half century of rural-to-urban migration. Policies that swapped agrarian collectivism for commercial agriculture created a push factor, while the prospect of new employment in industry pulled people to the city, especially Mexico City. The most significant alteration to the urban landscape came in the form of hastily constructed slums and shantytowns that overburdened the financial and environmental capacities of the rapidly swelling capital.[36] This phenomenon continued into the 1990s, making Mexico City at the time the largest urban agglomeration in the world. While average incomes rose and the urban middle sectors grew substantially, that growth proved to be highly unequal. Millions of new urban dwellers, pulled from their rural roots and dropped into an unfamiliar existence, faced the reality of endemic poverty. Those left in the countryside did not fare much better. The administration's embrace of large-scale commercial agriculture relegated the agricultural collectives known as *ejidos*—a totem of Cardenismo—to a secondary and increasingly distant status. The twin phenomena of widened social-economic inequalities and increased poverty formed the disturbing and often hidden underside of the economic miracle. During the boom years of the 1940s–1970s, these negative social outcomes were dismissed as unfortunate but temporary setbacks on the road to a better economic future. The assumption that growth at the top would result in across-the-board benefits served as one of the defining characteristics of Alemanismo.

Such assumptions tend to accompany situations involving the suffering of some segment of the population. In this case, the nation's poor bore the brunt of the Alemán administration's ambitious but disruptive plans. In Mexico and across Latin America, organized labor looked at the post–World War II era with optimism, as an aperture into renewed activity.[37] And Alemán, much like his contemporaries across the region, responded harshly. Intolerance for independent labor mobilization, usually justified as anti-communism, became a hallmark of Alemanismo. The administration purged Vicente Lombardo Toledano, the former leader of the Confederation of Mexican Workers (CTM), the party's working-class sector. Alemán replaced Lombardo Toledano and his allies with a cadre of loyal cronies who became associated with the image of the traditional cowboys known as *charros*. The nickname derived from to the propensity of the rail worker–union boss, Jesús Díaz de León, to wear chaps and spurs to union meetings. But it took on a bigger meaning as well. The labor charros, much like the actual cattle-rustling charros of the Mexican countryside, were known to be tough.

The toughest among them was not Díaz de León, but rather Fidel Velázquez, the new CTM chief, who oversaw the sharp and permanent rightward transition within the party's labor sector. Under Velázquez's tutelage and with Alemán's blessing, the leaders of various CTM affiliates carried out the infamous *charrazos* of 1948–1950, putting down several waves of strikes by railway, oil, and mine workers. In doing so, they permanently sidelined Lombardo Toledano and effectively ended the capacity of the CTM to advocate on behalf of workers.[38] The rural poor faced similar realities. Rank-and-file members of the CTM's rural counterpart, the National Peasant Confederation (CNC), learned quickly that their voice in the party did not carry as far as it once had.

Old Bottles, New Wine

The central initiatives of the Alemán years projected a national aesthetic of modernity and ambition to citizens and foreigners alike. Nevertheless, they also hid a host of negative social consequences, making the period one of sharp contrasts in experience. They also signaled a drift away from the revolutionary nationalism of the 1920s and 1930s. In the wake of the decade of armed conflict, officials had sought to renovate Mexico's national culture by exalting a mestizo (or mixed-race) and indigenous ideal through school curricula and in various media, including public art, music, literature, handicrafts, and film.[39] This cultural campaign to redefine the nation at the level of the citizen complemented concrete policies such as land, labor, and education reform that were designed to improve the material existence of the nation's poor. Beginning with Alemán, officials increasingly embraced an alternative vision of national development, one that took various forms—urban modernism that reflected avant-garde global trends; commercial agriculture that disrupted communal landholding patterns; middle-class consumerism that emulated the postwar United States[40]; and education policy that prioritized universities over rural schools. Officially, the Alemanistas and their successors remained committed to the revolutionary effort to create a new, inclusive national identity. But in reality, the post–World War II national leadership placed supreme priority on inculcating values consistent with industrial capitalism,[41] and this ultimately halted the momentum of Mexico's cultural revolution.

This did not stop Alemán or his successors from employing the myth of ongoing revolution to legitimate their actions. He and his advisers sought to establish political credibility by grafting his biography onto the political establishment's official version of the revolution. Since the inception of the National Revolutionary Party (or PNR, the first of the PRI's two institutional predecessors) in 1929, the nation's leaders, eager to attach themselves to the heroism associated with the revolution, had encouraged the transmission of a simplified nationalist history through nearly every conceivable broadcast, print, and artistic medium. This epic account de-emphasized the reality of lethal conflict among opposing revolutionaries, replacing it with a common heroes-and-villains narrative in which the rebels came together and delivered Mexico from the tyranny of the Porfiriato.[42] The PRI, so went the story, represented the institutional extension of that movement, giving it a popular mandate. In reality, the idea of institutionalizing a popular movement presented a paradox. Thus, monopolizing the most potent symbols of the revolution became a crucial component of the PRI's effort to discredit its opposition as counterrevolutionary.[43] Even the use of the capital letter "R" in Mexican Revolution helped to reify a complex movement—one that meant different things to different people—into an official concept (hence this study's preference for the lower-case form).

As the first president since 1910 not to have seen combat, Alemán had to work especially hard to convince the public that he was the torchbearer of the nation's ongoing revolution and not a fraudulent pretender. At certain moments, such as when he was named "Worker-in-Chief of the Fatherland" by the PRI's labor affiliate, or when he established a Day of Freedom of the Press, the party's claim to the revolutionary tradition came off as farce. Still, Alemán and his colleagues cast their policies, along with their nearly imperial power, as expressions of revolutionary benevolence. Alemán continued time-honored official rituals, such as the annual presidential address to the nation, while adding his own flourishes (the most noticeable being the revival of the vice-regal tradition of arriving for the speech in a procession under a series of triumphal arches, only in a Cadillac instead of a carriage).[44] In his attempts to pitch himself as the face of the next chapter of the revolution's constantly expanding story, he came to embody the contradictory image of a rapidly modernizing nation whose leaders still clung to the rhetoric of an ever-more-distant revolutionary heritage.

Alemán thus worked to cultivate a political style all his own. In a system in which revolutionary leaders had established their legitimacy through military campaigns and where hero cults of gritty revolutionaries became part of official propaganda and the popular imagination alike, Alemán presented a fundamentally new presidential ideal. Acting as the patriarchal head of the "Revolutionary Family," the title that the national leadership awarded itself, Alemán crafted an image as educated and debonair, physically vigorous, and even sexually appealing. His reputation as a "playboy president," fueled by reports of a fling with Golden Age starlet María Félix (so goes the pervasive rumor) and the nearly constant presence of female companions (a woman named Lenora appears to have been a long-term mistress, and whispers of a relationship with Nazi spy Hilda Kruger have recently surfaced[45]), underscored his sense of masculine vigor.

The conspicuous display of wealth further bolstered this new presidential image. Leaders from the revolutionary generation rarely entered military or political service with much wealth. If they gained it afterward, as was often the case, they tended not to indulge in the aristocratic lifestyle for which Alemán became famous. His large home and office in Mexico City, along with the mansion and yacht he owned in his beloved Acapulco, where he retreated to escape the capital's confines, conveyed the decadence he and his contemporaries enjoyed. Financial interests in everything from Cuernavaca real estate to Chihuahua forests to Veracruz hotels to an hacienda in Baja California, along with media stockholdings and countless untraceable investments kept under the names of front men (called *prestanombres*, literally meaning loaned names), all fed into his and his generation's image as the inheritors of the revolution's spoils. As the PRI increasingly moved away from a labor- and agrarian-oriented policy platform, the image of its leadership also grew more distant from that of the working class and rural poor. Alemán sought to spin that to his advantage: the qualities of a rapidly modernizing and prosperous country, his persona suggested, could be concentrated in one man.

With this in mind, Alemán and his generation crafted a political style that emphasized a high degree of administrative capability. The roundtable talks that Alemán hosted during his 1946 campaign showcased this objective. Whereas Cárdenas, the consummate populist, had traveled, sometimes on the backs of donkeys (and once by swimming across a lake), to remote pueblos to connect with villagers in his 1934 campaign, Alemán instead sought to project himself and his incoming administration as efficient and prepared for the technical challenges the nation faced. In this respect, the political style of Alemanismo foreshadowed the move toward technocratic leadership that would fully flourish by the 1970s. The roundtables allowed Alemán to engage only a limited number of representatives from various interest groups and forced them to come to him. Thus, while many of his Latin American contemporaries (especially populists such as Brazil's Getúlio Vargas and Argentina's Juan Domingo Perón and his most powerful weapon, his wife Evita) benefited from their ability to create a perception of empathy for the plight of the masses, Alemán instead developed a more distant, unapproachable presidential image.

Still, the campaign did have some folksy elements. Taking a page from Cárdenas, whose 1934 presidential campaign was accompanied by mariachis, Alemán brought a band to campaign stops to play *son jarocho*, the popular music of his native Veracruz. The genre's most famous tune, "La Bamba," became the campaign's theme song. These contrasting motifs—a businesslike, technocratic comportment set to the playful melody of "La Bamba," a bold modernizing message expressed in stale revolutionary language—serve to illustrate the transitional and polarizing nature of Alemán and his administration.

Mexico's Moment

This study analyzes the long-lasting implications of twin processes, as Mexico underwent substantial internal changes while simultaneously adapting to a new global context. Across the world, the austerity of World War II gave way to an optimistic if uncertain new era. In Mexico the revolutionary culture faded away, replaced by a fresh but also unfamiliar modernity. The nation, both in reality and official representation, began to look quite different. Its population began a long transformation from a predominantly rural to an ever-more urbanized society. Jet setters, both domestic and foreign, flocked southward to enjoy pristine beaches, while wealthy investors, again from within and outside Mexico, poured money into industrial and agricultural interests. Actors and actresses like Cantinflas, Pedro Infante, Dolores del Río, and María Félix shared the prestige of their Hollywood peers during the country's Golden Age of film.[46]

A new cultural ideal, modeled heavily on the image of the postwar baby boomers in the United States, guided the aspirations of a growing middle class. *La Familia Burrón*, the famous comic strip of cartoonist Gabriel Vargas, would later capture the comedy of the nascent lower-middle class's adaptation to this new urban life.[47] These cultural changes did not occur independently of political change. Rather, the two reinforced one another, and the Alemán generation's politicians sought to use their authority to promote their vision of a predominantly middle-class and urban society. Their efforts yielded real successes, but no amount of official rhetoric could mask the social consequences of such rapid development. While the burgeoning capital city underwent social, economic, and aesthetic changes through inward-looking development,[48] it also grew outward, making rising socioeconomic inequalities increasingly visible. While the affluent suburbs of Satellite City (Ciudad Satélite) and Jardines de Pedregal appeared overnight, slums formed in smaller pockets of the city, and shantytowns consumed the previously uninhabited surrounding hillsides.

Characterizing Mexico's performance during this time as a miracle, without exploring the limitations of that term, merely reiterates the official narrative utilized by the PRI leadership in the period. The contradictions in the ISI-based developmental model appeared early, offering an unflattering counterpoint to the period's otherwise promising economic statistics. Films such as Luis Buñuel's *Los Olvidados* (literally translated as The Forgotten Ones, but marketed to US viewers as *The Young and the Damned*)[49] and US anthropologist Oscar Lewis's controversial ethnographies *The Children of Sánchez* and *Five Families* contradicted the official version of the miracle. Crime, child abandonment and neglect, domestic violence, alcoholism, disease, and rampant poverty characterized the lives of a growing sector of urban slum dwellers (and of those who remained in the countryside), leading Lewis to theorize that the persistence of such problems could be attributed to a self-perpetuating culture of poverty.[50] His thesis did not sit well with citizens or with national leaders attempting to promote a new phase of development and progress, and, thus, they forced him to leave the country. Nevertheless, his work hit a nerve: stories like his remained conspicuously absent from the official rhetoric touting the success of the ongoing revolution. These contradictions gave rise to a cynicism that would grow and take on new forms over the next half century. From Abel Quesada's caricatures mocking a feckless new generation of political opportunists to groundbreaking novels such as Carlos Fuentes's *The Death of Artemio Cruz* and Juan Rulfo's *Pedro Páramo*, which both made unmistakable references to a failed revolution,[51] popular and elite culture alike began to reflect a growing discontent. By the time the generation born during Alemán's presidency came of age, Mexico was in the grips of a countercultural movement that drew inspiration from global trends but targeted local problems.[52]

None of this should suggest that these sentiments, positive or negative, had everything to do with Alemán or the generation of civilians who accompanied him to the highest perches of national politics. Yet more than any other group of political leaders, these men led their country down the path it would take over the next three decades—decades that encompassed a partially fulfilled economic miracle and a troubling Cold War. Thus, an explanation of their motivations and mentalities is crucial to understanding modern Mexico. That explanation begins in the critical decade of the 1920s, when these men first met one another as the fortunate sons of the 1910 revolution.

CHAPTER ONE

Coming of Age in Revolutionary Mexico City

THE NUCLEUS OF THE ALEMÁN GENERATION FORMED IN THE NATIONAL Preparatory School and the National University's law school during the 1920s, a quarter century before its members came to power. The men who later formed Alemán's political inner circle first met in these schools, and their early associations had a significant influence on their political careers.[1] More than any other factor, their formative experiences in Mexico City's elite institutions of higher education distinguished them from their military predecessors. While many of the students came from the provinces, often from families that suffered considerable hardship during the revolution,[2] in school they lived a remarkably different existence. During their time in Mexico City, they not only gained exposure to new ideas and ideologies, but also got a taste of a different way of life, one that was urban, cosmopolitan, middle-class in character, and devoid of both the rural strife of the revolution and many of the ongoing problems in the capital.

The image of Alemán and his generation as establishment political leaders later in the century conveys the sense that they had little actual experience with the revolution. For many, the mention of Alemán and his inner circle conjures an image of privilege and excess rather than one of revolutionary sacrifice. Yet most of the young men in Alemán's cohort had direct connections to the revolution, and they certainly did not begin their lives in the fortunate conditions they would later enjoy. In the capital, these relatively poor students witnessed a transformation of the revolution, from the devastating chaos of violence and death that characterized the 1910s to the constructive movement to address exigent social questions that took shape in the following decade. As politically active students, they participated in this moment of radical change at its epicenter. Being in Mexico City took them away from the grim circumstances of the provinces, exposing them to a capital city pulsing with optimism—the heart of a country that had just begun to rebuild and reform.[3] This allowed them to envision their country's future, and their own, in a fundamentally new way.

The combination of academic training and exposure to this atmosphere of political reformism set them apart from all previous academic and ruling generations. Unlike their military forebears, they experienced an eclectic set of intellectual influences that gave them a more worldly perspective. Unlike their academic predecessors, such as the celebrated Generation of 1915 (especially its "Siete Sabios," or Seven Sages, several of whom served as professors of Alemán and his classmates), they had a distinctly pragmatic orientation that served their political ambitions well. By the end of the decade, as they graduated and moved into their early careers, they had resolved to take control of the mechanisms of government, rather than merely to criticize them, as many of their professors had done.[4] Their political awakening came gradually and through various activities. Student publications, academic congresses, and literary clubs were among the most common.[5] The capstone came in 1929, first with a series of strikes that succeeded in persuading President Emilio Portes Gil to grant the National University full autonomy and rename it the National Autonomous University of Mexico, or UNAM, then with participation in the presidential campaign of former education minister José Vasconcelos. His campaign, which many of the students hoped would resuscitate a revolution dying at the hands of a self-interested clique of political opportunists,[6] ended in failure. Yet while it permanently embittered Vasconcelos, it ultimately drew many of the former students into lifelong political activism.[7]

The friendships these students formed in school were every bit as important as their political and intellectual activities. Most came to preparatory school in their late teens and left university by their late twenties. As young students, they devoted a good deal of time to social activity, especially dating. Their myriad social pursuits, which contributed to strong bonds of friendship, complemented their growing political and intellectual engagement and bolstered their formation as a generation. Many of their day-to-day activities revolved around what might best be described as a set of masculine rituals, such as drinking and pursuing young women,[8] which resulted in shared bonds of camaraderie. The intellectual and political pursuits of this generation were thus bound up in social activities typical of students. A night at a dance hall, for instance, might result in an hours-long conversation on the walk home about a new literary inspiration or plans for an upcoming issue of a student publication.[9] Both types of activity were important: one for defining the collective ethos of the group, the other for bringing its members closer together.

Alemán in School

Born in 1903 to a humble family that ran a small grocery, Miguel Alemán Valdés spent most of his first two decades in the tropical outpost of Sayula, Veracruz. Both of his parents, Miguel Alemán González and Tomasa Valdés de Alemán, had been married and divorced once before, and his father's previous relationship had given him a half-brother, Antonio. The youngest sibling, Carlos, would arrive some years later. Miguel's childhood bridged the waning years of the Porfiriato and the early stages of the revolution, the cause for which his father would ultimately lay down his life. From 1910 onward, he saw less and less of his father as the elder Alemán became drawn into nearly constant revolutionary struggle.[10] Thus, out of necessity, Miguel became accustomed to his father's prolonged absences and grew into his role as the household's proxy male authority.

To make ends meet the family relied on a number of means, including subsidies from family members and patronage from Alemán González's military associates. The boys worked in various occupations, ranging from mining to cattle ranching to office work, to contribute their share, while Tomasa made soap from beef suet. Miguel also pursued side jobs to stash away enough to see his father. At various points he sold milk, trinkets, or cigarettes, and he even smuggled stolen bullets to his father's battalion.[11] On one such mission, he was forced to rely on a military guard arranged by his father for safe conduct between Mexico City, where he lived as a student by the early 1920s, and his father's unit in Tampico. The decision for Miguel to enter school rather than follow in the footsteps of his father, whom he regarded as his personal hero, was made at the elder Alemán's behest.[12]

Miguel originally came to the capital to study, as his father had wished, in 1920. The National Preparatory School, the most selective in the country, held a level of prestige comparable to Phillips Andover or Exeter Academy in the United States, and Alemán owed much of his fortune in attending the school to his father and to widened access to higher education afforded by the revolution. While he failed to distinguish himself in the classroom, he quickly aligned himself with a group of energetic students who defined themselves as a distinct generation in Mexican scholastic life. For the majority of his time at prep school, he lived in the centrally located Colonia Santa María la Ribera in the house of fellow students Oscar and Carlos Soto Maynez. The Soto family had been prominent in Chihuahua, but ultimately fled the encroaching Division of the North, the legendary revolutionary army commanded by Pancho Villa, as it swept through northern Mexico. After initially relocating to Eagle Pass, Texas, the family ended up in Mexico City. Carlos Soto Maynez recalled Alemán being very poor, certainly too penniless to pay rent.[13] Victoria Soto de Córdoba, a sister of the Soto brothers, nonetheless remembered Alemán's four years in their house fondly. Both recounted the trying conditions: there were twelve living in the house, and all shared a single bathtub with an external heater. She recalled that Alemán functioned as the virtual head of his family since his father was frequently absent and his brother Antonio had died young. At the same time, he became a part of the Soto family, operating much like another sibling of the two brothers and their sisters. He frequently spent evenings dancing with the family, he occasionally joined the two brothers in playing pranks on the younger sisters, and he once even took the blame for Victoria when she snuck out instead of completing house chores.[14]

Integration into the Soto family anchored Alemán during those years when his father was away and his family was divided by geography. The Soto brothers and Alemán remained friends for the rest of their lives. Oscar ascended to the governorship of Chihuahua toward the end of Alemán's presidential term, and Carlos accompanied Alemán on trips to Europe and South America on official and personal business long after his presidency.[15] During their student years in the early 1920s, a number of other lifelong colleagues, including Raúl López Sánchez, Manuel Ramírez Vázquez, and Alfonso Noriega, all lived on the same street and studied together.

Alemán's father, who had been absent for much of his childhood because of his revolutionary pursuits across the country, corresponded with his son by writing letters from various parts of the republic. The correspondence reveals a closeness that the two maintained in spite of the long bouts of separation. General Alemán, known to his revolutionary comrades as "El Hule" (the rubber tree),[16] attempted to send Miguel money whenever possible. One letter from 1920 came with fifty pesos (about twenty-five US dollars[17]), to be split between Miguel and his brother, Carlos, so they could buy school supplies.[18] Others came with a promise of future payments.[19] Money rarely arrived, since the general often found himself in debt.[20]

The senior Alemán insisted that his son push himself in school. In another letter from 1920, the general alluded to an incident that Miguel had previously relayed, in which a fellow student had stolen his answers in an arithmetic class. Warning his son that he would encounter such cheaters throughout his life, he encouraged him not to let it deter his studies or morale. He also promised to send Miguel's mother enough money to provide the young Alemán with *huampole* or some other medicine to reinvigorate his health, which had become somewhat shaky.[21] By 1925 the general's correspondence took an apologetic tone. His letters arrived less frequently, and usually without money. In one he wrote that he had run into a flooded arroyo (a wash or creekbed) and damaged roads while moving horses and cars across the Nayarit countryside. He ended the letter by promising that his commission was coming soon, hinting that money would follow.[22] His letters, which expressed optimism and melancholy in equal measure, say much about Alemán's family life after he had moved from his hometown of Sayula to Mexico City.

Despite these frequent separations and the persistent lack of resources, Alemán grew up in a tightly knit family and regularly felt his father's presence, even in times of absence. His father's connections also proved beneficial to his budding legal career. In 1925, as Alemán entered law school, he was placed under the tutelage of Carlos M. Jiménez, a civil judge in Mexico City. Alemán's placement in his office began with Gen. Arturo Campillo Seyde, who recommended him to sub-chief of the Federal District's Office of Internal Affairs and penal judge Guillermo Schulz, who then saw to it that Jiménez employ Alemán. Seyde, who noted to Schulz that he was recommending the young Alemán as a favor to his longtime friend, General Alemán, was personally assured by Jiménez that he would employ Miguel.[23] It appears, thus, that Miguel's placement in a first-year law school practicum came as a direct result of his father's personal network. In this case General Alemán's high military rank provided valuable connections to both the judicial system and to the municipal government of the capital.

The elder Alemán's career briefly stabilized during his son's law school years, especially in comparison to the years when Miguel attended prep school. But in 1927, while serving as a deputy in the state congress, General Alemán joined the rebellion headed by Gens. Arnulfo Gómez and Francisco

Serrano. The Gómez-Serrano movement opposed the recent constitutional amendments allowing for non-consecutive reelection to the presidency, which would ultimately pave the way for former president Álvaro Obregón to run in 1928. Total prohibition on reelection had been one of the cornerstones of both the revolutionary movement of 1910 and the Constitution of 1917. Thus, the movement was based on an issue that many people saw as an egregious violation of the revolution. Their movement was put down with relative ease, but Alemán almost immediately attached himself to a subsequent rebellion, that of Gen. José Gonzalo Escobar.

Escobar's followers had the lofty ambition to destroy the political machine of former president Plutarco Elías Calles. They regarded Calles as the mastermind behind Obregón's political resurgence and correctly identified him as the dominant figure in national politics. The Escobar Rebellion, despite the questionable behaviors of its leaders (among them a succession of bank robberies), attracted a far greater following than Gómez and Serrano had been able to assemble. President Emilio Portes Gil put his estimate of the Escobar movement's membership as high as thirty thousand men, and Escobar himself claimed territorial control of massive areas ranging from several states in the far north to Oaxaca to Veracruz.[24] The rebellion, in addition to being the last major challenge to the dominant political establishment during the 1920s, also provided General Alemán a degree of stature he had not previously known.

As a follower of the Gómez-Serrano revolt, Alemán had become the chief of the movement's political party in Veracruz,[25] and one prominent outlet of the party, the Pro-Arnulfo R. Gómez Centro Antireeleccionista Panuquense, proposed him as its gubernatorial candidate.[26] By that time he had become one of his state's most vocal supporters of the effort to topple the national power structure. In a publication intended for nationwide distribution, General Alemán, who signed the document as "Chief of Operations of the State," pleaded for a rejection of the "triumvirate" of Álvaro Obregón, Plutarco Elías Calles, and Adolfo de la Huerta, accusing them of using Bolshevik-style terror tactics to establish their authority.[27]

Meanwhile, Miguel, who had a reputation for a disciplined work ethic and an introverted personality, rarely joined in the weekend trips that many of the students took together, nor was he known for indulging in excessive drinking.[28] Perhaps his unusually reserved behavior sprung from a constant and justifiable preoccupation with his father's military activities. Undoubtedly it arose, at least partially, out of his personal connection to the tragic side of the revolution. He had to leave prep school temporarily in 1921, only a year into his studies, to work as an office assistant in the El Aguila petroleum refinery in Coatzacoalcos, Veracruz, to support his family.[29] While the temporary disruption of his studies was a onetime occurrence, the necessity of providing his family supplemental income was more familiar. Even as a child, Alemán, whose father was a small-town grocer in Sayula before being drawn into nearly constant revolutionary activity, sold sundry goods and did odd jobs to be able to pay to see his father.[30]

Despite the improved circumstances of his career and relative stability of the country, General Alemán, who had established himself as the caudillo of southern Veracruz, was never far from battle. In 1929 he died fighting in the Escobar revolt. Overwhelmed by federal troops, who had been using scorched earth tactics to fight Escobar's allies across the country, General Alemán fell at Soteapan, Veracruz, in a raid called the "Slaughter at Aguacatillo."[31] While the precise details of his death remain unclear, the most reliable accounts point to a hasty suicide undertaken to avoid execution after he had been encircled by federal troops. For his son, the fact that his father had died came as less of a shock than the unceremonious way in which it happened.[32] Various sources also confirm the death of Miguel's brother, Antonio, once again most likely by suicide, at some prior point around the same time. According his own children, Miguel never openly acknowledged this fact.[33] Despite these challenges, Alemán forged on without allowing himself any time off from school. While not known as the most brilliant student of his generation, he pushed through his law program in three years, rather than the customary five, which appears to have been a record shared by only a few and never bested.[34]

Alemán relied on his friends to carry him through such trying circumstances. He must not have been alone in this respect, since many of his friends recounted their own turmoil during these years. These friendships, in turn, became the basis not only of their social survival, but also of their political awakening. Thus, the earliest expression of the Alemán generation came out of this formative context. Several of Alemán's closest school friends would follow him to Veracruz in the 1930s to occupy state-level executive and judicial positions while he was governor before ascending to higher political office at the national level when he became president.[35] Among them were Oscar Soto Maynez (later the governor of Chihuahua), Manuel Ramírez Vázquez (minister of labor), David Romero Castañeda (federal deputy from the State of Mexico), Gabriel Ramos Millán (director of the National Corn Commission), and Rogerio de la Selva (Alemán's professional secretary).

Other close collaborators in school went their own ways after graduation but were prominent in national politics during and after the Alemán years, largely due to the interpersonal relationships they cultivated in school. This group included Antonio Carrillo Flores (Alemán's director of Nacional Financiera, the public-development corporation, and later minister of finance and ambassador in a number of key posts), Antonio Ortiz Mena (twice minister of finance), Andrés Serra Rojas (minister of labor), and Ernesto Uruchurto (Mexico City's long-serving mayor). For a complete table of the Alemán generation, with more extensive biographical information, see the appendix of this book.[36] Examination of the daily social and intellectual activities of these young men reveals that they developed a common sense of purpose and unity that reflected the circumstances in which they found themselves. Their self-definition as a generation also fit within a long tradition of scholastic generations forming inside the higher-education system that began during the Restored Republic of the 1860s.

The Legacy of Scholastic Generations

The tradition of intellectual generations in Mexican higher education, with many later providing a springboard to national politics, originated in the crucial last third of the nineteenth century. From that point forward, at least three distinct generational waves prior to the 1920s group can be identified. The first example had its origins in a short-lived but highly influential publication, *La Libertad*, launched in 1878 by Justo Sierra (later minister of education in the regime of Porfirio Díaz) and several of his colleagues. According to Charles Hale, Sierra and the rest of *La Libertad*'s editorial staff shared common bonds of youth, personal ties, scholastic experience, and previous collaboration.[37] The group formed in the earliest days of the National Preparatory School, founded in 1867 by Gabino Barreda, Mexico's first disciple of French positivist Auguste Comte. Barreda, who applied Comte's scientific explanations of human development to the preparatory school's curriculum, had been awarded the task of creating the country's first viable secular institution of higher education by liberal reformist president Benito Juárez.

The group that formed around *La Libertad*, with Sierra as its intellectual leader, came to rely not only on Comtean positivism but also on a number of other influences, most notably the social-evolutionist theories of Herbert Spencer. Their publication conveyed disdain for the liberalism embraced by the administrations of Juárez and his successor, Sebastián Lerdo de Tejada, which the young students considered incompatible with Mexico's political realities. In its place, they promoted a "conservative liberalism" (as well as an "honorable tyranny"—both terms representing something of a creative exercise in contradictory semantics),[38] one that gave priority to utilizing a stronger central government and stimulation of capitalist development.[39] They regarded much of the mid-century liberal agenda, which sought to eliminate corporate privilege, secularize the government, and create a rural yeoman citizenry, as an abstract project based on a cult of the individual.[40] In their minds, Mexico's renaissance would come after solving social problems by curing the social body, even if this necessitated temporary authoritarian measures, rather than by focusing on affording people expansive rights that carried little practical benefit.

Several members of this group later became some of the most influential advisers to have the ear of dictator Porfirio Díaz during his reign from 1876 to 1911. They were known as the *científicos*, or men of science, due to their belief in the possibility of applying scientific principles to political and social questions. Their unremitting faith in science was a function of both their training in Barreda's preparatory school and the popularity of European positivist thought across Latin America at the time. These leaders eventually held considerable sway over many of Díaz's policy decisions. Indeed, they drew on their academic credentials to legitimate many of the repressive aspects of the regime, casting them as necessary in their society's ongoing evolution. At first glance, one can see a number of similarities between the Porfirian científicos and the Alemán generation. Both groups formed in part due to connections made in higher education, both identified themselves from a young age (in both cases, they were in their twenties) as scholastic generations and would later use their academic pedigrees to launch political careers, and both came to embrace a form of authoritarian leadership.

It remains unclear precisely how much this group influenced the Alemán generation's students. One of Alemán's longtime collaborators, Marco Antonio Muñoz, claimed that Díaz, Plutarco Elías Calles, and Alemán, all known for their authoritarian approach to political administration, represented the nation's three genuine statesmen.[41] Yet despite this statement likening Alemán to Don Porfirio, the subsequent two academic generations, whose influence spanned both the armed and reconstructive period of the revolution, left a far deeper impression on Alemán and his colleagues. Perhaps this was due to the fact that Alemán and his friends had felt the tragic effects of the struggle against the Porfirian establishment in their personal lives. Nevertheless, the *Libertad* generation had some kinship with Alemán's, since it set a precedent for the formation of political cliques in the National Preparatory School and served as a model for the future generations of revolutionary intellectuals who would serve as influential instructors in the 1920s.

The 1910 centennial of Mexico's independence from Spain gave Díaz an opportunity to showcase his nation's promising development and precipitous growth after three and a half decades under his watch. It also galvanized the opposition of several groups, differing in regional, class, and ethnic origins, to his repressive regime as the country moved further into the twentieth century. Francisco Madero's revolutionary movement later that year drew these myriad groups, each with their own distinct goals, into a devastating series of bloody struggles that lasted for more than a decade. What these rebels—representing sectors as varied as poor peasants, agricultural workers, the urban proletariat, the middle class, and provincial elites—all had in common was a dissatisfaction with the results of the Porfirian approach to economic policy and political administration.

Out of this conflict emerged the Athenaeum of Youth, a distinct intellectual group within the National Preparatory School. The Athenaeum's members repudiated the científicos' embrace of positivist education, which they regarded as intellectually stifling and dogmatic.[42] Instead, they pushed for a restoration of the arts and humanities in the curriculum of the nation's premier educational institution. Among the leaders of the Athenaeum were José Vasconcelos, Antonio Caso, and Alfonso Reyes, who all became luminaries of the revolutionary intelligentsia. Additionally, several of its leaders, especially Vasconcelos, became prominent instructors, administrators, and political functionaries in the education system of the 1920s.

The Athenaeum's members did not restrict themselves to waxing philosophical. Recognizing the importance of acting on their convictions to achieve broad-reaching change, they founded the Mexican Popular University in 1912. They organized the university to extend the benefits of higher education to the masses, a plan that embodied their desire to put the arts, culture, and humanities on the revolutionary agenda. Their efforts, though promising, were short-lived. The group disintegrated in 1914, largely because many of its members entered government ranks. In the wake of the

Athenaeum's dissolution, a successor generation, later known as the Generation of 1915, formed around a nucleus of prominent intellectuals later known as the "Siete Sabios," or Seven Sages. This group, which initially called itself the Society for Conferences and Concerts, would ultimately have the most direct influence on the Alemán generation.

Luis Calderón Vega, a founding member of the National Action Party (PAN) and father of president Felipe Calderón (2006–2012), was responsible for nicknaming the leading voices of the 1915 generation the Seven Sages.[43] Its members included Manuel Gómez Morín, Vicente Lombardo Toledano, and Alfonso Caso, the younger brother of founding Athenaeum of Youth member Antonio Caso. If the Athenaeum group began the move away from the positivist paradigm of the late nineteenth century, then the 1915 generation completed the mission through its members' professed desire to extend the benefits of the revolution to the realms of culture and the arts.[44] The group included various intellectuals who would go on to pursue vastly different careers. Three of them—Gómez Morín, Caso, and Lombardo Toledano—became influential instructors for the Alemán group.

Like their predecessors in the Athenaeum, these men were not bound to any single ideology, preferring instead to embrace a wide range of intellectual influences and to reject the orthodoxy of the late nineteenth-century positivists.[45] Moreover, their eclectic intellectual interests in the 1910s did not reflect the political ideologies or programs that they embraced later in their careers. Nevertheless, they, along with a number of other instructors, guided the intellectual development of generations of students, including Alemán's, in the 1920s. Their cohesion as a generation proved especially influential.[46] Many from Alemán's generation recalled the immense influence of Lombardo Toledano and Gómez Morín in their educational formation, a remarkable development given the later career trajectories of these two men. Lombardo Toledano, who served the ruling party and endorsed Alemán, was pushed out of his position within the Confederation of Mexican Workers (or CTM, the official corporate body representing the working class within the PRI) in 1947, and founded a leftist opposition party, the Popular Party, the following year.[47]

Gómez Morín, who became increasingly dissatisfied with the direction of the official party, became the founder and first president of the conservative National Action Party (PAN), which late in the century would align with Christian Democracy before finally wresting the presidency from the PRI in 2000. The intellectual orientation of these two leaders in the 1920s did little to presage their later political pursuits: Lombardo Toledano was known among his students as a spiritualist and had centrist political leanings; it was not until the 1930s that he fully self-identified as a Marxist-Leninist. Gómez Morín, the expert in banking and finance, onetime rector of the UNAM, leading founder of the Banco de México, and eventual leading voice of Mexican conservatism, was known as a leftist who taught Marxist theory in addition to courses on philosophy and ancient history.[48]

Members of Alemán's academic generation favored professors with whom they readily connected or collaborated. The names that most commonly appear, in addition to Lombardo Toledano and Gómez Morín, are Alfonso and Antonio Caso (the former taught anthropology and general legal theory, the latter sociology and philosophy), along with Narciso Bassols, who taught logic and constitutional law. Bassols would later become a devout Marxist and serve as minister of education in the early 1930s before occupying a number of diplomatic and other ministerial positions. Like the academic generations that preceded them, the students in Alemán's classes benefited from wide-ranging intellectual influences. Recalling his courses, Antonio Armendariz noted that they drew influences ranging from Karl Marx to Johann Wolfgang von Goethe to John Maynard Keynes to Georges Sorel. Poetry and literature, including everything from Spain's Generation of '98 to the great Russian novelists, also occupied a major presence in the curriculum.[49] Students complemented their exposure to these foreign works with those of domestic authors. In an interview, Alemán recalled some of their Mexican influences, ranging from the Flores Magón brothers, the anarchists who inspired countless revolutionaries, to the academic works of Lombardo Toledano, especially his "Etica," and those of Luis Cabrera.[50] In his memoirs he also noted the influence he drew from authors ranging from Plato to Erasmus. Other interviewees confirmed that their training was quite broad, and certainly not confined to one overarching ideology or school of thought. As Alemán put it, they were stuck between positivism and anti-positivism,[51] suggesting that while the Porfirian intellectual tradition had fallen out of favor with most professors, it had not been entirely buried. Another former student, Dr. Cardiel Reyes, reiterated his claim, noting that despite efforts to the contrary, the positivism so common during the Porfiriato had lingered. He even counted one self-proclaimed Spencerian (a reference to Herbert Spencer, a leading proponent of social Darwinism and a major influence on the Porfirian intelligentsia) among his professors.[52]

The professors of the 1920s, especially those at the preparatory school, tended to judge the revolution and its leadership in harsh terms. Francisco González de la Vega, who later became a professor upon nomination by Antonio Caso, said that the students who went on to attend law school at the National University actually had better professors at prep school, owing to their relative distance from the regime.[53] Sealtiel Alatriste, who served as treasurer of the Federal District through the majority of Alemán's term, went even further, noting that many of the students cultivated a critical view toward the revolutionary government as a result of their professors' influences. Some students even became embittered over certain professors, as was the case with the poet and writer Renato Leduc, a student in the group. Decades later, he regarded Vasconcelos as a reactionary and a "*cabrón*" (a vulgar insult roughly comparable to bastard or son of a bitch) and disdained the young Daniel Cosío Villegas as a crooked and prententious teacher who, as he put it, "dressed like an Englishman."[54] Nevertheless, Alatriste also noted that this same critical outlook shared by faculty and students ultimately convinced a significant number among the 1920s' generation to enter government in the hope that they could effect more constructive, substantial change.[55]

Beyond the myriad influences described by members of this generation, which ranged from political economy to philosophy to poetry, their most consistent source of cerebral stimulation was Russian literature. Numerous former students, in describing what they read outside of classes, recalled their fascination with Russia's great novelists, such as Tolstoy, Dostoyevsky, and Gorky. Additionally, Andrés Henestrosa and Manuel Palacios both recalled a lesser-known work, by a more obscure author, that also provided significant inspiration. Leonid Andreyev's realist novel *Sashka Zhegulev* follows the story of a young telegram writer who took up arms in defense of his fellow workers. Henestrosa and Palacios recalled that they wanted to be Zhegulev because they found parallels between their own experiences and those of the book's protagonist. The students found the broad themes of these novels—hope, rebellion, and social justice above all—to be particularly captivating.[56]

This sense of idealism was reflected in some of the students' earliest pursuits, including independent publications and student government. As the decade wore on, their political activities became more serious, especially in the student movements and presidential campaign of 1929. Along the way, their idealism not surprisingly gave way to hard-nosed pragmatism.

Nevertheless, the evidence of their early political awakening suggests that Alemán and some of his closest lifelong associates not only came into contact as young preparatory school students in the early 1920s, but also that they came to identify themselves as a generation in those early days.

A New Generation Forms

The arrival of a generation of civilian leaders in 1946 heralded a major shake-up in the personnel composition of the federal government. As Camp has demonstrated through an analysis of over seven hundred former law and preparatory school students who entered public positions in the middle and upper ranks of the national bureaucracy, scholastic training mattered immensely at various levels in facilitating contact and recruitment of political functionaries.[57] This begs the question of whether the members of the Alemán ruling generation had considered themselves part of a distinct generation of students while in attendance at prep school and university. Certainly some distinction should be made between the scholastic generation of the 1920s and the ruling generation of the 1940s. While there is substantial overlap between the two groups, they were not identical or interchangeable. It is nonetheless clear from both their documented activities and their later testimonies that through a combination of intellectual training, political activism, and personal friendships, this group cultivated a generational esprit de corps. Indeed, this commitment to the group, especially its members' tendency to reward political discipline and personal loyalty with financial perquisites, carried into their political careers in subsequent decades.

This generation comprised various members of several graduating classes within the National Preparatory School and National University in the 1920s. Alemán's law school classmates—those who entered in 1925—formed the nucleus of the group, but other members of his and subsequent administrations came to the schools in the years bookending Alemán's entering class. While each did not enter or leave at precisely the same time, their tenures in the schools overlapped, which facilitated contact and collaboration. Examination of the relatively small group that cohered around Alemán provides a richer picture of how this generation formed and how its members' collective experiences provided a foundation for later professional connections (for the full list, see the appendix).

From the outset, a nucleus of ambitious, active students fashioned themselves as a generation. In their first year in prep school, they designated themselves as the Grupo H, following a tradition of lettering one's clique in order to differentiate it from others past and present.[58] Most of the fourteen original members had nicknames. Alemán was known variously as "El Pajarito" (little bird), a somewhat oblique reference to his restless mind, and as "El Flaco" (skinny), a more obvious reference to his thin physique. Gabriel Ramos Millán, a lifelong friend of Alemán's, was known as "The Blind One," owing to his ophthalmia, and as "Jesucristo," because of his appearance.[59] Alfonso Noriega was "El Chato" (snub-nosed), Oscar Soto Maynez "El Chivo" (goat), and Raúl López Sánchez "El Conejo" (rabbit).[60] The boys within the H Group, which eventually came to include Alemán, José Pérez y Pérez, Leopoldo Chávez, David Romero Castañeda, Gabriel Ramos Millán, and Oscar Soto Maynez, among others, made a pact that if one member came into power or money, he would extend a hand to the rest.[61] Its opening statement reveals the extent to which they were aware that they were being groomed for lives as leaders: "Many of us—and we have faith in this—will come to occupy prominent positions in our country's social and political life. They will remain obliged to help those from the group who need it."[62]

The H Group's initial documents included the pact, as well as a manifesto that included thirteen statutes governing the group. Together, these documents made it clear that they intended to create a kind of fraternal organization. The group served no particular social goal and performed no service, nor was it bound to any guiding philosophical or ideological principle. Their expressed purpose, rather, was to ensure that their friendship provided a safety net for members in need. The group agreed to meet monthly; those who missed two consecutive meetings would be expelled, those who did not live up to their pledge of mutual assistance would be punished (the exact nature of the punishment was never specified), and those who wanted to leave had to appeal to the leadership, risking a denial of the request. The pact, which resembled a fraternity charter, points to a pattern of camaraderie and a culture of specifically masculine rituals that defined their social network. These early friendships, bolstered by these sorts of arrangements, laid the foundation for political connections and business associations later in life.

The most tangible evidence of their early politicization was a short-lived but sophisticated student publication, launched in 1924 by several of the prep school students. They called their publication *Eureka*, a reference to their desire to discover new possibilities, and funded the paper largely on the meager allowance that Alemán's father sent him while he was in school.[63] The students used this modest income to print the paper at an independent print shop on Marte Street.[64] How long the publication lasted and how many issues were printed remains unclear, because only the first and third have been preserved in archival collections.[65] These two issues nonetheless convey the optimism of these young students as they lived their salad days in Jazz Age Mexico City.

The editorial staff of the paper included many students who would later rise to prominence during the 1940s. Alemán, credited as the founder, took the position of manager, David Romero Castañeda worked as director, Gabriel Ramos Millán served as the publicity chief, Antonio Ortiz Mena as editor in chief, Adolfo Zamora as artistic director, Manuel Palacios as managing editor, and Oscar Soto Maynez as administrator. In all likelihood, many of the positions provided an opportunity for participation among those students who wanted to contribute. Their personal influence was not particularly apparent on the pages, even though they were responsible for selecting the contributions of a wide range of domestic and foreign writers, poets, and critics. The paper, according to the front page, could be purchased both in the school (for ten centavos) and in the street (presumably meaning newsstands, for fifteen).[66] José Vasconcelos, at that point the minister of public education, was so impressed by the publication that he ordered copies for the library of the ministry.[67]

The content of *Eureka* ranged widely. The paper, which averaged about twenty pages per issue, reserved a small section for news about events at the school and student politics. The rest of the paper reflected the eclectic intellectual interests of the group. Both well-known authors and obscure writers, including current students, received ample attention. Young luminaries with connections to the Alemán group, including future education minister, foreign minister, and UNESCO director Jaime Torres Bodet and prominent muralist Diego Rivera, were featured alongside foreign authors such as Henri Duvernois and Miguel Unamuno. Rivera's piece exemplified a tendency in the paper to celebrate the "*don racial*," the supposedly virtuous racial characteristics possessed by Mexicans.[68] This theme was replicated in an anonymous piece titled "El Flirt," which accused Anglo-Americans from the United States of having no time for the "flirt," an apparent reference to a mistress. Mexicans, by virtue of the "don racial," possessed the necessary spiritual and sensual characteristics to enjoy such company, according to the article.[69]

Both instances point to an embrace of the idea of a "cosmic race." While the notion of *mestizaje*, or racial mixing between Iberian, indigenous, and African populations, was not unique to Vasconcelos, his concept of a cosmic race, imbued with all of the best features of these groups, became the basis of official efforts to define national identity beginning in the early 1920s. In his capacity as education minister, Vasconcelos sought to indoctrinate successive generations with the idea that their culture and society would find its salvation in an embrace of mestizaje. He found substantial inspiration in the eugenics movement, which used ostensibly scientific methods to explain human development in terms of racial determinism (he later embraced Nazism and became an ardent anti-Semite). Indeed, the government continued to define Mexico officially as a mestizo nation until a 1992 constitutional revision recast the country as "pluri-cultural" with indigenous roots.[70]

The paper also contained a number of articles that provide insight into shifts in gender sensibilities and controversies over sex and sexuality that were emerging in the 1920s. The first issue included an exposé on the Escuela Hogar (roughly translated as Homemaking School or Housewives' School) Sor Juana Inés de la Cruz, an institution that trained aspiring housewives in the skills commonly found in home-economics courses, such as cooking, sewing, and table etiquette.[71] The article did not mention the irony that a school that existed to proscribe women's domestic roles was named after Sor Juana, an intellectual nun who in the sixteenth century railed against patriarchal Roman Catholic orthodoxy and who for many represents a feminist icon. Another article, attributed only to the nom de plume Moncrayon (in French, My Pencil), titled "Al margen de las pelonas" (On the Verge of Becoming Flappers), explored the implications of the short haircuts increasingly sported by young women in the 1920s. By comparing them to the iconic flapper girls of the United States, the article suggested that the look was not sufficiently feminine and thus could potentially alienate men.[72]

Esperanza Zambrano, in an article entitled "La mujer que trabaja" (The Working Woman), firmly repudiated the notion that intellectual work might de-feminize women, expressing particular disdain for what she identified as a tendency in society, especially among men, to define women as stupid or docile.[73] Another article in the third issue, called "El wildeísmo," mocked sycophantic imitators of Oscar Wilde. The article accused young men, wearing makeup and speaking in artificially high voices, of being pathetic, disingenuous "maricas" (a derivative of *maricón*, translated as queer) who betrayed the prevailing (and, by implication, more "authentic") macho masculine identity. The author, Albert Meural, did not treat Wilde himself as an aberration of masculine virtue. On the contrary, he regarded the Irish satirist as a noble intellectual, drawing into relief the lamentable behavior of those he regarded as vulgar imitators.[74]

This sampling of the paper's content suggests that it lacked thematic coherency. But what emerges from the pages of *Eureka*, beyond an interest in engaging some of the controversial cultural topics of the day, is the sense that these students were cultivating the self-image of a vanguard youth that would have both the practical skills and the intellectual fortitude to fulfill the promise of the revolution that their parents' generation had initiated.[75] The initial articles, especially those by students seeking to explain the paper's objectives, were written in a deliberately poetic language that emphasized the possibility of transcending the mediocrity into which they felt the country had fallen. This concern with the improvement of the nation's culture and politics found reflection in various places; for example, in attacks on a complacent middle class,[76] or on the philistine artistic tastes of uneducated consumers who, according to the editors, rejected the avant-garde muralists José Clemente Orozco and David Alfaro Siqueiros. The latter critique came in a response by the French artist Jean Charlot, who dedicated the majority of his career to producing revolutionary art in Mexico, to a lack of public outcry over an act of vandalism in which murals at the National Preparatory School painted by Orozco and Siqueiros were badly damaged.[77] The Union of Mexican Catholic Women and a group of conservative students claimed responsibility for damaging the murals. Even Salvador Novo, a poet of the same generation as Torres Bodet and later modern Mexico City's greatest chronicler, found the paintings to be full of anarchistic rage and vulgar depictions of the wealthy.[78]

Beneath the naïveté that one might expect from young students, the publication's importance lies in what it speaks about these students' self-identification as a new kind of generation, a group that had a shared purpose in taking the mantle of their nation's revolution. Years later, members of this generation would recall what they felt distinguished them from their predecessors within the preparatory school and university. In an interview from the 1970s, Antonio Carrillo Flores, Alemán's director of Nacional Financiera and minister of finance in the subsequent administration of Adolfo Ruiz Cortines, confessed that their generation lacked the brilliance of the Siete Sabios, but quickly noted that they had contributed far more to national development. He further asserted that he and his cohort shied away from dwelling on great and lofty ideas, and instead focused on practical solutions to their nation's ongoing problems.[79] Salvador Azuela, the son of famous revolutionary author Mariano Azuela and a fellow student, described their group as a "very civic" and "political" generation, further bolstering the notion that their collective mindset and priorities reflected practical rather than philosophical concerns.[80]

From this publication and the students' later recollections, it is clear that their idealistic tendencies were tempered by a deepening sense of pragmatism and responsibility. Alatriste noted that the harsh assessment of the revolution expressed by their professors helped to fashion their own views, ultimately inspiring them to enter government service. He recalled a course on rural economics, taught by a young Daniel Cosío Villegas, in which the professor noted his profound objection to the creation of an ejido-based rural policy to develop the agrarian sector.[81] Yet it was less a philosophical objection to this and other controversial revolutionary initiatives, and more a sense of pragmatism, that seemed to resonate most with the students. Julio Faesler, a law school contemporary of Alemán, perhaps put it best in noting that the students of his generation adopted the attitude that ideological dogma should have no place in public service.[82]

Many of the students, including several who would later follow Alemán to Veracruz when he became the state's governor in 1936, expressed an early interest in electoral politics. In 1924, in their final year at the National Preparatory School, they organized themselves as the Red Party to run as a slate for the student government. Led by David Romero Castañeda, the group promoted the following candidates: José Pérez y Pérez as president, Arturo García Formenti as general secretary, Manuel R. Palacios as vice president, Adolfo Zamora as secretary, Santiago Guevara as assistant secretary, Marina González as treasurer, and Lucia Cortez as assistant treasurer. The campaign flyer also designated a group of members at large: Miguel Alemán, Antonio Ortiz Mena, Felipe Garcia Ramos, León Gómez Díaz, Oscar Soto Maynez, and Augusto Zehnder. Aside from containing a large number of people who would become recognizable names (e.g., Alemán, Ortiz Mena, Palacios, Soto Maynez), the candidate slate also suggests an increasing presence of women both in political life and in the otherwise male-dominated school system.

The students campaigned on a series of demands that reflected the concerns of the student body. Several addressed the issue of student finances, circulating petitions to provide students free transfers on tramcars, reduced rail fares, more scholarships, discounts at theaters and movies, and tuition reductions in cases of financial hardship. This last demand reflected what former students said about their relative poverty in interviews,[83] something corroborated by school records housed at the UNAM's Center for the Study of the University and Education that document the extent to which students routinely sought temporary relief from tuition burdens.[84] The students also called for more literary conferences, scientific and athletic competitions, and invited talks by distinguished intellectuals. Their platform ranged widely: classes that formerly were held for six months that had been extended to one year were to be returned to the six-month format, and students could decide unanimously to expedite the finishing of a course by demanding an exam on the spot. The proposal also insisted that students get free medical consultation and hospital stays when necessary, and that they have the ability to bypass the physical education requirement with a successful fitness evaluation.[85]

Taken together, these activities demonstrate that the Alemán ruling generation of the 1940s and the scholastic generation of the 1920s, although not synonymous, did more than coincidentally overlap. Rather, the students, including many who rose along with Alemán through the ranks of the political system, formed as a unique generation through both scholastic and political activity. Nevertheless, this accounts for only a fraction of the process of socialization these young men and future leaders underwent. Their personal connections did not occur merely in the realm of formal politics, nor exclusively in the process of engaging in scholarly pursuits. Rather, they rested on a kind of fraternal bond that defined their bohemian existence for the duration of the 1920s. Their friendships deepened their personal relationships with one another at the same time that they helped instill in the group a more urban, middle class–oriented ethos.

Camaraderie and the Culture of Masculinity

The school experiences of these young men, however important they were in creating the basis for later professional connections, cannot be characterized merely as an exercise in political networking. Rather, their day-to-day existence, despite rigorous academic training, was defined by a myriad of social activities. The lives of these young men in their school years were typical of students. Indeed, numerous interviewees noted that they spent their time socializing at concerts, dance halls, political demonstrations, debates, the movies, the theater, cafés, and the residence halls and homes where the students lived.[86] Through these various activities they formed a tightly knit student community.

The rigors of preparatory school demanded that its students devote the majority of their time to study, so they took advantage of the infrequent off-hours. Many of the students set out on excursions at each chance they got. Ernesto Uruchurtu, most famous as the long-serving Mexico City mayor who came at loggerheads with President Gustavo Díaz Ordaz in the 1960s, became known among his student comrades because he had what they did not: access to a car. The automobile, it turned out, was on loan to him from the municipal government, for which he worked as a cabaret inspector. With enough peer pressure, they cajoled him into taking it to Cuernavaca for a weekend trip.[87]

In the city they passed their scarce leisure time in local restaurants, sipping coffee by day and drinking in cantinas at night. Several students recalled specific haunts they frequented—a *café de Chinos* (a café with Chinese-Mexican owners) called América near the Colegio de San Ildefonso (a former Jesuit boarding school that at that time served as the preparatory school's campus), a Russian eatery where they got bread and vodka on the cheap, the Cantina don Pepe, and a bakery on Belisario Domínguez where they discussed plans for *Eureka*.[88] These escapades inevitably led the boys to local girls. It was not uncommon for them to serenade young women with their guitars or to take dates to silent movies, dance halls, tangos, and the theater.[89] Those lucky enough for a second date often went to the girl's house for coffee and cake with her family. Andrés Henestrosa captured the essence of their existence: despite the bleak circumstances of their country after ten years of bloody revolution, they lived a bohemian existence during their time in the capital.[90]

Even with these intense scholastic demands, the students occasionally found themselves in trouble. Alejandro Gómez Arias, later the president of the National Confederation of Students, recalled an instance that led him to the office of José Vasconcelos, at that time the rector of the preparatory school. Gómez Arias, frustrated that he had been removed from the English class of a professor named Stein, hit the professor in a fit of rage. Vasconcelos meted out considerable punishment but ultimately ruled against expulsion.[91] Even Alemán, known for his innocent demeanor and quiet comportment, occasionally got wrapped up in mischief. In one example, he and Alfonso Noriega, after finishing a particularly grueling set of exams, stayed up celebrating in a cantina. They lingered beyond midnight, which appears to have been a curfew point, when the police came and informed the owner he would have to pay a fine for hosting paying customers beyond that hour. Alemán responded by claiming they were not patrons at all, but friends of the owner who were simply having a beer with him. The police, rejecting his alibi, promptly arrested them. Once in jail, they called Andrés Serra Rojas (who, a quarter century later, became Alemán's secretary of labor) to pick them up. The incident gave Serra Rojas the opportunity to hone his skills as an aspiring litigator. With the right combination of logic and charisma, he got the boys out of their incarceration.[92]

The political causes that many of the students pursued also led them into tricky or even life-threatening situations, as was the case with a 1924 movement against plans to install Lombardo Toledano as rector of the preparatory school. Vasconcelos, as education minister, intended to nominate Lombardo Toledano for the position. The students, according to Manuel Palacios, resisted the idea of someone as ideologically slanted as Lombardo Toledano in the position. By this point, Palacios argued, Lombardo Toledano had abandoned the idealism and intellectual freedom that had once motivated him when he was one of the Seven Sages in the 1910s in exchange for a hard-line version of Marxism-Leninism. The students marched to the offices of *El Universal* and *El Demócrata*, two large dailies, standing down a police force led by a particularly vitriolic commander, who suggested he ought to pump the students full of bullets. Palacios chalked the whole event up to cocky and smart-mouthed kids lashing out at authority.[93] In another instance, a number of students joined in solidarity with soldiers who revolted against their commander, a corrupt general. The conflict heated up when military officials loyal to the general beat up a student. According to Renato Leduc, the usually polite and reserved Alemán was so moved by the incident that he screamed, "*¡Que chinga a su madre, Gral. Fulano!*" (Screw your mother, Gen. so-and-so!).[94]

In their descriptions of these various episodes, several of which involved some measure of violence, the former students often wistfully reminisced that they could be so confrontational with police only in the hubris of their youth. To some extent this was true, but these activities, even the ones that seemed foolhardy in hindsight, helped to reinforce the camaraderie among the students as they moved from preparatory to law school, and as they entered the fray of the 1928 and 1929 presidential campaigns.

The Vasconcelos Presidential Campaign

The 1929 presidential contest between Pascual Ortiz Rubio and José Vasconcelos catalyzed the political aspirations of a number of students who would later enter government.[95] Many of the students of the National Law School supported Vasconcelos, who had inspired them both as their professor and as the architect of the revolutionary public-education program. According to testimony from several of the students, many joined because they saw Vasconcelos as the last hope to correct a revolution that had veered off course.[96] The long shadow that former president Plutarco Elías Calles cast over the political scene, not to mention the increasingly effective political machine and authoritarian government that he had helped to build, provided a source of frustration, even desperation, for the idealistic students. To them, Ortiz Rubio, the revolutionary general, official candidate, and eventual winner, represented just another of Calles's cronies. David Romero Castañeda described the general perception among students of the *callista* machine by saying that the revolution had been taken over by generals who, now comfortably in power, sat around drinking cognac and smoking cigars.[97] For many students, the campaign signaled a major turning point in their careers. Its disappointing results made a lasting impression on a number of them at the precise moment when they were leaving law school and entering professional ranks. In particular, the possibility of replacing a broken military establishment with a civilian candidate known for his intellectual prowess and educational achievements motivated these aspiring young leaders. The campaign thus served as both the culmination of their educational experience and a catalyst of future political activism. But well before the 1929 campaign had kicked off, the students had already undergone a long and multifaceted process of political formation over the course of their scholastic careers.

The 1927 movement to block former president Álvaro Obregón from being reelected to the presidency the following year provided something of a dress rehearsal for the 1929 Vasconcelos campaign. Many students, who aligned with those who considered themselves "old guard" revolutionaries, found Obregón's ambitions to reassume the presidency in direct violation of the sacred principle of non-reelection, a cornerstone of the revolutionary movement of Francisco Madero and a critical component of the 1917 Constitution. This anxiety was compounded by what many regarded as a plot hatched by Obregón and Calles to solidify their Sonoran Dynasty and to create an unconquerable political machine, over which they would preside as alternating presidents.

Fear of this outcome prompted the reactivation of an anti-reelectionist movement and party, modeled on Madero's original proposal nearly two decades earlier to prohibit elected officials from serving more than one term in any given position. Several students from the National Law School attended the fourth National Student Congress in Oaxaca, which had been convened to promote the anti-Obregón cause. In Mexico City, students went further than engaging in pacifist demonstrations and conferences. Palacios recalled demonstrations of more than ten thousand, and one gathering in which students, who had been threatened with death by local authorities, descended upon the *Jardín de San Fernando*, chanting "*¡Muera tu madre, Ortiz Rubio!*" (Death to your mother, Ortiz Rubio!) and carrying matches and gasoline to burn the garden in protest of the death of a fellow student.[98] Such tragedies reminded the students of the risks of political activism. Efraín Brito reminisced about the death of another fellow student, Ramón Armijo, who had been killed in the 1927 campaign while working for Col. Carlos I. Serrano, a venerable political figure from Veracruz who remained close to Alemán throughout his political career.[99]

Despite the efforts of the students and others, Obregón was elected, but he did not live to see his second inauguration. On July 18, 1928, the president-elect was shot to death at a luncheon in a restaurant in the suburban San Angel district of Mexico City. The assassin, José de León Toral, was a Catholic militant frustrated by the anti-clerical crusades of the Sonoran presidents. While the assassination became a national tragedy, it eased the preoccupation of many that the commitment to non-reelection had been eroded. Their relief proved to be temporary. Although Palacios recalled students dancing in joy upon hearing of the fallen revolutionary president, their excitement was tempered in the short run by the somber atmosphere following his death and in the long run by the ultimate result: a consolidation of Calles's informal power. Indeed, Obregón's death allowed Calles to strengthen his grip on his country's politics. In a masterful act that made him appear tactful and minimized his vulnerability to critics (and would-be assassins), Calles declared that he would not seek the presidency, and instead installed a temporary president, Emilio Portes Gil, who, he expected, would function as his puppet.

Recognition of the extension of Calles's power further galvanized opposition from the sectors that had already supported the anti-Obregón movement in 1927 and 1928. Thus, when the next presidential campaign began to heat up in 1929, many students threw their support behind Vasconcelos, the only remotely viable opposition candidate. In various interviews and writings, several students explained their reasons for joining up with the Vasconcelos campaign. The candidate, famous as a founding member of the Athenaeum of Youth and progenitor of the concept of a "cosmic race," had served the country through a distinguished career in education, in which he was director of the National Preparatory School, rector of the National University, and minister of education. In the latter capacity, he built thousands of rural schools across the republic, helping to extend the benefits of literacy and learning through a vigorous program of universally accessible secondary schooling that the government called socialist education. Thus, many students had at least some personal experience with Vasconcelos, and others who had not encountered him personally certainly felt the impact of his work. Some derived more selfish benefits from the campaign. For instance, Alejandro Gómez Arias, who served in 1929 as the president of the National Confederation of Students, rode with Vasconcelos through the opulent Bosques de Chapultepec neighborhood in the candidate's Lincoln (according to Gómez Arias, a very young Adolfo López Mateos, president of the republic from 1958 to 1964 and a member of a later scholastic generation, was also there).[100] Some students later claimed to have followed Vasconcelos merely because it seemed like the right thing to do, given his leadership role in the construction of the revolutionary socialist-education system.

Most had deeper convictions. Many students shared with "old guard" revolutionaries the idea that Vasconcelos could lead an effort to renovate the revolution. Large segments of society, especially peasants and workers in need of material improvement, veterans wanting to see their military efforts transformed into substantial reform, and students looking to see their idealism fulfilled, were deeply disappointed with the increasingly authoritarian Sonoran leadership. Vasconcelos, though far from perfect, was their chance at salvation.[101]

The students, despite forming a sizeable base for Vasconcelos, did not stand in unanimous support of the former education minister. Alemán, for instance, was among those who did not figure among his supporters. Palacios suggested that Alemán, despite his support of the anti-reelectionist cause, found Vasconcelos too romantic and too radical, and thus ill suited for the presidency. He further claimed that Vasconcelos had accused the students of representing a "bureaucratic generation," to which they collectively responded by asking, what was Vasconcelos if not a bureaucrat?[102] Some of those who did support him, such as Henestrosa, acknowledged that they knew he stood no chance against the Calles political machine.[103]

The resounding defeat of Vasconcelos at the hands of Ortiz Rubio left many of the students disillusioned. It nonetheless helped to guide them into politics.[104] Henestrosa claimed that above and beyond every other lesson the campaign provided, it made his generation aware of the paramount importance of winning in politics.[105] Antonio Carrillo Flores, who became Alemán's director of the public-development corporation Nacional Financiera and later minister of finance and minister of foreign relations, reiterated this sentiment, suggesting that while many students were attracted to the romance and optimism of the Vasconcelos movement, its failure ultimately taught them that to effect change, one must work with the instruments of power, not against them.[106] Several of the lessons that this group took away from the campaign—a desire to work within rather than against the system, a preference for pragmatism over abstract idealism, and a desire for a civilian system—directly informed their approach to public administration in the coming decades.

The same year that Vasconcelos suffered sound defeat at the hands of Calles and his chosen candidate, university students pushed temporary president Emilio Portes Gil to grant the National University total autonomy from the government. As Henestrosa would note decades later, some supported Vasconcelos because they felt obligated to do so. By contrast, the autonomy movement, which sprouted from a student strike in protest of a grueling trimestral exam schedule,[107] had more unanimous support, and students acted with profound conviction that only if the university were free from government control would it be able to foment free thought. The quick success of the university-autonomy movement, unlike the grueling and ultimately disappointing presidential campaign, buoyed the students' spirits as they began the transition from their student years to their early professional careers.

Conclusion

The 1929 Vasconcelos presidential campaign served as both the educational capstone and the political baptism of many of the students who would rise to national prominence in the 1940s. It gave many of them their first taste of the ruthless tactics and frequent disappointments inherent in political activity.

In doing so, it fostered a deep appreciation for the pragmatic tools necessary for political survival. But well before the 1929 electoral campaign, the experiences that the students gradually accumulated throughout their school years also prepared them for the demands of national politics and, at the same time, instilled in them an ethos that would prove to be remarkably different than that of their predecessors. Much of their political agenda would reflect this shared world view in subsequent decades.

These scholastic experiences, which took place principally over the decade of the 1920s, represented the first half of their political education at a critical time for their country. The 1920s encompassed a series of profoundly transitional experiences. On the one hand, lingering violence, including the de la Huerta revolt in 1923 and the Cristero rebellion of 1926–1929, combined with an increasingly authoritarian government, led many to question what the revolution had actually accomplished. On the other hand, the decade witnessed a period of rebuilding, one that gave many, including the students in Alemán's generation, a great sense of hope. This ambivalence, or perhaps this balance between optimism and discontent, swayed many of the students toward political activism. Subsequent developments, beginning with the creation of an official party in 1929, would draw them into public careers.

Thus the 1930s and the first half of the 1940s marked the second phase of the College Boys' political education. Now out of the classroom, most of the young men in Alemán's cohort embarked on private careers in law and finance. Many would continue to engage in private-sector activity for the rest of their lives, but they quickly entered public positions as well. Again, the context provided them new and unanticipated motivations. The new official revolutionary party quickly expanded into an expansive, corporatist entity, creating opportunities for young, civically engaged men to become public functionaries. The members of this growing bureaucracy, along with people who found careers in the growing urban-industrial sector in technical and professional fields, formed a large portion of the increasingly important urban middle class. Thus, the rise of the first civilian generation of leadership within the official party coincided with the rise of an urban middle class that, for the first time, grew to become the dominant voice within national politics by the late 1940s. This generation shared many of the same values with this group, and would later channel those priorities into concrete policy during Alemán's six-year term.

In this next span of time, the student group of the 1920s diffused into different regions and forms of employment. In the case of Alemán, a chain of events, some planned and others coincidental, helped him into a series of political offices in Mexico City, then in Veracruz, then again in the capital. For support he turned to a small group of his closest friends, most of them from school, bringing them to the state capital of Jalapa. They immediately earned an unflattering reputation as interlopers. Even though Alemán was born and raised in Veracruz, residents of the state nonetheless treated him otherwise—as yet another outsider from Mexico City who had come to take over state politics. Competence and luck allowed him to overcome those suspicions. On the surface, his governorship (1936–1939) does not seem as remarkable or colorful as a handful of others during the Cárdenas years (especially those that represented some form of opposition to national authority). Nonetheless, it represented a major period in his and his generation's evolution as leaders and prepared them for entrance onto the national stage.

CHAPTER TWO

Entering the Establishment

ALEMÁN, ALONG WITH TWO OF HIS CLOSEST SCHOOL COLLEAGUES, Gabriel Ramos Millán and Fernando Casas Alemán, established legal careers in Mexico City immediately following graduation.[1] Alemán's early victories in litigation, most notably a major suit he won for approximately four hundred mine workers afflicted with silicosis, suggested that his career in law held great promise. His advocacy for mine workers had a personal dimension: he had written his law school thesis on workplace accidents and workmen's compensation law,[2] his two brothers had worked as mine laborers in the early 1920s,[3] and his father had fought and died in revolutionary struggle. During this early phase of his career, he also served as a consulting attorney with the Ministry of Agriculture, giving him his first exposure to government service. Despite his successes as a litigator, his legal career endured only a short time, as business and political activity ultimately came to occupy the majority of his professional attention.

The transition from school to professional life came at a propitious moment for Alemán and his schoolmates. The collective educational and professional experience of their generation provided its members the opportunity to enter into the growing ranks of the nascent urban middle class. Alemán and his colleagues joined other aspiring young professionals in business, law, and technical fields, as well as the rapidly expanding public bureaucracy. Regardless of their family or class backgrounds, the members of this group thus adopted both the professional orientation and the everyday lifestyle of the urban bourgeoisie. Over the course of the next decade and a half, as the middle class grew from a comparatively minor interest group to the dominant voice in national politics, their early professional careers provided them the material support to pursue their political ambitions.

As students in the 1920s, Alemán and his friends had defined themselves as part of a vanguard generation. This gave them, as they saw it, a mandate to pursue lives in politics. As leaders within this scholastic generation, they assumed the responsibility of carrying their country into a new phase of political and social development. Alemán's experiences as an attorney, businessman, bureaucrat, governor, and cabinet minister provide insight into a moment that was fundamentally transitional both for the members of this group and for their country. The ambition, vision, and pragmatic skills that he and numerous others from his generation acquired in school during the 1920s, coupled with the opportunities for social and political mobility that emerged during the 1930s, allowed them to move from being poor students to powerful politicians in the decade and a half after their graduation.

Alemán's time as governor allowed him to apply many of the values that germinated in his scholastic years to the more difficult task of governing. During this phase of his career, he benefited from equal measures of astute planning and sheer luck. His term also overlapped some of the busiest years of the populist administration of Lázaro Cárdenas, allowing him to prove his loyalty to the president and to demonstrate his administrative capabilities as the state government's chief executive. His political acumen as governor caught the attention of the national leadership. Cárdenas's successor, Manuel Ávila Camacho, made Alemán his campaign manager and rewarded him with the powerful Ministry of the Interior upon taking office. Alemán's tenure as the ranking cabinet minister during World War II gave the population a glimpse of the combination of political skill and personal opportunism that he possessed. He used the post to convert his presidential ambitions into a reality by securing crucial alliances within the party. By the time Alemán became president, he had solidified his position not only as the undisputed figurehead of national politics, but also as the standard-bearer for a generation a quarter century in the making. The development of the political system, and of the group that would steer it into the Cold War years, can thus be traced through his experience.

Alemán in Transition

Alemán and Ramos Millán, best friends throughout their years in school together, teamed up to expand their earnings through investments. Together they formed Fraccionamientos México, a real estate–development company that operated under the slogan, "Don't fear the six zeroes,"[4] a catchphrase that conveyed their overwhelming confidence as they transitioned into professional life. They began by pursuing modest projects, first in small residential housing developments in Mexico City. Eventually, those investments grew to pay substantial dividends that they in turn reinvested.[5] In his autobiography Alemán described Ramos Millán's business sense as "clairvoyant,"[6] underscoring that his friend functioned as the principal financial strategist in the company. Longtime friend David Romero Castañeda claimed that Alemán, whose primary interest was always politics, functioned as something of a silent partner, while Ramos Millán acted as the real investment maven. In fact, Alemán's presence, while universally acknowledged, was rarely mentioned or acknowledged on paper.[7]

With a small but growing base of investment capital originating from their earnings as lawyers, they bought residential property in Cuernavaca, which soon emerged as a favorite weekend spot for prominent Mexico City residents. They also bought land in what later became the suburb of Satellite City, built during Alemán's presidential term. Along with Antonio Ortiz Mena and Carlos I. Serrano, they bought property in the Rincón del Bosque section of Bosques de Chapultepec, the increasingly upscale residential section of Mexico City preferred by the city's elite. At the same time, Alemán and several associates invested money into his home state, including the Hotel Mocambo and related tourist developments along the Veracruz waterfront. He kept the majority of those interests until ascending to the governorship.[8] These myriad investments allowed him to pursue his political ambitions without financial worries[9] and provided capital for future investments both during and after his presidency.

A number of important personal changes occurred in Alemán's personal life in these years. In 1929 his father died supporting the rebellion of Gonzalo Escobar. Within a year his brother Carlos and mother Tomasa moved to Mexico City. By this point Alemán had invested in several residential properties in the capital and was thus able to provide his mother housing.[10] According to Tomasa's brother, Pedro Valdés, Alemán was known to be especially protective of his mother, a sentiment that only grew after her husband's death.[11] During his political career, she would occasionally appear, often alongside his and other politicians' wives, to do charity work[12] (Alemán's wife, Beatriz Velasco de Alemán, would later help to found the Red Cross in Veracruz and establish a charity to help the children of poor refugees in exile due to the Spanish Civil War as the state's young First Lady).[13] In those years preceding Tomasa's relocation to Mexico City, when her son was off at school and her husband's military activities had once again picked up, it appears that she received very modest financial support from family and former associates of General Alemán.[14]

That first year after General Alemán's death proved difficult for the entire family. Miguel Alemán Velasco, the son of President Alemán, noted that he had a letter from his father's brother, Antonio, detailing their hardship and explaining that they would need to sell their cattle back home in Sayula in order to make ends meet.[15] Both of Alemán's brothers had worked in mining, living with their grandmother to avoid paying rent, in order to support the family, something Miguel had done at the El Aguila petroleum refinery in Coatzacoalcos.[16] Meanwhile, Miguel forced himself to continue to wrap up his law training and then to establish his career. This period, though hard on all the family members, was relatively brief, since his career, and with it his financial security, began to improve quickly.

In 1931 Alemán married Beatriz Velasco, a young woman studying home economics and known for her domestic proclivities.[17] Seven years his junior, Velasco was born in Guanajuato, but her family ultimately settled in Veracruz. The pair met in 1928 in Tampico, where Beatriz was living with her sister, Aurora, and two brothers, Luis and José.[18] After her father's death, the elder brother, Luis, became the head of the family.[19] Alemán became good friends with the entire family, especially her two brothers, and stayed in contact with Beatriz. The two reacquainted in Veracruz, where Alemán frequently had tea with the girl's family.[20] Eventually, she moved with Alemán back to Mexico City, where they lived together. Alemán recounted those years with fondness. The city had severe problems with crime and violence, but the two and their friends nonetheless enjoyed its parks, cinema, and *zarzuela* (popular musical theater) shows. Beatriz's mother, Columba, became a close friend of Alemán's mother, as well.[21] Even in these upbeat circumstances, the road to marriage occasionally proved rocky: Velasco once broke up with Alemán because it appeared he had no future, a feeling that was amplified when he spent their wedding savings on a new car.[22] Within a few years her hunch proved incorrect, and in 1931 they wed in a small, modest ceremony in Mexico City's Iglesia de San Cosme. Since neither family had much money to contribute, after the ceremony the attendees were rounded up and taken in rented cars to a restaurant called El Retiro, located in front of Chapultepec Park.[23] Following that, the two took a brief honeymoon in San Antonio, Texas, where they saw Charles Lindbergh's airplane, the Spirit of St. Louis.[24] At this point, Alemán, now comfortably married and professionally established, set his sights on politics.

Several of Alemán's friends recalled his early political ambitions. According to some accounts, those political leanings were coupled with a desire to make money. One of Alemán's close friends and later a political associate, Manuel Ramírez Vázquez, noted that as early as preparatory school, Alemán recognized that the Ministry of the Interior (of which he served as secretary from 1940 to 1945) was the ticket to "la grande," presumably meaning the presidency.[25] Of course, the idea was not entirely novel: a few presidents had served in the position, most notably Plutarco Elías Calles, prior to ascending to the nation's highest office. Yet it certainly was not the stepping-stone to the presidency that it became from Alemán onward (Alemán, Adolfo Ruiz Cortines, Gustavo Díaz Ordaz, and Luis Echeverría all served in the position before the presidency, and Ernesto Uruchurtu moved from the position to his long tenure as mayor of Mexico City), suggesting that his hunch about the ministry proved especially prescient. Another longtime Alemán associate, David Romero Castañeda, noted Alemán's early desire to obtain substantial wealth but remembered also that ever since their school days his primary interest had been politics.[26]

From 1932 to 1936 Alemán held a series of short-lived but crucial political positions that culminated in his ascent to the governorship of Veracruz. He and a number of associates first ran for office in 1932. All lost (Alemán having run for federal deputy), save for the veteran politico Gen. Cándido Aguilar, who would later be instrumental in supporting Alemán's bid as incoming governor of the state after the 1936 murder of governor-elect Manlio Fabio Altamirano in Mexico City.[27] Alemán's loss may nonetheless have done more to help than to hurt his career, because it gave him visibility and allowed him to establish valuable contacts, especially with General Aguilar.[28] When Lázaro Cárdenas came to power in 1934, he awarded the young, ambitious Alemán a seat on the Superior Court of the Federal District. Cárdenas had originally proposed that he serve on the Supreme Court, but age requirements disqualified him from serving on the high court. At this point still relatively obscure beyond a small circle of political observers, Alemán's political career had begun.

In 1935 Alemán, along with a group of Veracruz politicians, spearheaded the creation of the Socialist Group of Veracruz, an organization created to sponsor candidates under the umbrella of the PNR. The next year constituents elected him to the Senate as part of a slate proposed by his newly formed group. His career in the Senate had barely begun when a strange turn of events cut his time there short and unexpectedly put him in the governor's seat. This unanticipated development allowed his career to flourish under the aegis of Cardenismo.

A Mostly *Cardenista* Governor

As governor from 1936 to 1939, Alemán became one of president Lázaro Cárdenas's closest allies. Their productive working relationship in the 1930s has been overshadowed by the sharply contrasting ways in which scholars have interpreted their presidencies. At first blush, Cárdenas, the consummate populist, appears to have had virtually nothing in common with Alemán, the debonair businessman president. The former became known for an agenda that addressed the plight of the nation's poor, while the latter embraced the ideal of a modernizing, industrial society. These competing images, while simplifying and exaggerating their differences, nonetheless make Cardenismo and Alemanismo seem like polar opposites along the spectrum of the country's twentieth-century politics. Yet in the 1930s, the two had a mutually beneficial working relationship. Cárdenas found a governor capable of implementing national policies and bolstering federal authority, while Alemán sharpened his own political approach in part through his adherence to the six-year plan of the Cárdenas government.

Alemán oversaw a period defined more by consolidation than sweeping change in Veracruz. Compared to the more radical administrations that preceded his own, especially the non-consecutive terms of Gen. Adalberto Tejeda in the 1920s, Alemán's government was seen as relatively conservative. By the time he resigned his office and left for Mexico City to answer the calling of higher political office, rural landholders and urban capitalists had emerged as more powerful political actors, while workers and peasants had lost ground. On the surface this would seem to put Alemán at odds with Cárdenas, so often celebrated for his populist tendencies. Yet the two were close collaborators, and their relationship shaped not only the young governor's policies but also his political style. Alemán's three-year tenure in the governor's office allowed him to demonstrate loyalty and discipline by adhering to the president's six-year plan and to form an inner circle to serve as a prototype for a future administration. In doing so he clarified his political approach, and by the end of his gubernatorial term had emerged as a major presence in national politics.

As is so often the case in politics, Alemán's fortune came at the expense of another's tragedy. Alemán and the man originally elected governor in the 1936 election, fellow civilian Manlio Fabio Altamirano, had campaigned together on a PNR-sponsored slate, with Alemán as the Senate candidate. Altamirano possessed formidable charisma and used a stirring language of socialist reform aimed at the state's poor rural majority.[29] Known as a fervent orator, he, like Alemán, ran as a representative of a new generation attempting to distinguish itself from the military veterans who had controlled state-level politics since the earliest days of the revolution.

Yet while the state's landholding elite eagerly supported Alemán's political aspirations, they viewed Altamirano with disdain, regarding him as a radical out of step with the conservative direction they were anticipating in state and national politics. Thus, even if Altamirano commanded the support of the majority in Veracruz, a poor and predominantly agrarian state, he nonetheless created powerful enemies.[30] Veracruz became a study in the varying shades of Cardenismo. Altamirano, who had a personal friendship with Cárdenas, represented the most leftist streak to identify as *cardenista*. Others in the state, among them Cándido Aguilar and eventually Miguel Alemán, would remain loyal to Cárdenas but would nonetheless exhibit far more conservative tendencies.[31]

On June 25, 1936, Altamirano was gunned down in Mexico City's celebrated Café Tacuba. No precise narrative of the crime has ever been established, and no assailant was ever tried in court, but the most commonly accepted explanation implicates Manuel Parra. Parra, one part landed oligarch and one part cold-blooded gunslinger, was notorious for heading the informal paramilitary organization known as the Black Hand. The organization maintained a jail rumored to torture its prisoners and profited from an expansive network of contraband in liquor and sugar. In the case of Altamirano's assassination, various theories exist. The most dominant of them alleges that Parra provided 5,000 pesos to a pair of thugs, Gildardo Lobillo Martínez and the actual shooter, Rafael Cornejo Armenta, to assassinate Altamirano in the capital.[32]

While the precise details have never been unearthed, Parra's involvement is generally taken for granted. More surprising, given his shady reputation, is that in the years to come Parra maintained a supportive relationship with Alemán once he became governor. But Parra's interests closely aligned with

Alemán's. While Parra offered little in the way of transparency, he is rumored to have been instrumental in persuading Alemán to support the presidential candidacy of Manuel Ávila Camacho to succeed Cárdenas. Accounts also suggest that Parra further consolidated his influence within Veracruz under the governorship of one of Alemán's successors, Jorge Cerdán. According to one of the more disturbing anecdotes about Parra, when a local cell of the CTM (the PRI-affiliated organized-labor sector) accused Parra and Cerdán of being anti-worker fascists, he personally arranged for the deaths of eight hundred of the union's workers. Whether or not the story is true, Parra was a potent force in Veracruz politics and almost certainly displayed his influence through his involvement in Altamirano's assassination.[33]

The assassination left PNR leaders scrambling. For them, stabilizing the political establishment in Veracruz was a far greater priority than seeking justice for Altamirano's murder. Thus on July 9 the National Executive Committee of the PNR issued a statement saying that the state's party could hold an internal election to find its candidate within fifteen days.[34] A special election ensued, but by that point, Alemán's victory was all but assured, since he had secured the endorsement of the state's political elite. On the night of Altamirano's wake, the state's political elders met at the fallen governor-elect's house in Mexico City to determine who would replace him. A few representatives, most notably Fernando López Arias and José Murillo Vidal, objected to Alemán as the choice. As members of the PNR's State Executive Committee, they threw their support to Alemán's opponent, Veracruz PNR president Manuel Zorrilla Rivera.[35] Despite the objections of these two leaders, Alemán gained enough support to become the official candidate.

Alemán benefited from the endorsement of Gen. Cándido Aguilar, a former *carrancista* governor who maintained a position of considerable influence in state-level politics, more than from any other supporter. Some considered Aguilar to have been the state's most powerful person, and he quickly emerged as Alemán's patron.[36] Aguilar, along with Alemán, had reportedly attended the meeting held after Altamirano's wake, where he made a forceful effort to promote the young, promising son of a celebrated *jarocho* general.[37] Indeed, for most of the 1930s, Alemán was hardly known as anything other than his famous father's son. While this initially prevented him from establishing his own political identity, it also provided him an entry into state politics.[38] The younger Alemán and Aguilar could connect over the military legacy of Gen. Alemán, a fact that evidently helped him in his relations with President Cárdenas as well. Aguilar and Alemán had been associates since Alemán unsuccessfully ran for elected office in the early 1930s.[39] While his earliest campaigns immediately following school did not place him into elected office, they ultimately benefited his career more in the long run, since he began to cultivate his long-standing relationship with Aguilar.

Still, Alemán would later have to create some distance from the general as he became ever more domineering. As longtime colleague David Romero Castañeda noted, Aguilar's efforts to dominate Alemán only caused the young governor to push him further away from the center of decision-making in the state later in his career.[40] Nevertheless, the rift between the two would not happen for some years. In the crucial early phase of his governorship, when he needed to establish his legitimacy, Alemán thrived under the patronage of Aguilar. Their relationship smoothed the generational transition from a military-dominant to a civilian-based governing class at the state level.

Alemán proved adept at balancing the various political interests in the state and was particularly successful at placating the old hands of the state's political establishment. In particular, he maintained productive relations with the state's most powerful revolutionary military leaders. Beyond Aguilar, these included Gen. Heriberto Jara (the head of the 26th Military Division), Col. Carlos I. Serrano (a fixture of state and national politics and later a close friend of Alemán's as a PRI senator), and Gen. Adalberto Tejeda (the former governor of Veracruz). At the same time, he helped usher in a new cadre of young, primarily civilian leaders.[41] Jara, who became president of the PNR during Alemán's term, counted on the support of the young governor for the position. The case of Veracruz thus demonstrates that the arrival of a new political class did not happen all at once in the 1940s at the national level. Rather, the members of this ruling generation stepped into political office during the Cárdenas period, gradually moving the military generation aside without fundamentally or abruptly upsetting the balance of power.

The relations between the "old guard" revolutionary leaders and these emergent civilian politicians demonstrate that the process of transition in the 1940s from military to civilian leadership at the national level began a decade earlier, as leaders came to power at the state level. The national party leadership assisted in the process of introducing new functionaries, in large measure to cleanse the party of any lingering loyalties to exiled former president Plutarco Elías Calles. A 1936 circular from Emilio Portes Gil, the president of the National Executive Committee of the PNR and former president of the republic, instructed state PNR presidents to stamp out "*continuismos*" in politics, indicating that party leaders should welcome new—meaning non-callista—blood.[42]

By his own admission, Alemán, who did not have the extensive and loyal personal network of veteran allies that someone like Aguilar would have been able to summon, had to rely on the only one he had.[43] For that reason, he called on a number of the students with whom he had attended school in Mexico City to move to Jalapa, the state's capital, to help him govern. A few were originally from Veracruz, but the majority came from elsewhere. They came to be known as the Polacos (Poles or, more accurately, despite its contemporary pejorative connotation, Polacks), a reference to their status as outsiders that recalled a small community of Polish immigrants that had settled in Jalapa. Those opposed to their presence also labeled them *chilangos*, a reference to residents of Mexico City.[44] Their consternation is not altogether surprising. The nation's long tradition of regionalism was often expressed at the local level as opposition to perceived outsiders, and something that seemed like imposition from Mexico City would most certainly have been met with particular dissatisfaction.

The group was relatively small, and several noted that Gabriel Ramos Millán, Alemán's close friend and business partner, was the one who contacted and recruited them.[45] In this respect, he functioned much like a chief of staff for the incoming governor. Alemán appointed the majority as judges in the state court system. These included Fernando Román Lugo, who had not quite finished law school and came into office at twenty-two years of age.[46] He served alongside Oscar Soto Maynez, Manuel Ramírez Vázquez, David Romero Castañeda, Raúl López Sánchez, and Ernesto Aguilar Álvarez, all of whom had been close friends in school. Numerous others from his school circle received posts in both the executive and judicial branches: Ramos Millán served as an official (*visitador*) in the state's Superior Court of Justice; Enrique Parra Hernández, later Oaxaca's governor, was president of the Central Committee for Conciliation and Arbitration, while Marco Antonio Muñoz served as its general secretary; Manuel Heredia was director of the Department of State Assets (*Bienes del Estado*); Rogerio de la Selva was Alemán's personal secretary (a position he would hold from then through Alemán's presidency); and Fernando Casas Alemán (Mexico City's mayor during Alemán's presidency) became the general secretary of government, with Silvestre Aguilar serving as undersecretary.

From the outset the group generated skepticism and even some measure of scorn, especially from those who had been shunted aside by this new cadre of young leaders, which appeared to have been imposed from forces above and outside the state's traditional political circles. Several of Alemán's contemporaries made reference to the suspicions that the presence of these young outsiders, most of whom had no roots in Veracruz or its politics, created in the minds of citizens. Alemán in his memoir recalled that many from the group, especially the young Fernando Román Lugo, attracted a great deal of suspicion due to their age. He nonetheless defended his decision to hire Román Lugo in spite of his youth because of his political talents, though it is probable that their social and professional ties, coupled with Alemán's desperation for administrative personnel, played a significant role as well.[47] Even one of Alemán's gubernatorial opponents, the independent candidate Amado J. Trejo, expressed doubts about Alemán's relationship to Veracruz. In an article published by the Revolutionary Youth Front of Veracruz, he argued that Alemán's ascent to the governorship, if it were to occur, would be in violation of a state law that demanded that the candidate live full time in the state for five years prior to entering office. He also accused the pro-government newspaper *El Nacional* of a bias in support of Alemán. Since Alemán had been living in Mexico City almost continually since school, and since his business, legal, and political affairs and primary residence were all located in the national capital, in Trejo's eyes he was clearly ineligible for office.[48]

These criticisms certainly did not fall on deaf ears. Within two years Alemán had replaced many of the Polacos with leaders from Veracruz.[49] Decades later several contemporaries, including Andrés Henestrosa and Ezequiel Coutiño, accused the Polacos of having personal motives of their own, alleging that their primary motivation for coming to Alemán's aid when he was thrust into the governor's office was not only political but also financial gain.[50] Others claimed that Alemán's own plan all along was to use his good political fortune as a stepping-stone to the Ministry of the Interior.[51] Indeed, while some of the inner circle from Veracruz never ascended to the highest echelon of national politics, others, including Fernando Casas Alemán (who served as interim governor after Alemán left to run Manuel Ávila Camacho's presidential campaign in 1939 and then as the mayor Mexico City) and Rogerio de la Selva (who carried considerable responsibility as Alemán's presidential secretary), followed Alemán to the capital during his presidency, and underlings, such as future president Adolfo Ruiz

Cortines, rose higher within state ranks. But however coherent Alemán's plans may seem in hindsight, in reality there would have been no way of mapping out his political future in such linear terms. What is certain is that Alemán used Veracruz as a kind of "microcosm," as his friend and colleague Marco Antonio Muñoz put it, for his approach to governing the nation a decade later.[52]

By most measures Alemán's governorship did not look as noteworthy or as colorful as a handful of others during the Cárdenas period, but it nonetheless demonstrates how a disciplined and effective cardenista governorship functioned. In the first years of his presidential administration, Cárdenas sought to purge the country of leaders loyal to Calles. These included Rafael Villarreal in Tamaulipas, Tomás Garrido Canabal and his powerful *cacicazgo* in Tabasco, and Saturnino Osornio in Querétaro.[53] The president succeeded in eliminating these powerful allies of Calles, then Calles himself. Other governors could not be vanquished so easily, making the process of centralizing executive authority at the national level uneven and incomplete.

Cardenismo, often polemically exaggerated for either its mass-inspired or its authoritarian characteristics, proved to be a variable and dynamic program. During the Cárdenas years (1934–1940), popular radicalism combined with strong executive rule, while national centralization competed with stubborn regional intransigence, creating a period of governance fraught with contradictions. Several governors proved either unable or unwilling to tow the line for the president.[54] In certain cases, such as the Yucatán, where Cárdenas sought to implement one of his largest land-redistribution efforts, the governorship and state administration were not sufficiently stable to allow a productive linkage between national policy and state-level implementation.[55] In the case of other governorships, such as those of Román Yocupicio in Sonora or Juan Andreu Almazán in Nuevo León, the governors had sufficient local support to resist cardenista reforms and, by extension, the president's efforts to create a more centralized national government with increased presidential control.[56] Almazán, favored by conservative interests wary of the radicalism associated with Francisco Múgica, the presumptive favorite of Cárdenas for the 1940 election, maintained a loyal army in his home state. And the case of Saturnino Cedillo, the maverick caudillo of San Luis Potosí, proved that some leaders could mobilize loyal constituents to mount armed rebellion against Cárdenas, even if the *cedillista* insurgency ultimately failed.[57]

Despite the efforts of these governors to derail Cárdenas's six-year plan, the president, with the help of disciplined governors such as Alemán, succeeded in implementing an ambitious reform agenda.[58] Alemán spared no effort in demonstrating his loyalty to Cárdenas. Out of necessity, the president was equally eager to cultivate alliances with governors interested in doing business. As governor, Alemán undoubtedly derived political benefit from the general state of agrarian affairs in the second half of the 1930s. At the beginning of his gubernatorial term, the political organizations representing the interests of the rural poor were not only divided, but also prone to the violence that typified revolutionary agrarian conflict. By the end of his term he had managed to unite the disparate Red (radical, self-identifying as socialist and originally allied with Tejeda), Yellow (pro-reform and cardenista, but comparatively moderate), and White (conservative and explicitly anti-cardenista) agrarian leagues, and on March 28, 1937, he hosted the PNR-sponsored Congress of Campesino Unification in Jalapa.[59]

The language of agrarian unification put a positive spin on what was in fact a contentious process, one that arguably produced more losers than winners. While the quelling of rural political factions promoted a general state of peace, it also required that the more radical strains of the agrarian movement be cowed into submission. Moreover, while Veracruz saw a rapid acceleration of land reform in line with Cardenismo, as well as the construction of numerous public works such as highways and tourism installations,[60] large commercial landholders made the biggest long-term gains under Alemán's gubernatorial administration. Not all of this was due to Alemán. Rather, the Cárdenas administration offered exemptions protecting valuable banana, coffee, cocoa, sisal, and fruit plantations from agrarian reform. Alemán merely used these decrees, which had significant relevance to Veracruz and its wealthiest landowners, to his advantage.[61]

At first glance, a state-level agenda that put the interests of landed oligarchs over rural workers seems out of step with Cardenismo, so often celebrated for its populist character. In one sense there is some validity to that position, yet Cardenismo—and certainly the earliest version of Alemanismo in Veracruz—relied on corporatism, the process of drawing organized labor into disciplined organizations with strong linkages to the government. As governor, Alemán did precisely that by drawing rural laborers into the National Peasant Confederation (CNC). If his approach was more conservative than Cárdenas's, this was something the president could accept, given how much outright opposition he encountered from other state governors.

Thus, Alemán and Cárdenas maintained one of the most productive presidential-gubernatorial partnerships of the time, a demonstration of pragmatic sensibility on the part of both. The stability achieved at the state level allowed the federal government to carry out major land reforms. During his tenure as governor, Alemán also managed to promote the construction of significant public works (especially highways), to address ongoing literacy problems, and to provide a stimulus to the state's tourism industry.

Alemán proved to be skilled at the pragmatic responsibilities necessary for successful political administration. In certain cases, that meant smoothing over conflicts or accepting limitations placed on his authority, as he had to do in his relationship with Aguilar. In other cases, it meant demanding and exercising increased executive authority, something that happened concurrently at the state and national levels. On at least two occasions, he petitioned the state legislature for temporary but significant extensions of power. In June 1937 he proposed a new law that gave the governor unconditional authority over every executive department while the legislature was not in session. He explicitly stated his intention to resolve a rent-control law that had remained unfinished in the legislative term. The legislature granted him the request, and did so again in December of the same year, thus amplifying his authority in both cases.[62] Alemán contracted with an attorney from Guanajuato, Ernesto Arnoux Siqueiros, to write some of the centerpieces of his legislative agenda in 1937, including his Housing Law, his Law on Public Assistance and Pensions, and his Law on Expropriation.[63] The ease with which Alemán set his legislative agenda into place suggests an efficient, responsive gubernatorial administration. This, along with his loyalty to Cárdenas, set Alemán's governorship apart from many of the others of the period.

The rent-control law extended from a political debate that Alemán inherited. In 1922, during the administration of Tejeda, protesters in the port of Veracruz, and afterward in the state's other major cities, took to the streets to demand justice from usurious landlords.[64] While their protests prompted only minor reforms and ultimately led to repression, the issue remained alive through Alemán's term. His law put a ceiling on urban rents, ostensibly a pro-worker gesture, but in reality strengthened the position of homeowners by making legal eviction for non-payment of rent far easier than it had previously been.[65] In the end, the rent-control legislation fell into the pattern of favoring capital over labor that would become a familiar facet of Alemanismo.

The most dramatic opportunity to display unity with Cárdenas came in 1938, when the president expropriated the assets of all foreign oil companies operating in Mexico. While in the early 1930s Alemán, along with Luis I. Rodríguez, at that time the president of the PNR, originally opposed moves toward expropriation, by 1938 it appeared both logical and necessary due to ongoing disputes between foreign oil companies on one side and organized labor, the Mexican government, and the Supreme Court on the other.[66] Alemán, along with Rodríguez, acted decisively in organizing a conclave of governors in solidarity with Cárdenas's expropriation and nationalization of the petroleum industry. The governors of Tabasco, Tamaulipas, and Puebla were the first to join the effort. Alemán, who only two years earlier was a relatively minor figure in state-level politics, presided over the governors' meeting, giving him wide national exposure. His aggressive efforts to align with Cárdenas on the petroleum question in order to recruit others to the cause endeared him to the president. It also gave Alemán a boost with his own constituents, since Veracruz possessed the nation's largest oil reserves.

In later years Alemán faced criticism for displaying opportunism in his support of the expropriation. Before the end of Cárdenas's term, he had retreated from his initially enthusiastic position, a switch that Antonio Carrillo Flores described as an astute, pre-meditated maneuver.[67] Suspicions about his motives as governor increased after his administration in the following decade altered the charters that governed PEMEX, the state-run corporation in charge of all oil-related operations, opening it to private investment, including foreign capital. In his posthumously published autobiography, he rejected any implication that his support of the expropriation had been a politically calculated move, explaining that the expropriation, in the context of Cardenismo, had been an appropriate measure that represented the culmination of a long social, economic, and political process. Furthermore, he correctly noted that by the 1940s PEMEX had become an inefficient drag on an economy that was experiencing a temporary slump after the Second World War.[68]

The fact that Alemán initially supported the expropriation as governor, only to retreat from that support as president, reflected more than anything else the shifts in geopolitical circumstances that occurred between the Cárdenas era and the postwar years. Moreover, the partial privatization of PEMEX during his administration formed part of a broader objective to secure credit from the United States. As with most major policy decisions, doses of realpolitik, compromise, personal commitment, and political loyalty all factored in the decision. Thus, characterizing the changes in his position over time as a demonstration of a lack of political principle ignores the significant structural changes that occurred over the course of more than a decade. The reorganization of PEMEX represented less a betrayal of the revolution and more a prudent decision to correct the administrative shortcomings of the agency that had emerged by the mid-1940s.

Alemán succeeded in creating an administration that proved efficient, disciplined, and relatively popular, but he could not escape all criticism. Letters written to national officials provide some insight into the types of concerns harbored by citizens. The ones relayed back to Alemán, usually by the Ministry of the Interior, indicate those that the federal government considered worthy of a response. One citizen accused Alemán, upon leaving the governor's office, of accepting numerous bribes, including 500,000 pesos (about US$94,300) from the Jalapa Power and Light company and another 100,000 pesos (about US $18,900)[69] from an association of coffee growers to ensure that their property would not be expropriated, along with another 500,000 pesos from beer manufacturers seeking to keep their product categorized as a "bebida refrescante" (soft drink) to avoid the high taxes levied on hard liquor.[70] Some critics alleged that his inner circle made money by manipulating the licensing and taxation of alcohol, and others claimed that his administration favored capitalists and large landowners at the expense of the state's poorest residents.[71]

Another letter sent to Alemán by the undersecretary of the Interior contained a complaint about the extent of nepotism in the state government. The author listed numerous members of the Alemán and Valdés families in government: Juan Valdés, the governor's uncle and municipal president in the capital, who had been the official candidate of the PRM; Dr. Carlos Alemán, the director of Public Assistance (*Beneficiencia Pública*) and secretary of the Regional Committee of the PRM; Fernando Casas Alemán, the general secretary of government (an erroneous claim—Casas Alemán had no actual familial relation to Miguel Alemán, despite the coincidence of name); Xicoténcatl Ley Alemán, the governor's cousin, who had been the only candidate in Cosamaloapam; Frocopio Alemán, the municipal president of Hueyapam de Ocampos and a relative of the governor; Alejandro Alemán, another of the governor's uncles, the municipal president of Santana Rodríguez; and Gilberto Alemán, another relative of the governor and president of the Muncipal Council of Puerto México.[72]

Similar complaints from citizens can be found in the public files of nearly every governor or other major public official and thus must be regarded with a high degree of skepticism. But complaints from high-profile public figures merit special attention. In one such example, former governor Adalberto Tejeda, a popular and influential public figure, wrote directly to Cárdenas, complaining about the extent of corruption in the state's government.[73] He wrote his letter in mid-1939, just after Alemán had resigned as governor to run Ávila Camacho's presidential campaign, leaving Casas Alemán as the interim governor. Even if Alemán had left Veracruz, Tejeda's letter nonetheless can be regarded as an indictment of the administration of Miguel Alemán, since Alemán had brought Casas Alemán and the majority of public officials at the state level to power. Indeed, Casas Alemán remained part of Alemán's inner circle through his presidential administration and years later was considered a possible presidential contender.

The criticism extended beyond Alemán. A military official, Captain Manuel Hernández, also wrote to Cárdenas, alleging that longtime Alemán colleague Col. Carlos I. Serrano had robbed the state's treasury and was flaunting his wealth by purchasing two cars and living on his own hacienda. He extended his accusation by saying that Alemán could not intervene in these illegal affairs because Serrano had provided his gubernatorial campaign with 50,000 pesos (about US$13,900[74]) the prior year.[75] This and the other accusations suggest that Alemán not only generated criticism, but that the criticism was over many of the same issues (especially cronyism and corruption) that would damage his reputation during his presidential term and his legacy long afterward.

Alemán's commitment to Cárdenas was cemented in 1938, first with the national oil expropriation, then with the revolt of Saturnino Cedillo in San Luis Potosí. Alemán took an immediate lead in opposing Cedillo's movement. In *El Dictamen*, a leading Veracruz newspaper, Alemán's picture appeared next to Cárdenas's, alongside a manifesto signed in San Luis Potosí by every other governor of the republic denouncing Cedillo's actions.[76] By uniting disparate agrarian leagues in 1937, Alemán was also able to align the League of Agrarian Communities and Peasant Unions of the State of Veracruz with Cárdenas over the issue of Cedillo the following year. In a manifesto released on May 23, 1938, the confederation denounced Cedillo as a money-grubbing, counterrevolutionary, anti-proletarian, pro-imperialist fascist.[77] The pileup of adjectives only underscored Alemán's efforts first to centralize the state's agrarian interests, then to keep them committed to the president's interests. Beyond these gestures of alliance with the president, Alemán on numerous occasions demonstrated an ability to appeal to the president's pragmatic sensibilities.

As governor, Alemán faced increasingly aggressive demands for women's suffrage. In a memorandum that he sent to the incoming governor, which was also published as an article in *El Nacional*, former president of the republic and then-PNR president Emilio Portes Gil noted that women had begun to demand the same advances that the working class had achieved with the revolution.[78] At the state level, Alemán and other politicians at the time faced a movement for women's enfranchisement that had gained momentum both from the international suffrage movement and from the revolutionary efforts to increase political incorporation across society. A 1936 letter to Alemán from the Municipal Feminine Committee of the PNR in Veracruz, for instance, demanded that women in public office should also be members of the PNR. They claimed that Cárdenas supported their position.[79]

According to Fernando Román Lugo, the longtime Alemán collaborator who had been part of the original *Polaco* group, the young governor also attempted to incorporate former opponents into his government. In the case of Fernando López Arias, a fellow student who had originally supported Zorrilla, Alemán succeeded in drawing him into his fold.[80] Alemán appointed him to serve first as a magistrate, before he ascended to the position of president of the Regional Commission of the PNR.[81] During Alemán's presidential term, López Arias would again become an objector: he helped found the Popular Party alongside former CTM head Vicente Lombardo Toledano, the new party's leader. However, during the late 1930s the two worked closely in Veracruz while Alemán was governor. Their relationship suggests that the student group, while close, did not guarantee cooperation between all alumni.

Román Lugo and Rodríguez both claimed that Alemán ultimately talked Cárdenas into selecting Manuel Ávila Camacho as his successor.[82] According to both of them, Alemán correctly simplified the situation for the president: Juan Andreu Almazán had gained considerable ground, but was too conservative and anti-cardenista. Francisco Múgica, one of the radical voices within Cárdenas's cabinet, would be too polarizing a choice at a time when powerful interests had grown tired of the administration's aggressive reform efforts. Alemán therefore recommended that the president consider a moderate candidate who could generate broad popular support and find a middle road between the two extremes. Ávila Camacho fit the bill. It also appears that Ávila Camacho, as Cárdenas's secretary of defense, had sized up Alemán while the latter was governor, asking the president what he thought of Alemán and his leadership. Alemán and Ávila Camacho eventually cultivated a personal relationship, to the point that the general got Alemán to ride horses with him, an activity not normally associated with Alemán's urbane lifestyle. This process of mutual vetting led Alemán to the conclusion that Ávila Camacho had the mettle to succeed Cárdenas, and Ávila Camacho to the realization that Alemán should run his campaign and sit in his cabinet.[83] Alemán resigned in 1939 from his position as governor to run Ávila Camacho's campaign, moving with his family to a new home on Durango Street in Mexico City.[84]

During his term as governor of Veracruz, Alemán matured quickly as a politician. By the time he left, he had developed a series of political traits that served him well in his positions of national leadership, first as minister of the Interior and then as president. Above all, he understood the role of the governorship as one that should be powerful within the realm of state politics but subordinate to presidential authority. This became a persistent theme in his later public offices. In the coming years, Alemán would transform the position of interior secretary to one of major influence within the executive branch partially through his relations with governors.[85] As president, he demanded discipline from governors, and he helped to orchestrate the removal of several who did not fall in line.[86]

Beyond his insistence on discipline, Alemán also honed his skills in political networking and public administration to survive and benefit from a difficult political transition. His ability to navigate the simultaneous rise of a new civilian generation and the gradual diminution of the revolutionary veterans as a political force proved difficult in practice, since the generals did not simply wither away at once. The task of managing existing political networks, populated primarily by the military generation and containing more than a few dominant and charismatic personalities, at the same time that he tried to build his own circle, required a high degree of improvisation on his part. This was all the more true given his rapid ascent to the governor's office, which necessitated a kind of on-the-job education.

The Alemán governorship, in sum, proved to be important on a number of levels. First, it produced a balance of positive and negative practical results. Rural peace came at the expense of autonomous labor organization, while a decline in militarism in state politics made way for a cadre of ambitious young civilians eager to reward themselves with the spoils of political office. Second, it reflected the context of Cardenismo. While scholarship has emphasized the more obstinate governorships, such as those of Cedillo and Yocupicio, Alemán's comparatively stable gubernatorial term embodied the twin forces of national state consolidation and state-level implementation of national policy that together solidified single-party rule. Thus, Alemán's term from 1936 to 1939 made him into a model cardenista governor. Third, the strategies that Alemán pursued as governor foreshadowed the kind of leader he would become at the national level. The qualities that he would bring to his presidency were thus born in his school days and incubated in Veracruz. The next step in his political evolution would come in the first half of the 1940s, when he occupied the powerful position of minister of the interior.

Back to Mexico City: The Ministry of the Interior during World War II

Alemán, despite his close and mutually supportive relationship with Cárdenas, would ultimately play a part in orienting national politics away from Cardenismo. His support of Ávila Camacho's selection as the official candidate represented the first step in that process. The general, known more for his administrative capabilities than his battlefield prowess, proved to be a moderate, transitional candidate and president, possessing neither the radicalism of Múgica, his leading competitor within the party, nor the opportunism and conservatism of Almazán, the most threatening of the opposition candidates. These qualities, coupled with a personality that conveyed a sense of competence, if somewhat blandly, made Ávila Camacho a superb choice in the eyes of Cárdenas and an acceptable one for the electorate. In spite of the momentum that Ávila Camacho was able to build, problems persisted: the campaign and election day both saw considerable violence, including an attempt on Almazán's life in Monterrey and several other skirmishes,[87] and it is widely acknowledged that while he most assuredly won the election, Ávila Camacho's results were nonetheless padded by fraud.[88]

Beyond the day-to-day management of the campaign, Alemán's responsibilities extended to official business for the presumptive incoming president. From the outset, Ávila Camacho placed a considerable amount of trust in his hands. In August of 1940, just after he had become president-elect, Ávila Camacho sent Alemán to Washington. During his visit, he assured undersecretary of state Sumner Welles that the radicalism of the Cárdenas period would not be replicated under Ávila Camacho. His trip earned him and Ávila

Camacho kudos from the United States. To express his government's positive impression, Vice President Henry Wallace attended Ávila Camacho's inauguration that December.[89] Alemán's trip to Washington, as well as the vice president's presence at the inauguration, signaled both an opening in US-Mexican relations and the confirmation that Alemán had arrived as a major figure in his country's politics. Indeed, a diplomatic mission of this sort would normally fall under the jurisdiction of a country's foreign minister; since Ávila Camacho was still president-elect, he had more flexibility in his choice of personal emissary. Consequently, Alemán moved into the view of US officials, something that he worked to his advantage after Ávila Camacho threw Mexico's support to the Allies during World War II. For his efforts in managing the campaign, Alemán was rewarded with the powerful Ministry of the Interior. Heading the most important cabinet ministry during World War II allowed him to make a series of astute decisions that ultimately resulted in his ascent to the presidency.

Ávila Camacho's decision to declare war against the Axis precipitated a series of internal and external political changes. Numerous members of his administration, as well as a majority of the public, had expressed hesitation over entering the conflict, which they regarded as something external to the national interest and to the revolutionary government's goals.[90] Nevertheless, mutual security and economic concerns almost inevitably drew the United States and Mexico closer together, and after German U-boats sunk the Mexican oil tanker *El Potrero del Llano* off the Florida coast in May 1942, then the *Faja de Oro* later that month, Ávila Camacho issued a formal declaration of war. His government's support of the Allies helped to end three decades of turbulent bi-national relations that included two maritime invasions and a punitive expedition led by Gen. John G. Pershing, as well as lingering tensions produced by the Cárdenas administration's oil expropriation.

Mexico and Brazil were the only Latin American countries to provide direct military support during the war, with Ávila Camacho sending the air unit known as Squadron 201 to the Pacific theater. The squadron, which included around thirty pilots, known as the Aztec Eagles, along with approximately three hundred ground crew personnel, toured the Philippines in the final weeks of the war. Its participation represented a largely symbolic gesture of support to the United States. Mexico's other contributions, on the other hand, which included metals, foodstuffs, inexpensive manufactured goods, and temporary migrant laborers, proved invaluable to the war effort.

The economic and military arrangements between the two nations also brought domestic benefits, providing simultaneous impetus to Mexico's nascent industrial base and to its export sector, both of which had flagged through the prior decade of global economic recession.

The circumstances of war increased the relative authority of the executive branch. Ávila Camacho, like many of his counterparts throughout the world, assumed emergency wartime powers. His wartime authority permitted him to quell factional struggles within the official party and to thwart opposition from outside it. Above all, his National Unity campaign sought to undo the polarizing aftereffects of Cardenismo by reuniting opposing factions of the Revolutionary Family, beginning with the orchestration of a public détente between former presidents Plutarco Elías Calles and the man who sent him into exile, Lázaro Cárdenas. The exigencies of the war also allowed Ávila Camacho to bring organized labor in line with presidential authority.[91] The CTM, which once exerted considerable political influence on behalf of its working-class membership, agreed to declare a moratorium on strikes in order to ensure a successful war effort. Finally, the military, despite the role of the officer corps in persuading Ávila Camacho to go to war, diminished considerably in its political authority during the war years. While Cárdenas had made the military a corporate sector with the party's reorganization in 1937–1938 in order to keep a lid on potential dissent or rebellion by drawing it closer to presidential authority, Ávila Camacho took the opposite approach, stripping it of its corporate status entirely. By the end of his term, its political role had been circumscribed considerably. The reduction of the military's presence in national political affairs coincided with the rise of a largely civilian-based political class during the Ávila Camacho years.

The process of consolidating and extending executive authority was not confined to the presidency. During the first half of the 1940s, Alemán redefined the Ministry of the Interior.[92] Indeed, his tenure as the ranking cabinet minister shaped the position into the most reliable stepping-stone to the presidency and extended the reach of its authority in ways that would become crucial during the Cold War. The extensive formal powers and informal influence he accumulated owed much to the context of the war and benefited his political ambitions considerably. As interior minister, Alemán oversaw national intelligence and security services. The domestic intelligence community was transformed during the war from a relatively ineffective presence to a professionalized force, and security functions once belonging to other ministries such as treasury fell under the control of the interior minister.[93] In the process, the intelligence service and its central agency prior to 1947, the General Directorate of Political and Social Investigation (DGIPS), also became more politicized.[94] Through the 1940s, its agents increasingly came to serve the interests of the ruling party and the national leadership, allowing Alemán to track political trends and the activities of opposition groups and various social sectors. The expanding intelligence and security apparatus also helped Alemán to solidify his relationship with fellow Veracruz native Adolfo Ruiz Cortines. As the Ministry of the Interior's *oficial mayor*, its third-ranking position, Ruiz Cortines oversaw the coordination of police intelligence-gathering activities, allowing the two future presidents to work together within the ministry.[95]

The Ministry of the Interior was charged with overseeing the business activities of foreigners and held responsibility for the immigration services. Under Alemán's watch, German and Japanese-owned enterprises and property were confiscated by the government, which provided a steady revenue stream during the war years.[96] The ministry was also responsible for setting up a concentration camp at Perote, Veracruz, for German and Japanese prisoners of war and people with family or ethnic backgrounds of the Axis countries. Despite the hard rhetorical line against the Axis and the punitive measures taken against both foreign nationals and Mexicans of German, Italian, Austrian, and Japanese descent, the Ministry of the Interior nonetheless made a number of exceptions to its anti-Axis policies. Alemán and other officials in various departments of the Ministry of the Interior benefited from their relationships with individuals who officially qualified as enemies. In other cases, there was considerable gray area. The wealthy Swedish industrialist Axel Wenner-Gren, for example, invested considerable sums of money in Mexico, even as he was blacklisted by the Allied powers due to suspicions about his relationship to the Axis.[97] Subsequent evidence has suggested that the claims about Wenner-Gren's Nazi connections were false, with some indicating that he opposed the führer. Nevertheless, it is surprising that such a high-profile figure, one who had been blacklisted by the United States and Great Britain, was such a welcome presence in Mexico.

Alemán's relationship to German nationals in Mexico, especially prior to the formal declaration of war in 1942, stirred both domestic and foreign suspicions about his allegiances. Along with a majority in Ávila Camacho's cabinet, Alemán had privately opposed Mexico's entrance into the war.[98] Still, throughout its duration he benefited from association with both sides. His relationship with German nationals living or traveling in Mexico can be traced back to an incident that occurred during his last year as governor of Veracruz. A yacht from the United States, called the *Blue Eagle*, was apprehended in Veracruz by port authorities after its captain appeared to evade their requests to board the ship. In the midst of investigation of the ship, which turned out to have been full of morphine and opium, Alemán intervened and ordered the Coast Guard to allow the ship exit.[99] No further inquiries as to why a yacht full of narcotics would be allowed exit at a governor's request were made, bolstering existing evidence of a Nazi-funded narcotics ring that operated in Mexico in the late 1930s.

Other instances corroborate the pattern of allegations of association between Alemán and individuals representing the Axis. One pervasive rumor suggests that Alemán accepted a ship full of Jewish refugees from various European countries fleeing the Nazis. After being turned away at New Orleans, as the rumor has it, the ship first sailed to Cuba and ultimately to the eastern seaboard port of Tampico, where the interior minister accepted the passengers in exchange for a substantial bribe.[100] Even Alemán's romantic associations drew criticism. There is strong evidence that he (along with Ramón Beteta, who would go on to become Alemán's treasury minister) had an affair with Hilda Kruger, a German dancer and alleged Nazi spy. While Kruger's Nazi contacts were never proved during her time in Mexico, the potentially embarrassing romantic entanglement between her and Alemán raised eyebrows at home and abroad. Kruger was eventually arrested by US authorities while visiting New York on a dancing tour following her time in Mexico City.[101]

The Ministry of the Interior charged Alemán and other high-level officials with the responsibility to decide who could enter the country and to determine the status of Axis nationals living in Mexico. Their positions on these matters were inconsistent. Alemán and other Ministry of the Interior officials, including Ruiz Cortines, earned a reputation for accepting bribes from Axis nationals to allow them to avoid prison sentences in the Perote concentration camp or forced resettlement in Mexico City. In doing so, Alemán and other political leaders allegedly accumulated cash for future campaign war chests.[102] Similar allegations against other Ministry of the Interior officials abound. While not directly linked to Alemán, they point to a pattern of cooperation between various departments within the Ministry of the Interior and Axis nationals. The presence of Abwehr (German intelligence) spy rings in Mexico also occurred largely as the result of relaxed regulations and a culture of bribery within the Ministry of the Interior.[103] Two close associates of Alemán's, Jorge Viesca from the Ministry of the Interior's legal department and a Secret Service agent named Schoeninger, were implicated in a plot to sell arms and manufacturing tools on the behalf of a Japanese firm in Shanghai. Viesca later arranged the departure of Arthur Jost, ex-captain of the *SS Orinoco*, and then collected 50,000 pesos (about US$10,400[104]) in connection with the release of the ship's interned German and Italian crews. Oscar Peralta of the ministry's immigration department was also accused of allowing suspected Axis agents to remain in the country, and Secret Service agent Alfonso García González also allegedly had improper dealings with Axis nationals in Mexico.[105]

The news magazine *Proceso* made a similar accusation. According to one of its editors, Miguel López Azuara, Alemán offered protection to Dr. Kisso Tsuro, a Japanese magnate acting as an Axis spy in Mexico, because of Alemán's direct interest of more than 2.2 million pesos (about US$460,000[106]) in Tsuro's petroleum, mining, and commercial enterprises in the country.[107] While each of these anecdotes of improper dealings would be impossible to substantiate, when taken in sum Alemán's various associations with Germans in Mexico and pro-Axis agents point to a pattern of shifting wartime alliances. His ability to remain officially committed to the Allies while exploiting opportunities for personal gain with the enemy exemplifies his shrewdness as he set his sights on the presidency.

An examination of Alemán's career from 1940 to 1945 reveals the ways in which he grew as a political operative within a changing political climate. The Ministry of the Interior positioned him at the center of national politics, giving him access to everything from foreign business contacts to confidential intelligence. By the end of his term, he had made behind-the-scenes arrangements with the majority of governors for their support and had gotten similar commitments from the party's critical sectors that they would pledge their support for his candidacy when the time came. Even Cárdenas, who was rumored to have favored Gen. Miguel Henríquez Guzmán,[108] agreed that maintaining party discipline and unity within the Revolutionary Family was more important than pushing for his own preferences. Through the campaign, the popular former president's public support of Alemán never wavered. As the world moved from global war to a restoration of peace, Alemán emerged as the likeliest candidate to lead Mexico into a new phase of internal development and international engagement.

The most peculiar feature of Alemán's transition from interior minister to presidential candidate was the fact that, despite holding a highly visible public office and having extensive formal authority, he was a mystery to most. To this day, many of his activities during this period remain the topic of speculation and rumor. His personality, especially his reputation as a debonair playboy, was a source of fascination, yet his unclear wartime political sympathies made him something of an unknown quantity. In the first half of the 1940s, he remained officially pro-US while avoiding being painted as a US lackey, something that plagued his only serious presidential opponent, the foreign minister Ezequiel Padilla. At the same time, while officially committed to the war effort against the Axis, he in fact benefited politically and financially from his ties to German interests in Mexico. His background and previous positions on domestic issues made him unpredictable. By most counts, he was considered a reform-oriented, liberal (though by no means radical) leader who sought improved economic and diplomatic cooperation with the United States (but within some boundaries, unlike Padilla).[109] Again Alemán displayed a consummate sense of political tactics and foresight. Unlike the majority of his opponents, as well as failed former candidates for the official party's nomination and opposition leaders, it was nearly impossible to pin him to any controversial position. Through the duration of his term at the Ministry of the Interior, his politics kept observers guessing, which minimized his vulnerability to criticism from any one interest group, at home or abroad. Yet as his presidential ambitions became public knowledge, Alemán had little choice but to clarify in his campaign the kind of president he intended to become.

The 1946 Presidential Campaign: Establishment Politics with a Folksy Touch

Alemán's time as interior minister provided him an opportunity to build support for a run at the presidency. A number of factors aided his rise. The first of these factors was the fact that his principal opponent for the party's nomination, Ezequiel Padilla, generated far more popularity abroad, especially in the United States, than at home. The left dismissed him as too pro-US; the right reviled him for his vigorous prosecution of Catholic militant José de León Toral, the assassin of Álvaro Obregón, when he served as attorney general in the 1920s.[110] While Obregón's death was seen as a national tragedy, Catholics saw Padilla's pursuit of the death penalty for the pro-Cristero assassin as an excessive measure. The most vigorous support that

Padilla's campaign received came from the US ambassador, George Messersmith, who praised the foreign minister, a personal friend, as competent and effective. His views of Alemán were decidedly more negative. In his estimation, Alemán was an opportunist with little political skill and even less personal virtue.[111] His criticisms, which he rarely substantiated with concrete evidence in his correspondence to the State Department, were coupled with a more valid concern over Alemán's dubious relationship with the Axis during the war. Despite Messersmith's protests, Alemán had secured the support of higher authorities within the State Department, who recognized that he had the selection locked up.[112]

The second factor that smoothed Alemán's road to Los Pinos, the presidential residence, was the death of Maximino Ávila Camacho, the outgoing president's mercurial brother. Maximino, the brooding, boastful former governor of Puebla and the state's undisputed political kingpin, had routinely embarrassed his brother with his public vulgarity, chronic womanizing, and violent temperament. He publicly declared that he felt entitled to the presidency, owing to the fact that his brother (whose presidency he found preposterous; he once called Manuel a steak with eyes) occupied the post. He also possessed a formidable hatred for Miguel Alemán, to the point that he promised to kill him if his brother were to choose him to be the next president.[113] As minister of transportation and communications in his brother's administration, he grew wealthy from privileged access to information about soon-to-be-lucrative investments and cuts from private contractors.[114] Therefore, he certainly would have had the financial resources for a campaign. Nevertheless, he had failed to piece together a base of political support during his brother's administration, as Alemán had done meticulously. Therefore, it is unclear what kind of presence he would have had in the 1945–1946 campaign. In either case, his death removed a notoriously loud obstacle to Alemán's political ambitions.

Despite the antipathies that Maximino Ávila Camacho displayed toward Alemán, the two had worked together while they served as governors of their states. Ávila Camacho, in one instance, wrote directly to Alemán about a plot to place dynamite under a train moving from Orizaba to the city of Veracruz. He reported that other men had been arrested previously for similar reasons, and that another man had been taken in for spreading pro-Cedillo propaganda along the line, drawing an apparent link between the Cedillo revolt, railroaders, and the bombing suspect.[115] A reply from the state's Confidential Services office in Jalapa informed Ávila Camacho that it would open an investigation into the event.[116] While no final report has been located to confirm how the situation ended, the episode nonetheless demonstrates a temporary measure of cooperation between the two governors that would eventually fade into mutual animosity.

The third factor that aided Alemán was his success in securing the support of organized labor. Vicente Lombardo Toledano, whom Ávila Camacho had removed as head of the CTM in 1941, nonetheless remained on the Executive Committee and also served as the moral leader of the union confederation, making his support invaluable. Lombardo Toledano was by no means especially enthusiastic about Alemán, but he had reason to be cautiously optimistic: Alemán had a personal and professional background in pro-labor politics, self-identified as a pragmatic reformist, and came from a revolutionary family. Moreover, during World War II, he displayed his official support for the Allies, but he was never especially vigorous in his support of the United States. Above all else, the simple fact that he was not Padilla, a man Lombardo Toledano regarded as little more than a yes-man for the United States, gave Alemán credibility with organized labor.[117] Therefore, Lombardo Toledano threw his support to Alemán as a last-ditch effort at political survival and because he could not stomach the idea of Padilla in Los Pinos.

Even though Alemán had secured the support of critical party sectors, governors, and Cárdenas, he nonetheless feared that Padilla might end up as the more appealing option to Ávila Camacho, since his international prestige stood at high tide. At the conclusion of the war, Padilla represented Mexico at the 1945 San Francisco conference that laid the foundation for the formation of the United Nations. As he had done before, he made a positive impression on US leaders, generating especially effusive praise from Messersmith. Alemán, troubled by the possibility that Padilla might gain ground, made a shrewd maneuver: by resigning in June 1945, he forced the hand of Ávila Camacho, even as the president had insisted that possible candidates avoid what are known in Mexico as *futurismos*—open attempts to gather information and drum up support. Since his resignation could signal nothing except a declaration of candidacy, Alemán in essence forced various groups to show their cards early.[118] When it became immediately evident that he had the support of sector leaders and governors, along with a positive public image, the rest of the field gave up. Padilla ran a weak opposition campaign for a hastily formed new party, the Mexican Democratic Party (PDM), while the other candidates, including Federal District mayor Javier Rojo Gómez and

Gen. Miguel Henríquez Guzmán (who launched a more formidable effort six years later, in 1952), faded from the electoral scene. Ávila Camacho was left with little choice, and Alemán's path had been cleared from the beginning of all major obstacles.

The twenty-one official roundtable conferences conducted by the Alemán campaign in 1945 and 1946 served both pragmatic and symbolic objectives.[119] In practical terms, they allowed the candidate, whose victory was assured in the upcoming July election, to meet with representatives of the party's corporate sectors, along with industrialists, technicians, and engineers. Moreover, they permitted the incoming president to gain specific knowledge of local conditions as well as the desires and needs of constituents throughout the republic. For many reasons, the roundtable discussions provided a two-way benefit for the new president and the citizenry. He succeeded in gaining technical knowledge and in clarifying the six-year plan his administration would pursue, while citizens gained an understanding of the person who would navigate his country into the post–World War II period.

Symbolically, the roundtables underscored the incoming administration's efforts to fashion itself as efficient and modern.[120] In particular, they allowed Alemán to juxtapose his own style and approach to that of his predecessors, especially Lázaro Cárdenas. Whereas Cárdenas forged his populist image by traveling deep into the remotest villages, often on horse or donkey, to pose while eating tacos and hearing peasant demands, Alemán made one stop per state, usually in the capital city. Rather than reaching out to the masses, he received a representative from each sector who had been nominated by the organization. To convey a sense of personal appeal to counteract the impersonal qualities of the roundtable talks, Alemán's campaign relied on the sound of son jarocho, the typical popular music from his home state. The bands that played at campaign events always struck up the genre's most iconic tune, "La Bamba," creating a connection between the candidate and the music of Veracruz. In sum, the roundtable conferences contained equal measures of practicality and political theater.

Some, especially those from the opposition, saw the events more as propaganda than as genuine efforts to engage citizens and provide a campaign that was responsive to their interests and demands. Writing to Manuel Gómez Morín, the ideological leader of the National Action Party (PAN), fellow party leader Efraín González Luna commented from Guadalajara in February of 1946 that his city was on the verge of being exposed to the "well-known routine" of the PRI campaign.[121] He also referred to the roundtable meetings as little more than gatherings of businessmen that wreaked havoc on the host city.[122] González Luna expressed dread about what would happen: blocked streets, halted public services, closed schools, and a flood of paid shills in the streets.[123] At the conclusion of the campaign stop, his bitterness was unconstrained. He considered the roundtable discussions to be nothing more than a "masquerade" put on by the Alemán campaign, and estimated that the whole ordeal in Guadalajara alone had cost over one million pesos (about US$208,000[124]) and that some forty thousand people had been brought in to cheer for the official candidate. He alleged that the campaign paid them ten pesos a head, unless the person had had to ride a horse into town from the countryside, in which case he earned thirty.[125]

Despite González Luna's cynicism, the roundtable discussions had genuine technical purposes at the same time that they helped Alemán establish a certain type of persona and dialogue with the population. More importantly, they became the culminating events of a decade and a half of political development for Alemán and his generation prior to his presidency. By the time the campaign drew to a close, the roundtable discussion had clarified what type of leader Alemán promised to be.

Conclusion

Miguel Alemán and his generation underwent a process of political evolution during the period from approximately 1929 to 1946. Their rise from idealistic students to powerful government functionaries and prosperous businessmen represented the practical application of the values and priorities they accumulated in school. Alemán's professional trajectory helps chart this transformation almost perfectly. As a young lawyer, he made his name, and the initial basis of his fortune, by advocating for workers. In doing so, he took up one of the central causes of the revolutionary movement. Investing a portion of his income in real estate and other ventures gave him financial stability and laid the foundation for considerable wealth later on. His professional successes, education, and family background catapulted him into a series of bureaucratic, judicial, legislative, and executive positions, signaling his and his generation's entrance into public life.

His three-year term as governor of Veracruz and the five years he spent as minister of the interior allowed him to clarify his own governing approach. In both cases, the strategies he pursued foreshadowed many of the features of his presidency. Alemán's years in the governor's office exemplified this shift and incorporated many of the later tendencies of Alemanismo in great measure. He proved himself to be especially astute at placating the state's dominant military personalities while simultaneously circumscribing their authority,[126] a task he would again face once he assumed the presidency. The combination of administrative competence, subservience to executive authority, and preference for civilian rule reflected many of the central elements of his presidential administration and presaged the kind of leadership that he and the members of his inner circle would bring to the presidency in 1946.

The first half of the 1940s saw a continuation of Alemán's evolving political approach. As he transitioned from the Ministry of the Interior, which had broad but nonetheless highly specific powers, to presidential contender, it became evident that he had used his time in the ministry in crafty ways. At the same time, his governing style and policy priorities owed much to his predecessor's efforts to move his country's politics in a new, rightward direction. Many of the hallmarks of his campaign, and subsequently his presidency, bore the stamp of the Ávila Camacho administration: a more open relationship with the United States, a decrease in the political influence of the military and organized labor, an increased political role of intelligence services, and new state efforts to foment industrial production. While these changes provoked controversies that he would have to confront during his presidency, they nonetheless formed the bedrock of what would become his greatest successes once in office.

The process of creating a civilian-dominant system thus began in the early 1930s and culminated after World War II, and the leaders of the Alemán generation became the central protagonists of this change. This transitional period, from their days as students to their rise to national prominence, allowed these leaders to envision the possibilities of government to serve their professional objectives. While 1946 remains the pivotal year in the shift from a military to a civilian ruling group, the process leading up to that change took place over the better part of the intervening decade, as the new generation moved into the political system and then moved upward within it. Miguel Alemán emerged as the most cunning, and undoubtedly the luckiest, of that generation. His political calculation in the crucial, transitional first half of the 1940s made him the undisputed leading figure of the official party's first civilian generation.

CHAPTER THREE

Alemán's Revolution

ALEMÁN'S TRANSITION INTO THE PRESIDENCY FORETOLD LITTLE OF what the next six years would bring. The 1946 election, despite the occasional flashiness of his campaign, was uneventful compared to prior electoral cycles, which were almost invariably accompanied by bouts of violence. Moreover, various groups had substantially different ideas about what kind of president he was going to be. For his part, Alemán did more to encourage those expectations than to temper them, mainly to establish a broad and diverse base of support on his road to the presidency. Most of his rhetoric thus consisted of vague and generally appealing promises, rather than specific and potentially controversial plans. His generation's lack of adherence to any particular ideological or intellectual trajectory, while consistent with the nation's political traditions since 1910, set it apart from the ruling cadres of virtually all other single-party systems in the twentieth century, and even from prior generations within prerevolutionary national politics. It also made the future president all the more unpredictable. Consequently, at the time of his inauguration, competing interests in Mexican society, from the working class to the business community to foreign governments, did not have an entirely clear picture of what to expect.

Despite the lack of clarity about the incoming administration's plans, Alemán and his colleagues wasted no time in setting their agenda in motion once in office. Part of that process involved aligning Mexico with the rest of the larger nations of Latin America, which they did in two important ways. First, the administration shared much in common with its counterparts in Brazil, Argentina, and Chile in its aggressive turn toward state-supported industrialization. The region-wide embrace of protectionist policies, aimed primarily at stimulating the production of consumer goods for the domestic market, stemmed from dependency theorists' conclusion that the region needed to become more economically self-reliant and diversified. Second, Alemán's crackdown on independent labor organization and mobilization, and his subsequent embrace of an authoritarian corporatist approach to labor relations, reflected similar moves by his contemporaries in the aforementioned countries. For these reasons, it is important to recognize that Alemanismo was, like any other political approach, a product of its time, and that it had considerable kinship with political trends in the rest of Latin America.

Yet an overemphasis on the similarities between Mexico and the rest of the region risks understating the uniqueness of Alemán's agenda. Alemanismo was many things: a set of policies designed to promote urban industry and commercial agriculture; an economic philosophy that favored growth over wealth redistribution; a vision of the nation as a self-sufficient middle power; a governing approach that demanded political discipline and subservience to executive authority; a tendency to put pragmatic sensibility over ideological consistency; a preference for rewarding the urban middle classes, often at the expense of other populations; and a personal style that conveyed a sense that these men belonged to a political class defined by privilege. This combination of forces gave Alemanismo considerable potency. While Alemán and his colleagues borrowed the same rhetoric of revolutionary nationalism from prior decades, in practice they treated the revolutionary movement as something that belonged to their predecessors. Their contribution, by their own estimation, was evolutionary.

The administration's major initiatives projected the values of this new generation of officials, who had been socialized in more fortunate circumstances. In the capital, the government invested in bold experiments in urban planning and suburban development that used a modernist aesthetic to appeal to a growing middle class. In the countryside, the administration built massive public works to improve crop yields, irrigate previously underutilized land, and produce hydroelectric power. Their efforts were suffused with the attitude that Mexico was poised to move from being a poor and predominantly agrarian society to a prosperous and urbanized power. Hardship for the poorest segment of the population, they reasoned, was the unfortunate but necessary cost. The decisions that stemmed from these sentiments led to the most significant changes to Mexico's political economy and social development since the onset of the 1910 revolution.

The *alemanista* agenda gave some hints of the problems that would balloon in coming decades, but for the most part the administration's policies showed a high degree of initial success. This, not surprisingly, emboldened Alemán and his colleagues, but it also led them to become trapped in what might best be described as a middle-class paradigm. Consequently, their urban- and rural-development strategies combined to create a cycle in which the material existence of the urban poor, whose ranks were multiplied by a seemingly unending stream of rural-to-urban migrants, was aggravated by neglect. Those left in the countryside fared no better, and subsequent administrations were left to confront the plight of both populations.[1] In sum, the central projects of the Alemán era left a record of considerable accomplishments that nonetheless were incongruent in many ways with national needs.

Mexico's Industrial Revolution

The Alemán administration's approach to economic management deviated sharply from the reformist agenda of the Cárdenas years. Whereas Cárdenas focused on confronting the nation's social problems through direct spending aimed at ameliorating poverty and redistributing wealth, Alemán, by contrast, discarded such efforts to balance wealth and income. Instead, his administration devoted its attention to promoting rapid industrialization. Operating with the basic logic that social conditions would improve across the board only after national wealth expanded, the Alemán administration directed its efforts toward the buildup of industry-supporting infrastructure and direct investment in new domestic manufacturing.[2] This new economic orientation, precisely because it endured far beyond Alemán's six years in office, marked a watershed in the nation's development. This did not mean that it was entirely unique. While Alemanismo contained various elements that made it exceptional, it also shared a great deal in common with the rest of the region.

Above all, Alemán fully embraced the development strategy known as import substitution industrialization (typically labeled ISI), a new form of state-supported industry buildup that economists developed in response to the global depression of the 1930s. While the first inklings of state-led industrialization occurred in the late nineteenth and early twentieth centuries, for the most part that period saw an expansion of Latin America's long-standing position as primarily an exporter of raw goods.[3] During this period, the landed interests in different parts of the region, such as those selling beef and wheat in Argentina, coffee in Brazil, fruit in Central America, or minerals in Mexico, had grown ever more wealthy, leaving the region's economies highly unequal in their distribution of wealth and highly dependent on export earnings to pay for the necessary imports of capital goods and finished consumer products. The 1930s global depression, which saw a sharp decline in global demand for numerous commodities, exposed the region's economic vulnerabilities. The crisis, in much the same way that it spurred the Keynesian revolution in economic thought in the United States, gave impulse to new economic thinking in Latin America.

Proponents of ISI, with the Argentine economist Raúl Prebisch as their chief spokesman, sought to correct the structural deficiencies facing Latin American economies. Working through the United Nations Economic Commission on Latin America (called ECLA, or in Spanish CEPAL), which Prebisch headed, the supporters of ISI argued that the region needed more economic self-sufficiency to blunt the impact of periodic crises in the world economy, such as the one in the 1930s.[4] To that end, they proposed that Latin American governments take the initiative in supporting industrialization, since it would go nowhere if left to a private sector dominated by landed interests. Beyond the buildup of productive industry, their proposition rested on the growth of a domestic market for consumer products. The need to create a symbiotic relationship between domestic production and consumption made ISI as much a cultural process as an economic or political one. Thus, the culture of consumerism so commonly identified with Alemán went hand in hand with the development of ISI. This paradigm shift—away from the laissez-faire logic of dependent export-based trade and toward an embrace of inward-looking development and state-supported industrialization—led the region into a four-decade experiment with ISI.

For Mexico, the first half of the 1940s, which was consumed by World War II, involved limited recovery. The recovery came in the form of export stimulation through a series of trade agreements with the United States. Mexico, dedicating its support to the Allied forces at a late stage in the war, was able to export minerals, foodstuffs, and small manufactures to support the war effort. Nevertheless, it could not devote much attention to supporting industrialization, since its wartime agreement with the United States demanded that it avoid tariff protection or any other hindrance to free trade.[5] It was not until the immediate postwar years that Mexican industrialization took off, and for this reason, the shift toward state-led industrialization is most closely associated with Alemán.[6]

During his term, Alemán, like his counterparts across the region, embraced a number of policy instruments to promote rapid industrialization. These included protectionist import controls and high tariffs designed to make domestic manufactures competitive vis-à-vis foreign products, along with state subsidies and tax incentives for domestic investors. These measures, aimed at providing an impulse to domestic industry, required a considerable amplification of the presence of the state in economic affairs. Beyond requiring considerably more direct government spending, the nascent industries that emerged in this period relied on state-owned enterprises, the most notable Mexican example being Petróleos Mexicanos, or PEMEX, the state-owned oil corporation. Other industries, especially economies of scale such as natural gas, water, and transportation, followed a similar pattern across the region.[7]

Beyond direct ownership of scale industries, the Mexican government also financed numerous ventures. It did so largely through the public financing corporation Nacional Financiera (NAFIN), headed by longtime Alemán friend Antonio Carrillo Flores. NAFIN became the majority owner under Alemán of the national steel industry, Altos Hornos, borrowing money from the US Export-Import Bank to acquire its share.[8] In subsequent years, NAFIN would pursue similar investments in Mexico's national railcar industry and in Diesel Nacional, among whose investors was Bruno Pagliai, a longtime collaborator with Alemán. The company, which used Fiat technology to build diesel trucks, had gone nearly bankrupt by building shoddy vehicles ill adapted to Mexican roads, but following NAFIN's intervention, Diesel Nacional became a profitable partner of General Motors and International Harvester. NAFIN also invested in enterprises that were subject to "Mexicanization" laws requiring majority ownership (often 51 percent) of the industry, as was the case with numerous foreign interests. In some respects this presented a loophole: a foreign-owned company could operate in Mexico under Mexicanization law by having the government, represented by NAFIN, front the capital, with little or no Mexican private investment.[9]

These examples point to the fact that statist intervention was as much a necessity as it was a choice in Latin America's turn to industrialization. While the production of cheap, non-durable consumer goods—the so-called "easy phase" of ISI—was achieved early, the prospect of encouraging domestic private investment in more capital-intensive industries proved to be dimmer. And in cases such as Diesel Nacional and SOMEX, a private industrial financing bank later taken over by NAFIN to ensure its long-term stability, the state could rescue fledgling or failing companies.[10] In sum, state ownership became one of several vehicles to achieving what economists and policymakers envisioned in the long view as a fundamentally capitalist path of economic development.

The benefits of the ISI-based development model were immediate and profound. Across the region, average living standards went up, as did a host of other indexes, including per capita income, literacy, and life expectancy. Above all, growth stood out as the signal benefit of ISI, and nowhere was this more true than in Mexico, where observers called it an economic miracle. Over three and a half decades, growth averaged between 3 and 4 percent, and double that through the 1960s. Such promising statistics were a boon to Alemán, both during his presidency and afterward, since they helped remove the tarnish that his reputation for corruption had left on his legacy. Under his administration's program of aggressive import substitution, new industries cropped up and existing ones expanded dramatically. Domestic appliances such as refrigerators, electric washing machines, and gas stoves were built in Mexico for the first time. A sprawling range of other industries—sulfuric acid, steel, cement, metallurgy, chemicals, pharmaceuticals, consumer electronics, paper, textiles, publishing, canned food, beer, carbonated beverages, shrimp, sugar, cotton, mining, and cacao—all underwent manifold expansion.[11]

Over time, prohibitions on foreign ownership were relaxed (and, in cases where the law became an obstacle, Mexican prestanombres could be used as fronts for foreign capital; or, as discussed above, the state assumed partial ownership through Nacional Financiera). Thus, foreign-owned companies, including General Motors, Ford, Chrysler, Volkswagen, General Electric, Kodak, Sears, Anderson Clayton, and Dow Chemical, increased their presence in the economy.[12] For many, this seemed to be precisely the opposite of the revolutionary mandate for more national self-determination. Warnings about the economic stress posed by outflowing profits seemed to go unheeded, largely because growth remained so robust. The fact that the economic boom only got bigger in the 1950s and 1960s provided officials, first in the Alemán administration and then in those of his successors, reason to share in the optimism of the postwar years.

Yet even with statistics suggesting that Mexico and the rest of Latin America had finally found a pathway toward sustained economic growth, the problems that would ultimately bring ISI into crisis showed themselves early. Those problems took on multiple dimensions. First, contrary to orthodox ISI and unlike many of his contemporaries across the region, Alemán depressed the wages of workers. While conventional economic thinking had it that higher wages would equal more consumption of domestic products, and while populists such as Argentina's Juan Domingo Perón, as well as Lázaro Cárdenas in the prior decade, had relied on wage hikes for political support, Alemán took a different path. Part of the Alemán administration's problem with inflation had to do with its inability to address the nation's regressive taxation system. Alemán staunchly opposed the idea of raising taxes on businesses, arguing that it would stifle investment incentive.

The president did attempt a somewhat halfhearted attempt to reform the tax system, using a strategy of federal centralization to achieve increased tax revenue. The plan largely backfired, as cash-strapped state governments found it impossible to generate sufficient amounts of their own revenue while the national government increased its capacity to collect taxes. Forced to choose between provoking tax protests or being left unable to do much of anything, state and local authorities turned to informal measures, ranging from the use of forced labor to reliance on local church parishes, to fulfill their responsibilities, particularly in the area of public-works construction. In achieving one gain—a political architecture that could, in theory, correct Mexico's deficiencies in tax collection—Alemán created a scenario that encouraged corruption, weakened the political legitimacy of the PRI, and failed to provide reliable tax revenue in the long-term.[13]

Alemán's tax policy endured beyond his administration and made Mexico exceptional, to the extent that the country had the lowest tax burden of any country in Latin America by the late 1960s. As an alternative to building any progressive mechanism of generating government revenue through taxation, his administration printed money to pay the costs of the government's expenditures, something that invariably leads to inflation. In more practical terms, the effect of raising the money supply was higher prices for goods.[14] This hit workers hard. The fact that Alemán staffed the CTM, the party-affiliated labor sector, with conservative loyalists meant that workers could not count on much relief from rising prices. The lack of government revenue, combined with costly investments in public works, also limited the Alemán administration's ability to invest in social programs, as discussed above.

Second, the buildup of ISI put severe stress on the balance of payments in most of the nations of the region. ISI, despite its ultimate goal of minimizing dependency on imports, in fact required a higher balance of imports, largely because the production of non-durable consumer goods required capital inputs, such as large factory machinery, from abroad. In this moment of inward-looking development, export earnings, which would otherwise have been used to pay for the imports, were unable to keep pace, leading to an imbalance of trade. The fact that ISI, a program specifically designed to make the region's economies more self-sufficient, ended up making them more dependent on foreign imports of capital goods, proved to be a major paradox.[15] This imbalance, moreover, resulted in central banks losing a greater and greater share of their foreign-currency reserves. The Banco de México was no exception. To compensate for this stress on the balance of payments, officials resorted to a number of measures, many of which were undertaken on the misguided assumption that they were short-term efforts that would result in more stable economic footing.

Currency devaluation and external debt were the two most common responses to this pressure on the nation's balance of payments. The Alemán administration devalued the peso at the recommendation of the International Monetary Fund (IMF) in 1948, and Alemán's successor, Adolfo Ruiz Cortines, grudgingly did so again in 1954, citing his predecessor's excesses as the reason (see chapter 4). Devaluation proved effective in doing what it was intended to do: to slow imports by making them artificially expensive, thereby shoring up currency reserves and stimulating domestic industry. External debt, which brought an immediate injection of money into central banks, provided an even more direct remedy to the negative balance of payments.[16] Washington was eager to provide the capital, either directly through the US government (especially the Export-Import Bank of the US Treasury) or through the IMF, since debt cemented political alliances in the region and tethered Latin America to US economic interests.

Mexico, as part of Latin America's "big three" countries (along with Brazil and Argentina, both because of the overall size of their economies and because of their full-scale embrace of ISI), had a difficult experience with each of these mechanisms. Devaluation, despite its effectiveness, nonetheless brought with it the high social cost of more inflation. For the nation's poor, this was nothing short of devastating, as masses of people were left unable to buy basic goods, including food. Debt proved costly in the short and long run. From the outset, payments to service debt put strain on the economy, and in the long run, debt got the better of Latin America. While 1982, the year Mexico defaulted on its foreign debt, is generally seen as the tipping point, the region's troubles were apparent through the 1970s, as the Arab nations responsible for fixing global oil prices dumped money into Western banks that in turn farmed out that money as loans to willing debtors, among them Latin American nations. But when global recession hit in the early 1980s and the US government responded by raising interest rates, the region was unable to keep pace.[17] This period marked the next fundamental turning point in the region's economic development. If the 1930s depression spurred a new approach based on state-led development, then the 1980s saw a sharp turn toward free-market policies.

It is worth emphasizing that this outcome—the onset of debt crisis and subsequent turn to neoliberal privatization and austerity in the 1980s—cannot be ascribed entirely to what Alemán did in the 1940s and 1950s. Rather, the intervening decades were characterized by distinct economic trends, often punctuated by extreme shifts. The program of "Stabilizing Development," which followed the Alemán years, attempted to maintain growth while tamping down inflation by replacing direct government intervention with private-sector investment. The administration of Luis Echeverría in the 1970s changed course again, devoting massive sums of state funding to the nationalization of industry. His successor, José López Portillo, went on a massive spending spree leveraged against what turned out to be temporarily robust oil export revenue.

While the dynamics of each of these programs is beyond our scope here, one salient point emerges: each failed to correct the social consequences of the economic agenda that was largely established under Alemán. This fact points to the third major problem with the ISI model: despite its hypothetical promise to do the opposite, it led to a terribly lopsided distribution of wealth. While this problem was anything but new to Mexico, it in fact got worse under ISI, as unemployment skyrocketed to 25 percent and the informal economy became a means of survival for more and more people.[18] All of the economic factors discussed above—the absence of a beneficial tax structure, the lack of social investment, the myriad inflationary pressures, the decline in organized labor's potency—are reflected in the social reality of the era. By the end of Alemán's term and across the economic "miracle" that continued over the next two decades, Mexico ranked dead last among Latin American nations in terms of what the government did for the poorest quarter of the population.[19]

The social consequences of the ISI model were thus substantial. The overall composition of the social pyramid changed considerably: at the top, large landholders, once the oligarchs of the old agro-export economy, were replaced with a new industrial elite.[20] In Mexico, a small segment of large landholders, the so-called *neolatifundistas* of the Alemán era, managed to achieve considerable wealth, but the new cadre of industrialists were nonetheless firmly in control of the economy's commanding heights. This lent itself to close relations between the government and certain sectors of the business community (other segments, such as the Monterrey Group, instead backed the opposing National Action Party, or PAN[21]). Alemán was particularly noteworthy for having personal business connections that made him exceptionally wealthy. In most other cases during the years of single-party rule, the political networks out of which the presidents emerged and the nation's business networks remained distinct.[22] With Alemán, who turned industrialization into an official priority, government and business were at their closest. His government favored various businessmen, such as Carlos Trouyet, Bruno Pagliai, Eloy Vallina, and Luis Aguilar, and Alemán used others close to him, including Carlos Serrano, Jorge Pasquel, and Enrique Parra Hernández, as intermediaries between the political and business communities. The wealthy industrialist Antonio Ruiz Galindo even made it into his cabinet as minister of national economy,[23] and his personal relations with major foreign investors, such as Conrad Hilton, went far in attracting capital from abroad.[24]

Alemán and his colleagues were particularly encouraged by the "trickle-down" effect that ISI had on the middle class.[25] As the dynamic center of the national economy moved away from large landholders and toward urban industrialists, a new entrepreneurial class emerged. Urban industry spurred demand for managers, engineers, architects, scientists, technical experts, lawyers, professors, and other typically middle-class professions. This, coupled with expanding opportunities to build a career in public service through affiliation with the PRI, stimulated the growth of the postwar middle class. The emergence of a visible and powerful middle class must have emboldened Alemán and his colleagues. These leaders had, after all, acquired a distinctly middle-class sensibility as early as their college years in the 1920s, and the postwar years in which they governed provided them a benchmark of comparison in the form of the new baby boomer generation in the United States. Yet for all the visibility and potential of Mexico's growing middle class, its promise was left unfulfilled. While government officials and citizens had good reason to believe in the potential of upward mobility at both the national and individual levels from the late 1940s through the 1960s, by the 1970s the idea of a "new middle class" had become something of a farce.[26]

The most troubling developments were at the bottom of the pyramid. From the 1940s to the 1980s, the benefits of ISI failed to reach the poorest classes. Instead, those benefits were divided between domestic and foreign capitalists, along with a fortunate segment of the middle class. Rather than providing a basis for broad-based prosperity, the combination of rapid industrialization and commercialization of agriculture resulted in a rapid influx of rural residents into the cities. These troubling developments were compounded by reduced death rates that resulted in a subsequent increase in population. While those developments had little to do with Alemán's policies, his administration's general economic orientation certainly exacerbated their effects. In spite of the growth of labor-intensive urban industry, employment opportunities could not keep pace with the number of rural-to-urban migrants.

The result was persistent unemployment, a growing informal economy, and a host of infrastructural, financial, environmental, and public-health consequences, especially in the capital. Those left in the countryside fared no better. Indeed, the combined forces of the green revolution and the expansion of commercial agrobusiness left Mexico's agrarian sector dominated by foreign multinationals and its peasants severely in debt and endemically unemployed.[27] By 1970 Mexico was as sharply divided between rich and poor as it had been in the Porfiriato.[28] The structure of the pyramid may have changed, but the twin realities of highly concentrated wealth and extreme inequality had not.

These changes to the nation's economic orientation carried political implications as well. The rise of a state-supported, urban-centered industrial economy went hand in hand with a set of broad political changes in the major nations of the region, including Argentina, Brazil, and Chile, during the first half of the twentieth century. Each had its own particular dynamics, but together they followed a common trajectory. These nations' export-based economies, which had taken root in the colonial period and had endured through the nineteenth century, converted into urban-industrial powerhouses. Their political dynamics followed suit: whereas small landed oligarchies had previously controlled national affairs, increasingly the working and middle classes demanded political incorporation and official attention to their interests.

Consequently, from the 1920s through the 1960s, and especially after the Latin American economies turned to ISI as a response to the economic depression of the 1930s, populism as a style of leadership flourished. Some of Alemán's most noteworthy peers in the region, especially Juan Domingo Perón of Argentina (whose wife, Eva Duarte de Perón, popularly known as Evita, served as a liaison between workers and her husband's government during his term from 1946 to 1955[29]) and Getúlio Vargas of Brazil, stand as some of the region's most important populists. These and other populist leaders sought to harness the political support of previously marginal and disenfranchised groups. They did so by coupling broadly appealing anti-elite and nationalist rhetorical themes with policies that balanced the competing demands of the majority. Often they monopolized mass communications and benefited from a healthy dose of charismatic leadership to establish personal connections with the society's humbler classes, even if that meant alienating established elites.[30]

In general terms Mexico followed this pattern, but its experience differed both in form and timing. Its shift from oligarchic to mass-based politics came earlier, in the form of the 1910 revolution, and its "populist period" occurred in the 1930s, during the Cárdenas administration and prior to the Cold War. By the Alemán years, just as other populists in the region were perfecting their strategies of engaging the masses, Mexico's government had abandoned this form of personalist leadership in favor of a more centralized, bureaucratized system under the PRI. The corporatist institutional structure of the ruling party helped to ensure that the system held together and that it could be used to push the population into supporting the regime's constantly shifting economic and political goals.

Single-party corporatism had its origins in the Cárdenas reforms of the 1930s. The population was organized into class-based sectors that had official linkages to the ruling party (the working classes were represented by the Confederation of Mexican Workers, or CTM; the peasantry by the National Peasant Confederation, or CNC; in the 1940s, another sector, the National Confederation of Popular Organization, or CNOP, was created to represent the growing middle classes, and the military was dropped as an official body within the party). These organizations provided different segments of the population an institutional channel through which to voice their demands and grievances. At the same time, they helped to block out political opposition by drawing constituents into the party's fold.[31] But over time, the party's sectors functioned less as avenues for grassroots political empowerment and more as instruments of presidential power. By the early 1940s the system had hardened into a pyramidal bureaucracy, with the president issuing decrees that were then carried out by loyal functionaries through the party's main institutions and their subsectors. National leaders, adopting a carrot-or-stick approach, with clear preference for the carrot, provided incentives for loyalty and acquiescence. Those who fell in line were rewarded, although the greatest rewards were reserved for those closest to the top of the pyramid. Predictably, those who did not fall in line were subjected to repression. The arrangement resulted in one of the world's most stable and least violence-prone authoritarian models in the twentieth century.

Despite the considerable differences between the overwhelmingly bureaucratic system in Mexico and the more personalist regimes elsewhere in the region, Alemán and his populist contemporaries did have some things in common. Both sought to choke out political opposition and independent unionization through strong patron-client linkages. Across the region, organized labor saw the end of World War II as a political aperture, which spurred the working classes to ramp up mobilization. Yet within only a few years, most of the region's governments, including those of populists who were ostensibly committed to worker interests, had minimized the capabilities of independent unions and brought the working classes under stricter state control, which they viewed as crucial to the success of nascent industry.[32] Mexico's version of this rightward shift was among the most severe in the region, precisely because other leaders (particularly the populists) maintained a commitment to meeting a portion of proletarian demands and positioned blue-collar workers at the center of their rhetoric. By contrast, Alemán and his civilian colleagues took an especially hard line against labor militancy and placed the middle classes at the center of their agenda. This general orientation led Mexico into a period of extremes. On one side, political stability and economic growth emerged as its most visible benefits. On the other, widening socioeconomic inequality, lack of attention to the interests of the poor, and structural problems in the economy came together to threaten—and ultimately destroy—these substantive gains.

The Urban Revolution

The ambitious urban projects undertaken by the Alemán administration represent a sizeable share of its legacy. The administration's most stunning urban developments included a sprawling university campus conceptualized as a city unto itself, an experimental suburb built to attract a growing middle class, and several enormous housing and commercial complexes designed to offer every possible amenity and service to their residents. Collectively, these achievements made a dramatic statement about the Alemán generation's vision of a middle class–oriented society. The development of the beach resort destination of Acapulco, fed by an efficient new highway from Mexico City, underscored this priority.

These projects served both practical and symbolic objectives: new infrastructure prepared the capital to support large-scale industrialization, while modernist planning and architectural schemes were designed to showcase the forward-moving trajectory of a nation in the throes of modernization. Many of the projects that the administration supported or funded were unprecedented in scale and with few exceptions remain intact and functional today.

By making urban planning one of its policy centerpieces, administration officials acknowledged the need to confront urban population growth head on. The initiatives the administration pursued appealed above all to the growing urban middle classes, composed of public functionaries from the expanding bureaucracy and of private-sector professionals associated with the growing urban-industrial base. A palpable optimism fueled the efforts of administration officials, as well as the architects, engineers, and planners responsible for these projects. Yet for all the optimism for the future that these grandiose projects conveyed, they also masked a hard reality: that even as the middle class grew, working-class and other poor sectors grew far more precipitously. As a result, the administration's urban-planning strategies, which favored the middle sectors at the expense of the working class and the impoverished, did little to anticipate the widening social-economic inequalities that characterized the 1940s through the 1970s, a period described in official rhetoric as an economic "miracle." Ultimately, the pattern of urban development pursued by Alemán reflected the priorities of his generation more than the needs of the majority of the nation's urban residents.

Much like the alemanista economic agenda, the administration's urban construction plans were simultaneously new but also based on at least some existing precedents. Development of urban infrastructure, services, commercial zones, and residential areas—all major features of the Alemán era—had also been major priorities during the 1920s and 1930s. As one historian has pointed out, the mentalities of the era and its leaders found reflection in the built environment. The Cárdenas years in particular saw a flurry of construction initiatives that showcased the contradictions of the revolutionary state. One the one hand, a generation of "socialist architects," drawing on both the utopian prescriptions of Swiss architect and urban planner Le Corbusier and the more practical reference point of the Soviet Union's five-year plans, expressed a progressive vision of proletarian housing. At the same time, the federal government invested considerable sums of money in educational and healthcare facilities.[33]

Despite these gains, the pattern of urban construction in the Cárdenas period showcased and perhaps exacerbated much older patterns of socioeconomic inequality. Residential development, left almost entirely to the private sector, tended to favor the middle and elite classes, leaving the growing sectors of the city's poor with usurious landlords and dreadful infrastructure. Despite the government's investments in services, as well as good-faith regulatory efforts aimed at protecting impoverished residents from rent increases, for the most part the 1930s saw widening inequality. The urban landscape thus exposed a revolution inadequate to the task of easing the miseries of the urban poor.[34] More importantly for our purposes, it presaged much of what was to come during the Alemán years.

Mexico City in the Alemán era looked nothing like the present-day megalopolis. Far smaller at the time than London, Paris, New York, Tokyo, and many other major metropolitan centers, it would not emerge for several decades as the expansive megacity of the sort that has since become a common feature of contemporary Latin America. Still, the 1940s saw the beginning of a gradual process that transformed a comparatively small national capital into one of the world's largest urban agglomerations. Immediately following World War II, as the combined demographic pressures of import substitution industrialization and rural modernization programs thrust people from the country into a new urban existence, and as population growth at all social levels picked up, Mexico City grew.

Characterizing the capital before the post–World War II economic boom as a place of minor importance would be misleading. Mexico City had long stood as a place of great significance—as the innovative island capital of the Aztec empire, the epicenter of the sprawling Spanish American colonies, and the showpiece of Porfirian modernity. The 1910 revolution interrupted much of the progress made in the capital during the turn-of-the-century "metropolitan revolution."[35] Across the nation, the material toll, seen as burned buildings and piled rubble, hinted at the extent of the human toll:

approximately two million, about one in seven Mexicans, perished in the decade of armed combat.[36] The 1920–1940 period witnessed a process of gradual rebuilding punctuated by periodic violence. While peace gradually took hold, Mexico City hardly experienced an urban renaissance. This was largely due to the fact that federal programs and expenditure were directed at rural priorities, ranging from the quelling of the Cristero Rebellion of Catholic militants in the late 1920s to the massive redistribution of rural land to peasants a decade later. Not until the 1940s did the city again become the priority it had been in the Porfiriato.[37]

Above all else, the administration's urban-development programs reflected the sincere aspiration held by Alemán and his closest collaborators to usher in a golden age for Mexico's middle class. Projects such as the University City (Ciudad Universitaria, or CU), the Multifamiliares Miguel Alemán and Benito Juárez (large-scale, middle-class apartment and commercial complexes), and the suburban Satellite City (Ciudad Satélite) showcased the president's grandiose plans to embrace not only a modernizing ethos, but also a modernist approach to urban design shared by the nation's leading architects, who drew influence from Le Corbusier. These projects, along with infrastructural developments such as the construction of the Viaducto Miguel Alemán (the large, circular viaduct that rings the Federal District) and tourist destinations such as Cuernavaca and Acapulco, constituted a strategy to lay the groundwork for what government officials envisioned as a middle-class, urbanized society. More than any other individual, the architect Mario Pani was responsible for the forms that the administration's urban-development projects took.

Pani was the progeny of a well-connected family. His uncle, Alberto Pani, was twice finance minister in the 1920s and 1930s and a prominent associate of President Plutarco Elías Calles in a period that saw the construction of numerous public works, especially an extensive national system of roads.[38] His mother descended from a prominent Porfirian family that held on to its wealth and prestige through the revolution. Over the course of the twentieth century, Pani built numerous large-scale projects, especially in Mexico City, but his most productive years were under Alemán. Pani rose to prominence as one of Latin America's first disciples of modernism to gain international renown. A contemporary of modernist luminaries Lúcio Costa and Oscar Niemeyer, the Brazilians most famous for their collaboration on the unprecedented construction of the planned inland capital of Brasília, Pani embraced many of the principles of modernist architecture and urban planning and his architectural vision of urban development flourished under the tutelage of Alemán.[39]

The construction of the massive University City campus, arguably Pani's crowning achievement in the Alemán era, signaled a shift in educational priorities. Since 1921 the Ministry of Education, under the leadership of José Vasconcelos, had oriented its efforts toward the creation of a universally accessible education system with the goal of promoting basic literacy, cultural inclusion, and political incorporation (especially among rural indigenous populations).[40] Although Alemán did not officially abandon this effort to expand the nation's primary and secondary school system, he decreased the percentage of the federal budget it previously occupied.[41] Instead, he devoted far more attention to the university system, diverting staggering sums of money into the construction of the CU. Various presidents, beginning with Emilio Portes Gil, who granted the National University full autonomy in 1929, had grappled with the possibility of creating a single campus to encompass the sprawling UNAM. Alemán's predecessor, Manuel Ávila Camacho, even expropriated the land and signed legislation authorizing its construction, but during the war years he never found the resources to fund it.[42] Alemán, on the other hand, placed considerable priority on carrying out the project, however detrimental the financial consequences may have been.

Alemán secured the credit through the Banco de México, providing it directly to the university's rector, Salvador Zubirán, to expropriate the remaining land and build the site. Securing the land was the first hurdle, but the peasants who lived on it also had to be relocated. To do this, Alemán utilized a legal provision known as the *permuta* (literally exchange) to swap their land for an equivalent amount somewhere else.[43] Abuse of this loophole (which bears a striking resemblance to the eminent domain law in the United States) forced officials to revise it after Alemán's *sexenio* (the name given to Mexico's six-year presidential terms). Nevertheless, with this obstacle removed, the project proceeded. The leadership structure of the initiative emanated directly from Alemán, helping to ensure that his pet project moved according to schedule. Carlos Novoa, head of the Banco de México, served as the *presidente del patronato* (roughly chairman of the board), while another prominent architect, Carlos Lazo, oversaw the construction site.[44]

Lazo, part of the same generation as Pani, had originally worked at the US firm Delano & Aldrich, which made its mark by planning several Tennessee Valley Authority projects. Despite an offer to remain at the firm, he returned to Mexico after World War II, where he used his foreign credentials to advance professionally. Alemán named him head of the CU project, reportedly to the chagrin of Pani, who had expressed an interest in overseeing it. Nonetheless, Lazo, as the former oficial mayor (third in command) of the Ministry of National Assets, took on the project, gaining a reputation for his paternalistic approach to worker-management relations. A staunch Catholic, he brought in clergy and nuns to hold Sunday masses and offer classes to workers. Following Alemán's term, Lazo was rewarded with the Ministry of Communications and Public Works, where he was instrumental in convincing President Adolfo Ruiz Cortines to finish the CU project, despite the increasingly burdensome costs it presented.[45]

The campus marked a radical departure from the previous installations of the UNAM, which occupied various buildings in the downtown sector. In contrast to the previous collection of buildings, the winning design by Mario Pani and fellow architect Enrique del Moral represented a major achievement in modernist architecture. For a building site they chose El Pedregal, an extensive basalt-covered lava bed that had broad cultural significance for local indigenous peoples following the Spanish Conquest and that hosted a number of unique species of animals, lichens, trees, and grasses.[46] The installations that made up the CU included not only buildings for the various departments within the university, but also recreational spaces, residential dormitories, and athletic facilities, including the large stadium used for the university's professional soccer club, the Pumas. To this day, the shaded areas and wooded trails make the university attractive to visitors, even those with no official university function.

The idea of a self-contained and self-sufficient space, a kind of total environment that harbored facilities for every social aspect associated with it, served as a cornerstone of the architectural movement that Pani and his fellow CU architects put into practice. Pani, del Moral, Lazo, and the rest of the architects associated with the project also adopted an approach known as plastic integration, which sought to integrate the functionally oriented buildings with aesthetic improvements. In this case, the government commissioned a series of striking exterior murals and mosaics.[47]

Similar to many of the murals that were commissioned to adorn public spaces as part of the revolutionary cultural project, the installations at the CU conveyed nationalist messages and epic historical themes. In aesthetic terms, they also helped to "Mexicanize" a set of buildings that were otherwise austere and rectangular. In many ways, the visual interplay between the modernist architectural forms and the mythic pictorial content of the murals captured what the site was meant to represent: a symbolic space where an ancient past would be acknowledged and celebrated, but ultimately where a forward-looking nation would see its best ideas cultivated.[48]

Prominent domestic and foreign intellectuals participated in the opening ceremony of the CU in 1952. José Vasconcelos, Alfonso Reyes, Ángel María Garibay, Enrique Gonzáles Martínez, Manuel Gamio, and Jaime Torres Bodet were among the first to receive honorary degrees at the event, which was also attended by foreign scholars Norbert Wiener, John Dewey, Paul Rivet, Alfred Kidder, Otto Struve, and Jean Sarrailh.[49] The stunning murals adorning many of the most prominent buildings, which tended otherwise to have a stark, boxy quality, created an impressive setting. Especially important were David Alfaro Siqueiros's mural on the rectory and Juan O'Gorman's iconic wrap-around installation on the main library. Diego Rivera, the nation's best-known muralist, designed the mural adorning the stadium the following year. The campus also contained a massive statue of Miguel Alemán, draped in a toga signifying *Doctor Honoris Causa*, as a monument to his role in the construction of the campus. The statue, drawing controversy in subsequent decades as Alemán's reputation darkened in the collective memory, was vandalized with dynamite and subsequently removed during the tumultuous student protests of the 1960s.[50]

Beyond the statement of public support for higher education that it made, the project also yielded a few unforeseen benefits. In the initial stages of his work, O'Gorman replaced his original plan to install a mural with one for a mosaic. After securing approval for the proposal, Lazo asked each state governor to supply local stones. He received everything from dump-truck loads to shoeboxes full of rocks. The arrival of the stones became the basis for the first national inventory of its mineral resources. Another positive byproduct of the CU project was a reunion between Siqueiros and Rivera arranged by Lazo. According to his son Lorenzo, Lazo claimed credit for mending the tempestuous relationship between the two muralists, who up to that point had been sworn enemies.[51] In spite of his contribution to the project, Rivera nonetheless criticized the architecture of the CU, complaining that the boxy architecture of the buildings gave students the feeling of being on prison grounds. He was especially vociferous in his criticism of the Rectory, which appeared to him to look like four serapes (woven poncho-like garments worn especially by rural men) hanging on a clotheshorse, and the library, which abandoned the original proposal of using Le Corbusier's innovative layered design to conform to the box-like forms of the rest of the buildings. On the whole he judged that the project blighted the pristine grounds of El Pedregal, the giant lava bed on which the CU was built.[52]

The fanfare of the new facility belied the controversies that were to follow. The initial project was not actually completed until 1953 (major additions were added in subsequent decades). By that point Adolfo Ruiz Cortines had become president, inheriting a shakier economy than the one Alemán had enjoyed and encountering the overextended commitments that his predecessor had left him. As former treasury minister and Nacional Financiera director Antonio Carrillo Flores noted, the expenditure from the CU's construction contributed to the peso crisis of 1954, and the debt the government incurred (absolved only by decreeing the CU national patrimony) helped to precipitate the adoption of various austerity measures.[53]

Others complained that the relocation of the UNAM from its central downtown location to a more isolated plot in the southern margins of the city debilitated the student body as a political force. More precisely, critics argued that students became disempowered as an interest group because they could not organize and militate at the center of the city, where government offices were located and where their visibility would be greatest. While government officials did not expressly admit to this motivation, it is plausible that defusing student political activism formed part of the equation.[54] Many of these critics further argued the downtown sector lost vitality and resources when the large student body moved to the southern part of the city.[55] In addition, some architects, particularly those who were most committed to the modernist movement, complained that the murals and mosaics not only disrupted the avant-garde quality of the architecture, but also served as little more than official propaganda for the benefit of the PRI.[56]

While the government was decisive in carrying out the planning and construction of the CU, its legacy from the moment of completion onward proved to be contested. On one side, the impressive campus represented a monumental achievement in its scope and audacity. On the other, it came at a great cost, prompting observers to question whether the ends justified the means. Ejido-dwelling peasants, who only a generation earlier had benefited from land reform under Cárdenas, were relocated; students lost the opportunity to learn and mobilize in the city's vibrant center; and the public absorbed the effects of the venture's sizeable financial cost over the ensuing decade. The problems the CU engendered notwithstanding, it stood as one of Latin America's boldest applications of urban modernism. Above all, it represented the product of collaboration between the political will of Alemán and the vision of Pani and the rest of the architects who contributed to the project.

If the CU was Pani's most expansive project, then the multifamiliares he built during the Alemán years (as well as the even larger Unidad Habitacional Nonoalco-Tlatelolco, built during the 1960s and most famous for surrounding the Plaza de Tres Culturas, site of the 1968 student massacre days before the city hosted the Olympics) stand as his most direct attempts to incorporate the complete ethos of Le Corbusier's Radiant City concept. In much the same way that he intended the CU to encompass the educational, social, and residential needs of its students, Pani designed the enormous housing complexes to contain commercial and social outlets. Within the boundaries of the complexes (the Multifamiliar Miguel Alemán still stands and is fully operational; the Benito Juárez facility was demolished after it suffered major damage in the 1985 earthquake), there were numerous social services, including schools, medical clinics, and child daycare facilities. Numerous commercial centers were constructed within the complexes, including grocery stores, dry cleaning and laundry services, butcher shops, bakeries, and banks. Recreational sites such as community swimming pools and full-sized cinemas abounded, while public gardens and walking paths covered the grounds. Basketball and other sports leagues offered school-age residents a chance to socialize and exercise. Residents even watched games from the windows that looked inward toward the center of the complexes.[57]

Pani intended the multifamiliares to function as cities within the city.[58] Aside from their innovative philosophical foundations and daring scope, they simultaneously came to represent government plans to confront expected growth and the expectation that this growth would occur in the ranks of an upwardly mobile middle class whose members were still modest in taste and resources. They immediately became symbols of the audacity of a modernizing government and exemplars of the progress of a booming capital city. If urban slums became the backdrop for films such as Luis Buñuel's masterpiece *Los Olvidados* and the ethnographies of Oscar Lewis, then the petit bourgeois surroundings of the multifamiliares (often called *vecindades*, literally neighborhoods within one complex) served as the setting for films such as *Maldita Ciudad*, *La Ilusión Viaja en la Tranvía*, and *Amor sin Barreras*,[59] as well as Gabriel Vargas's celebrated comic series, *La Familia Burrón*.[60] These large projects are among the most recognizable material expressions of the ambitions of the Alemán era.

Pani regarded Satellite City as the suburban conceptual counterpart to the multifamiliares. The former was a city within the city; the latter a city outside the city[61] but, by virtue of its name, one within its orbit.[62] Alemán approved the plans for Satellite City in 1948. Residents did not begin moving there until the last year of his term, and construction continued into the late 1950s. In similar fashion to the CU and the multifamiliares, Pani and his fellow architects, especially José Luis Cuevas and Domingo García Ramos, built Satellite City according to an experimental design that owed a great deal to various applications of modernist architecture. Beyond Le Corbusier, these architects drew inspiration from the Austrian-born architect Herman Herrey, who conceptualized an urban plan based on circular designs that prevented the need for interaction between pedestrians and automobile drivers. They also looked to Radburn, a city built in 1927 outside New York City by architects Clarence Stein and Henry Wright, as a model worth emulating. Stein and Wright, known for pioneering the concept of superblocks with so-called green belts, built their city to contain self-sufficient subdivisions.[63]

Le Corbusier, Herrey (who had changed his name from the original Zweigenthal to help launch a career in New York[64]), and the Radburn project all influenced the design of Satellite City, located in the Naucalpan area to the northwest of Mexico City proper. Pani and his associates designed the city around large, self-sufficient complexes (*supermanzanas*, or superblocks) bounded by arcing boulevards. Within each, civic, administrative, residential, and commercial spaces formed a social nucleus. In instances where places of employment were attached, the architects considered them wholly self-sustaining spaces.[65] In each case, the arcing thoroughfares and roundabout intersections made halting crosswalks and traffic lights unnecessary. This effort represented a practical application of Le Corbusier's dictum of "death of the street," an expression of his hatred for the seemingly disorganized, improvised, and confined nature of streets, which he viewed as cluttered with sidewalks, cars, trees, and other things he regarded as disorderly.[66] Just as large murals adorned the buildings of the CU, so too did the planners of Satellite City employ public art to convey a sense of modernity and progress. At the city's entrance on the Periférico freeway that dissects the capital, the towers of Satélite, consisting of five cement towers, alternately painted either in bright colors or white, greet visitors. The towers, designed and built by the sculptor Mathias Goeritz and the architect Luis Barragán, said much about the project and the architectural movement that underpinned it. The angular lines and bold stature of the towers prioritized confidence over subtlety, while the bold colors conveyed a sense of optimism. The simple forms, devoid of ornate decoration, simultaneously suggested unapologetic ambition and straightforward logic.

The austere aesthetic character of each of these major installations reflected the inherently authoritarian nature of Le Corbusier's plans. For him as well as his disciples in Latin America, major urban architectural and planning initiatives, like the ones built during Alemán's term in Mexico, would ensure that order and rational planning overtook disorder, irrationality, and constant improvisation.[67] This ethic reached its maximum expression in the construction of Brasília in the 1950s and 1960s. In both the Brazilian and Mexican cases, the authoritarian nature of the architecture visually reinforced the equally authoritarian nature of the governments that supported their construction. On a more practical level, the projects also represented the priority of the federal governments in both countries to invest public funds in grand projects that, if not aesthetically pleasing, were nonetheless impressive and served both ideological and practical objectives.

The construction of Satellite City marked the first major effort to use government funds to reduce urban congestion. Over the course of the six years Alemán was in office, his administration developed a political apparatus to study urban-development issues and initiate planning endeavors. In addition to building the CU, the mulifamiliares, and Satellite City, the administration devoted efforts to a number of other projects: during Alemán's sexenio, the Ministry of National Assets supported plans for forty port and border cities. Additionally, in 1952, just prior to his departure from office, Alemán also established the Dirección General de Planificación (General Directorate of Planning), which conducted studies related to electrification and the construction of communication and transportation networks.[68] Urban population growth and congestion, along with the presence of adequate services and infrastructure, represented critical priorities, but the government's concerns did not stop there. Since one of the hallmarks of the Alemán agenda was to bring foreign commerce in the form of tourism, his administration utilized its capabilities in urban planning to attract foreign visitors.

The project that drew the most international attention was the new stretch of high-rise resorts overlooking the glimmering bay of Acapulco on Guerrero's Pacific coast. The city had long been the victim of political and geographic isolation, which gave local caciques (political bosses) unchecked power. But renewed interest in the port during the 1940s prompted Alemán to make it the centerpiece of his extensive efforts to promote tourism.[69] As he did with the CU development, Alemán created a chain of command that extended from him directly to those on the ground. He utilized the Junta Federal that existed prior to his presidency, vesting it with increased authority to undertake urban planning to support the administration's tourism agenda. The Junta operated under the command of another modernist architect, Carlos Contreras, who originally planned to build worker housing and related facilities to support the low-income service employees associated with the burgeoning tourism industry.[70]

Alemán also charged Ramón Beteta, his treasury minister, with appointing local political kingpin Melchor Perusquía as head of the Committee for the Material Improvement of Acapulco and as chief of maritime customs. In this capacity Perusquía served as the chief mediator between the business community, the national government, and local residents. Officials in government, including Alemán and Minister of National Economy Antonio Ruiz Galindo, had considerable investments in Acapulco, making direct oversight of the project an understandable priority. As part of the government's effort to promote the port's development, it awarded generous subsidies and tax incentives to a number of companies to build hotels, golf courses, and commercial zones.[71]

Again in similar fashion to the construction of the CU, the process of development meant disrupting the lives of the rural residents who inhabited the land. To achieve its objectives, the federal government shielded larger estates from being divided into collectively owned ejidos, and relocated existing ejidatarios who lived near pristine coastline to make way for high-rise resorts and the dramatic Costera Miguel Alemán promenade. Evidence exists that officials on the ground resorted to terrorist violence, including machine-gunning, to drive indigenous residents from land to which they had ancestral ties.[72] Moreover, police forced ejidatarios, many of whom resisted relocation, to vacate their land by burning crops and houses.[73] As a consequence of these harsh measures, Acapulco shared with the CU a legacy of extremes.

Acapulco represented a monumental achievement: a modern tourist destination that delighted domestic and foreign travelers with its combination of natural splendor and luxurious amenities. It nonetheless came at a high social cost. Many of the initiatives proposed on behalf of the city and the municipality's poor populations, including potable water systems and *colonias populares* (working-class neighborhoods with subsidized housing) for rural residents who worked in tourism, never came to fruition. As part of a broader effort to promote hygienic facilities, many local vendors' food stalls were moved to make way for cement facilities. Moreover, local fishermen had to move farther off the coast as high-rise hotels began to dot the beach in front of the Costera Miguel Alemán.[74] In sum, the development of Acapulco formed part of a broader effort to cater to middle-class tastes and aspirations, focus on urban construction, attract foreign attention, and pursue projects of financial interest to members of both the private and public sectors. As with the development in Mexico City, its success belied the hard truth that such development efforts contributed to socioeconomic inequality and victimized those on the losing side of a widening social divide. Despite this uneven development, the city's heyday as a resort destination lasted several decades, during which time the jet-set destination attracted throngs of visitors, ranging from ordinary travelers to actors, politicians, and businessmen from the United States.

The uneven outcomes of Alemán's urban-development agenda reflected the overall pattern of mixed results that Alemanismo left. The period's lasting achievements are impossible to deny, but so too are the considerable costs—in human, social, and financial terms—required to implement such an ambitious set of plans. Most glaringly, Alemán's efforts proved to be out of step with the reality of mass population growth among the urban poor that had become apparent during his term. The demographic shift that resulted in sustained rural-to-urban migration over four decades, and ultimately the rapid urbanization of Mexico's population, came as the result of policies set in motion by the Alemán administration. Alemán's efforts to foment domestic industry and commercialize the agrarian sector were symbiotic and brought the most enduring social changes since the 1910 revolution overturned the Porfirian oligarchy.

From Agrarian Revolution to Green Revolution

During the Alemán years Mexico's rural majority faced changes every bit as profound as those experienced by urban residents. These changes took on multiple dimensions, disrupting and reconfiguring rural existence at all levels, from macro-level economic structures to the predictable rhythms of daily life. The abrupt shift away from collectivist ejidos and toward commercialized private agriculture, justified on the grounds that it would increase productivity, went hand in hand with ISI. In the eyes of officials a spike in agricultural production was not merely desirable, but indeed necessary, since the nation had to feed a rapidly growing population and simultaneously provide the export earnings required to pay the heavy costs of industrialization. The alemanista agrarian program also required a considerable amount of legal wrangling to free the administration from various constitutional constraints. Alemán not only slowed the already moribund agrarian reform to a virtual standstill; he also altered the previously sacrosanct twenty-seventh article of the constitution to clear the way for his administration's ambitious plans.

The president's most consequential act in the agrarian sector was to change the definition of what constituted a "small" farm, thereby protecting a greater number of landholders from expropriation of their land. While Article 27 had previously stipulated that any farm exceeding 100 hectares (247 acres) could not be deemed small (except in unusual situations, such as extreme aridity, rainfall, or mountainous terrain, in which case the law provided various alternative calculations to offset those factors), the new amendments amplified that number substantially: 150 hectares (370.5 acres) for cotton, and 300 hectares (741 acres) for bananas, sugar cane, coffee, henequen, olives, vanilla, cacao, rubber plants, and fruit trees.[75] For arid grazing land, "small" now meant up to 50,000 hectares (approximately 123,550 acres), or enough to hold 500 head of cattle.[76] By redefining the limits of small property, Alemán exempted all but the largest farms and most undesirable land from further agrarian reform. The administration also revived the defunct *amparo*, a writ of appeal designed to protect landholders through judicial recourse. The amparo offered them the opportunity to have proposed expropriations reviewed, and thus potentially to be deemed unjust, by the court system. These dual changes allowed Alemán to oversee a dramatic reversal of the revolutionary agrarian reforms that had reached their apex in the 1930s.

Mexico also became the first site of what later came to be known across the world as the green revolution. The nation's experience with the green revolution had its origins in US vice president Henry A. Wallace's six-week visit to the country in late 1940. During that time, he attended the inauguration of Manuel Ávila Camacho. Wallace was eager to demonstrate the intention of the administration of Franklin Delano Roosevelt to cultivate positive relations with Ávila Camacho, who had promised to exercise more moderation than had his predecessor, Lázaro Cárdenas. Wallace, touring the countryside in his own Plymouth, became especially interested in corn production.

The deteriorating conditions he witnessed compelled him to approach Nelson Rockefeller, then head of the Office of Inter-American Affairs (OIAA), about the issue.[77]

The encounter led to the creation of the bi-national Mexican Agricultural Project (MAP), funded by the Rockefeller Foundation and adopted by Mexico's Ministry of Agriculture in 1943. The MAP established research centers that gave US scientists a chance to experiment with corn and wheat yields. A year later, as Mexico's entry into World War II on the side of the Allies drew the two nations closer together, their governments created the US-Mexican Agricultural Commission, underscoring both countries' mutual agricultural needs. Through the 1940s and into the 1950s, the establishment of research initiatives and the importation of hybridized seeds, chemical fertilizers, insecticides, and mechanical equipment came together to form the first major application of the green revolution.[78] US researcher Norman Borlaug, who went on to win the Nobel Peace Prize in 1970, working alongside fellow scientist J. George Harrar, led research efforts to develop high-yield grain that was less susceptible to inclement weather or variations in ecological conditions. Borlaug, later hailed as the father of the green revolution, earned acclaim for creating a model for developing countries with widespread hunger. His work offered a potential corrective to widespread malnutrition around the world. To Mexican officials, it also offered the possibility of stimulating the country's insufficient production of staple grains. Yet despite the almost utopian promise of his green revolution, Borlaug also received criticism for creating an environmentally devastating form of mono-crop agriculture that imposed a commercial agricultural model onto a country that had just begun to adapt to an ejido-based land-tenure system. Notwithstanding these critiques, which have grown over time, the green revolution proved to be compatible with the alemanista development objectives. Just as it had in the city, the administration's agenda also included a set of enormous public works in the rural sector.

The showpieces of Alemán's rural public-works projects reflected the global economic context in which he governed. Emboldened by the idea that his administration could replicate the successes of the Tennessee Valley Authority, Alemán invested in projects that were unprecedented in their scope. Efforts such as the massive Papaloapan River basin development project, especially its new hydroelectric facilities, dazzled domestic and foreign observers. The Morelos Dam on the Colorado River and its massive irrigation network, which supplied water to new wheat-producing regions in

Sonora, represented a practical application of new thinking in economic management: government intervention, whether used to protect domestic industry, correct market imbalances, encourage consumption, or build infrastructure, could aid the development of an advancing capitalist economy. The Falcón Dam, a joint US-Mexican undertaking in the lower Rio Grande Valley to irrigate crops, control flooding, and provide electricity, highlighted a new era in bilateral cooperation. New, expanded, or modernized highways, including the trans-Isthmian and Pan-American routes, connected Atlantic to Pacific ports, cities to the country, and domestic markets to the United States. Alemán also adapted to the post–World War II economy by utilizing large sums of foreign credit and capital from the United States, and further underscored his efforts at US-Mexican cooperation by joining a bilateral initiative to eradicate hoof-and-mouth disease.[79]

The enormous irrigation projects in the country's north fed expansive wheat farms, including those that formed the nucleus of Borlaug's research. The investment in increasing wheat yields also followed the increasingly prevalent theory that wheat presented a preferable alternative to corn as a staple crop, an idea advocated by scientists in both the United States and Mexico. The idea that wheat was a preferable cereal grain had appeared before, as early as the sixteenth century, but the distinction took on greater urgency in the twentieth century.[80] For instance, the anthropologist Manuel Gamio, who held considerable influence within the Alemán administration, advocated such a shift from corn to wheat consumption.[81] Consequently, wheat production, especially in the northern state of Sonora, exploded in the 1940s and 1950s.[82] The misguided scientific argument that wheat was a better base dietary starch found its way into consumer culture as well. As the urban middle sector grew, its members sought to distinguish themselves from those whom they viewed as their social inferiors. Thus, corn came to be seen by many within their ranks as something eaten by poor, rural, and especially indigenous populations. This, aside from reinforcing a notion of indigenous backwardness that revolutionary reformers in the 1920s and 1930s had so eagerly sought to overcome, created an important niche market for commercially produced wheat.

The embrace of wheat production, despite its origin as a strategy to combat hunger, was thus fraught with class implications since it represented something desirable to the upwardly mobile urban middle classes. It also did nothing to subtract from similar efforts to produce more corn. On the contrary, the administration created a new agency, the National Corn

Commission, to oversee production increases. Alemán appointed his longtime friend and associate, Gabriel Ramos Millán, as its director. Ramos Millán, a native of Oaxaca, coordinated the interactions between private landholders, ejidatarios and other rural residents, and government officials necessary to carry out increased corn production.[83] In Oaxaca's Papaloapan River basin, the creation of the Miguel Alemán dam permitted not only hydroelectric production, but also controlled flooding that previously impeded corn production (with the relocation of local peasant populations as the unfortunate byproduct). The development of the Papaloapan basin showcased Alemán's efforts to adopt a TVA-inspired rural-development program.

Alemán's rural initiatives led to a permanent pattern of favoring large-scale commercial agriculture over ejido-based and other collective arrangements. By the 1950s the green revolution had firmly taken root. Officials saw its potential in pragmatic terms, above all as a way to increase yields. Their US counterparts, eager to support the endeavor, also saw in it an ideological potential: if it could help foster broad-based prosperity by producing food, creating employment, and fueling economic growth, then it could help stave off communism by reducing its appeal among the rural poor.[84] Thus, the green revolution reflected the anti-communism of the Truman administration, which took an approach (later called the Truman Doctrine) aimed above all at containing the influence of communism, especially in places with poor majorities that might otherwise be drawn to it. Precisely because of the combined commercial and geopolitical interest that the United States had vested in the green revolution, its critics in Mexico saw it as yet another form of US imperialism eroding the nationalist gains—and the hard-fought material benefits for the poor—of the 1910 revolution.[85]

The changes in land-tenure patterns and production modes introduced in the Alemán years resulted in substantial social and political changes in the coming decades. As was true of his urban-development agenda, these changes produced inconsistent results. On the one hand, production of foodstuffs and electricity underwent a manifold increase. The reforms associated with the green revolution helped agricultural production increase sixfold, besting international averages across the board.[86] Yet those positive gains belied a host of grave consequences. Over the next three decades land became more concentrated, an outcome all but foretold in Alemán's revisions to Article 27 of the constitution. Large landholders, including old families of the Porfirian oligarchy that had survived the revolution intact, extended their investments, while foreign companies like Ralston Purina and Anderson Clayton established a presence that ultimately resulted in an outflow of profits. While these changes helped to spur an increase in productivity, more and more of that production was destined for export, making Mexico a net importer of food. This put even more pressure on its balance of payments, which were already under strain due to ISI's unanticipated costs.[87]

While large capitalist interests, domestic and foreign alike, shared the spoils of this turn toward large-scale commercial agriculture, those on the bottom of the social ladder were denied the opportunity to experience the benefits of cardenista collectivism. Instead, they f aced declining employment due to labor-saving agricultural mechanization and fell into a cycle of severe debt due to lack of access to ejidal credit.[88] This situation drove peasants in record numbers to pull up roots and move to urban areas, above all Mexico City. This push factor was every bit as strong as the pull that came from new jobs in urban industry. For many, life under the new rural political economy introduced by Alemán was simply untenable: private farmers were given subsidies not available to credit-poor ejidatarios, while federal troops and the old "white guards" were on occasion forced to deal with intransigent peasants by inflicting violence.[89] To them, Alemanismo was tantamount to neolatifundismo—a reversion to the abusive and semi-feudal latifundio system that took root in the colonial period and endured until the 1910 revolution.

Conclusion

The rural and urban construction projects of the Alemán years stand as monuments to an era of great optimism. If the symbols of the prior era had been rural schoolhouses and revolutionary murals, then Mexico's post–World War II existence conveyed a sense of something altogether more grand. Yet the outward expressions of national success—from the expansive University City to the innovative multifamiliares, the powerful hydraulic installations of the Papaloapan River to the glittering beachfront promenade of Acapulco—masked harder realities. The alemanista agenda, which moved the nation definitively away from its revolutionary days, was of course not formulated as an attack on those from the ranks of the poor. After all, the mid-1940s represented the beginning of the nation's economic "miracle"—a period of ambition and promise. Yet for those who did not share in the bounty produced by the multi-decade economic agenda established by Alemán and continued by his successors, it must have felt that way.

Alemán and the men of his generation did not consider themselves revolutionaries, at least not in the way that the term had come to be understood by Mexicans after 1910. But even if the term does not apply in the strictest sense, the changes at mid-century were no less transformational than the ones the revolutionaries brought in 1910. The combination of the post–World War II and early Cold War context in which they governed and the consequential decisions that they made within that context led to a fundamental and long-lasting shift that had political, economic, social, and cultural dimensions. The juridical component of this change is most readily identifiable in the Alemán administration's revisions to the 1917 Constitution, while its economic dimensions are most apparent in the replacement of expenditure on social programs with public investment in industry. Yet despite how telling these indicators are, they also reduce such significant changes to a handful of abstract numbers. The most visible legacy of the Alemán era resides in the enormous construction projects funded by the administration. Those projects provide a visual record of the ambitious but only partially realized vision that Alemán and his like-minded collaborators had for their nation.

Figure 1. Young Miguel, standing at left, with his family in Veracruz in the early twentieth century. Seated is his father, Gen. Miguel Alemán González, and his younger brother Carlos. Standing are his mother, Tomasa Valdés de Alemán, and, at right, his older half-brother Antonio (courtesy of Biblioteca Mexicana de la Fundación Miguel Alemán, AC).

Figure 2. (above) As the young governor of Veracruz (1936–1939), Alemán (second from right) aligned himself with populist president Lázaro Cárdenas (1934–1940), seen (center) visiting the state. Cárdenas's expropriation of the oil industry was a popular move in Veracruz, which housed some of the nation's largest petroleum deposits in places such as Poza Rica (courtesy of Biblioteca Mexicana de la Fundación Miguel Alemán, AC).

Figure 3. (right) Alemán's service to the Cárdenas administration and overall competency as governor led President Manuel Avila Camacho (1940–1946) to appoint him as Interior minister, a position Alemán held until launching his own campaign in 1945. The powerful ministry made Alemán head of the nation's intelligence, security, and immigration services, among others (courtesy of Biblioteca Mexicana de la Fundación Miguel Alemán, AC).

Figure 4. Alemán's presidential campaign had its share of large demonstrations, such as this one in Culiacán, the capital of the northwestern state of Sinaloa (courtesy of Biblioteca Mexicana de la Fundación Miguel Alemán, AC).

Figure 5. Alemán took a particularly vigorous personal interest in the construction of the University City (CU) of the National Autonomous University of Mexico (UNAM). Here he is seen touring the construction site, led by supervising architect Carlos Lazo (courtesy of Biblioteca Mexicana de la Fundación Miguel Alemán, AC).

Figure 6. The Central Library of the UNAM, with its signature wraparound mosaic and mural by artist Juan O'Gorman, became one of the most iconic installations of University City. The white statue of Alemán, later vandalized and ultimately dismantled, can be seen faintly at left (courtesy of Biblioteca Mexicana de la Fundación Miguel Alemán, AC).

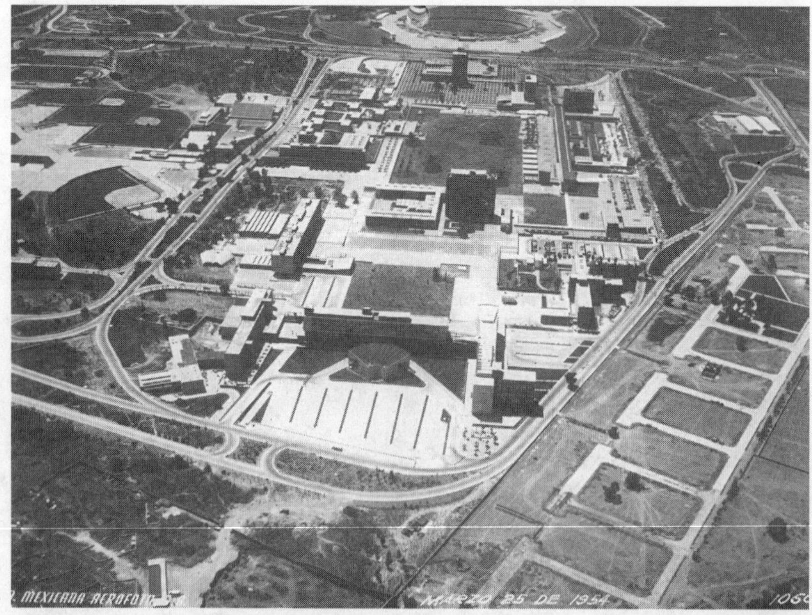

Figure 7. (above) This aerial photograph from 1954 provides some indication of the scope of the CU's construction. The two most iconic buildings, the main library (center) and the rectory (top of photograph) are visible, as are various other installations, including the stadium, dormitories, and classrooms (courtesy of Biblioteca Mexicana de la Fundación Miguel Alemán, AC).

Figure 8. (opposite top) Similarly, this aerial shot from between 1947 and 1949 reveals the scope of the Centro Urbano Presidente Alemán (more commonly known as the Multifamiliar Miguel Alemán). The installation, designed by modernist architect and close Alemán associate Mario Pani, was the first of several massive lower-middle-class housing and commercial complexes built during or immediately after his term. Often called vecindades, literally meaning neighborhoods, the multifamiliares offered amenities ranging from health clinics to laundromats to movie theaters. Their all-inclusive and self-contained qualities reflected an embrace of urban modernism, which can also be seen elsewhere, such as the planned suburb of Satellite City (courtesy of Colección de Fotografías Fototeca Tecnológico de Monterrey, Guillermo Zamora, 1947–1949, All Rights Reserved ©).

Figure 9. (opposite bottom) The mutual state visits of Harry Truman and Miguel Alemán in 1947 represented historic firsts in both cases and went far in generating both goodwill and concrete benefits for US-Mexican relations. Here the two appear together in a parade, with Alemán holding what appears to be a key to the city (presumably Washington, DC) (courtesy of Harry S. Truman Presidential Library).

Figure 10. (top) Alemán boarding the Sacred Cow, the US president's official plane, to visit Harry Truman in 1947. Behind Alemán, on the stairs, is Miguel Alemán Velasco, his son, who would later serve as senator and governor in Veracruz (courtesy of Biblioteca Mexicana de la Fundación Miguel Alemán, AC).

Figure 11. (left) Alemán, seen in 1952 inaugurating the monument to the Niños Heroes, the boy cadets who became national heroes due to their valor in the US-Mexican War. US president Harry Truman earned goodwill when he honored their memory during his 1947 visit. The monument, which stands in the capital's Chapultepec Park, has six pillars to honor each of the fallen cadets (courtesy of Biblioteca Mexicana de la Fundación Miguel Alemán, AC).

Figure 12. Alemán, visiting a cornfield with longtime personal friend Gabriel Ramos Millán, who headed the National Corn Commission until his death in a plane crash in 1949. The Alemán administration devoted considerable effort to the promotion of corn production through public-works projects, green-revolution initiatives, and constitutional amendments that benefited large commercial landholders (courtesy of Biblioteca Mexicana de la Fundación Miguel Alemán, AC).

Figure 13. Alemán, seen here in 1949 testing out fumigation chemicals used to eradicate the citrus blackfly, which threatened crop yields. Alemán oversaw the introduction of chemical fertilizers and pesticides as part of the commercialization of agriculture and green revolution during his term (courtesy of Biblioteca Mexicana de la Fundación Miguel Alemán, AC).

Figure 14. Alemán inaugurating the Solís Dam in 1949, on Guanajuato's Río Lerma. The dam was one of several major hydroelectric installations built during his term (courtesy of Biblioteca Mexicana de la Fundación Miguel Alemán, AC).

Figure 15. Alemán inaugurating another hydroelectric installation, this time in the northern state of Sonora (courtesy of Biblioteca Mexicana de la Fundación Miguel Alemán, AC).

Figure 16. Alemán and his entourage at the inauguration of another hydroelectric facility. Date and location unknown (courtesy of Biblioteca Mexicana

Figure 17. Inspection of a newly constructed site, most likely hydroelectric operations (courtesy of Biblioteca Mexicana de la Fundación Miguel Alemán, AC).

Figure 18. The years immediately following World War II saw the beginning of several decades of mass-scale industrialization, especially in Mexico City. In the photograph, Alemán visits in 1951 a factory built by metal-goods manufacturer Worthington Industries (courtesy of Biblioteca Mexicana de la Fundación Miguel Alemán, AC).

Figure 19. Alemán inaugurating a new Ericsson telephone connection. During his term, the corporation Telmex bought the Mexican operations of the Swedish company, along with those of the American ITT Corporation. The consolidated company would become a government monopoly in the 1970s and would again be privatized in the 1990s (courtesy of Biblioteca Mexicana de la Fundación Miguel Alemán, AC).

Figure 20. Construction taking place along the pristine waterfront in Acapulco. During Alemán's term, Acapulco was transformed from a distant outpost to a major jet-set tourist destination both for Mexicans and for foreign travelers, especially from the United States (courtesy of Biblioteca Mexicana de la Fundación Miguel Alemán, AC).

Figure 21. Alemán and his associates were known for indulging in a luxurious lifestyle. Here, Alemán (seated at center) dines with Nuevo León governor Ignacio Morones Prieto and members of elite Monterrey society. Seated to his left, in white, is socialite and art collector Lydia Sada (courtesy of Biblioteca Mexicana de la Fundación Miguel Alemán, AC).

CHAPTER FOUR

Toward a Better Good Neighbor Policy

ALEMÁN TOOK OFFICE AT A CRITICAL JUNCTURE IN MEXICO'S RELATIONS with the United States. He inherited from his predecessor, Manuel Ávila Camacho, the benefits of an upswing in bilateral cooperation that occurred during World War II. He also faced the task of determining the shape that his country's relationship with the United States would take in the immediate years following the war. The Ávila Camacho administration had taken a number of domestic- and foreign-policy measures that many viewed as out of step with the goals of the revolution. In nearly every case, those policies were characterized as temporary responses to the exigencies of the war. Alemán, on the other hand, encountered an entirely different set of circumstances in the postwar context, ones that provided him greater flexibility in his approach to foreign relations.

On both sides of the border, expectations for the incoming administration were hazy. As interior minister and presidential candidate, Alemán had staked out a middle ground on the issue of US relations. This shielded him from domestic criticism from anti-imperialist voices, a trap that his primary presidential opponent, Ezequiel Padilla, had walked right into. But upon taking power, hazy expectations gave way to a clear vision of national development that would draw Mexico much closer to the United States. Alemán's decision to embrace US government loans and private capital reflected the opportunities and constraints of the early Cold War period as well as the priorities of his generation.

The Alemán administration put supreme emphasis on fomenting industrial development and agricultural productivity, drawing federal resources and attention away from the social programs that originated in the 1910 revolution. To achieve their objectives, officials recognized the need to draw on the economic resources of the United States as it solidified its position at the center of the new global economy. Alemán's approach to bilateral relations, which oscillated between concession to US demands and exploitation of its vulnerabilities, allowed him to carry out his ambitious domestic agenda. Many of his administration's most ambitious and controversial initiatives, including the decisions to convert the Bracero arrangement into a peacetime program, to revise the charters of PEMEX in order to secure foreign credit, and to quell labor activism to attract foreign investment, reflected the fundamental shift in Mexican-US relations that occurred in these years.

As the United States made the transition from wartime victor to postwar superpower, its leaders sought with increased urgency to reaffirm its hemispheric alliances to confront what they perceived to be the growing threat of international communism. Inter-Americanism, safeguarded by a renewed commitment on all sides to the Good Neighbor Policy, underpinned their efforts. Emphasizing the importance of regional solidarity under US leadership, several inter-American conferences were held from 1945 to 1947, first in Mexico City, then in Bogotá, San Francisco, and Rio de Janeiro. Beyond these hemispheric matters, the US government also sought to resolve issues specific to Mexico. The shaky economic climate of the immediate postwar years compelled US officials to recognize the strategic importance of securing a stable oil supply and a reliable influx of temporary agricultural workers. In both cases, they looked to Mexico. US Ambassador George Messersmith, writing to newly inaugurated US President Harry Truman shortly after Franklin Roosevelt's death, described Mexico as "a key country and the key country in the Latin American picture."[1] Underscoring the importance of their nations' relationship, Truman and Alemán both paid official state visits to the other's country in 1947. The reciprocal diplomatic missions showcased the potential for mutual cooperation in the early Cold War period.

A Tale of Two Visits

Harry Truman surprised everyone, including his own personal staff and a skeptical Mexican public, when he interrupted his tour to pay tribute to six of the nation's most celebrated martyrs. During his visit to Mexico City in 1947, he laid a wreath before the monument to the *Niños Heroes*, the fallen boy cadets who, in the last moments of the last battle of their country's disastrous war with the United States a century earlier, threw themselves off of Mexico City's Chapultepec Castle in a dramatic display of national pride. Truman's symbolic act had not been included in the official itinerary of his visit, and when asked by a reporter why he did it, he beamed, "Brave men do not belong to any one race or country. I thought they ought to have the wreath. I respect bravery wherever I see it."[2] The press and public alike were struck by this spontaneous gesture of goodwill. His move to recognize the young soldiers was especially timely, since his visit coincided with the centennial of the US-Mexican War of 1846–1848, which still lingered in the population's collective memory.

Truman's folksiness and warmth, which so often contrasted with the patrician airs of his predecessor, captivated the Mexican public. He set his diplomatic mission off on the right foot within moments of disembarking from the presidential plane, known then as the Sacred Cow. In a brief statement to an enthusiastic welcoming crowd, he tripped over the daunting word Tenochtitlán, the name of the ancient Aztec city located where the capital now stands.[3] The good-humored attempt won the crowd's affection, and above the din one could hear a woman shout "Viva Missouri!"[4]

Truman's charm offensive lasted the duration of his trip. He made particular efforts to emphasize the virtue of peace. When flying over the region's numerous volcanoes, including Michoacán's smoke-belching Paricutín, he proclaimed, "It's a terrible thing when nature takes it out on human beings, but it's even more terrible when human beings take it out on other human beings. And that's just what we've been doing." He reiterated a similar point when visiting the ancient pyramids of Teotihuacán, warning that if a permanent peace were not achieved, modern human civilization would be doomed to the same ruination that befell the Aztecs.[5]

For his part, Alemán went to great lengths to impress upon the US president his country's progress. He treated Truman to full military reviews, parades, and banquets. A lavish ceremony at the National Stadium showcased the dance, music, and indigenous clothing of his nation's various regions, allowing Truman to see plume dancers from Oaxaca, bow dancers from Nayarit, and rattle players from Jalisco.[6] A marimba band played Veracruz's "La Bamba" and the "Missouri Waltz" at a packed US Embassy the next day, showcasing the folk music of the home states of the two presidents.[7]

The visit had high stakes. Alemán's economic ministers had already submitted a detailed six-year plan to the US government, which included the utilization of significant quantities of capital from the Treasury's Export-Import Bank. They intended the money to go toward a range of ambitious development projects in the areas of hydroelectric power, irrigation, highway construction, industry, and agriculture.[8] The most controversial component of the plans, at least from the US perspective, pertained to investment in oil, which had been managed since the 1938 oil expropriation by the public corporation PEMEX. Negotiations on temporary migrant labor, civil aviation, and a number of other strategic and commercial issues loomed over the horizon. The 1947 presidential summit in Mexico City, and its counterpart later that year in several US cities, helped resolve many of those issues.

Alemán's visit to the United States three months later reciprocated the success of Truman's trip to Mexico City. While US Ambassador Walter Thurston had suggested early on that his country would be unable to provide the same degree of ostentation to Alemán,[9] the two stays in fact shared much in common. Alemán traveled on the Sacred Cow and received an official welcome at the White House. He then proceeded to Arlington National Cemetery, where he laid a wreath before the Tomb of the Unknown Soldier, a clear reciprocation of Truman's prior gesture to the Niños Héroes.[10] The same day, he gave a well-received speech to a special session of the US Congress. The final leg of his Washington visit included a boat trip up the Potomac to Mount Vernon, George Washington's home, accompanied by Secretary of State George C. Marshall.[11]

Alemán next flew to New York, where an estimated one million people, undeterred by rain, turned out to wish him well as his motorcade paraded through the city en route to meet Mayor William O'Dwyer. He also made a quick trip upstate, to West Point Academy, where he reviewed troops and delivered a flag from his country's *Colegio Militar*. The tour's next segment took him to the projects of the Tennessee Valley Authority, on which he hoped to model his administration's six-year plan for electrification, irrigation, and energy production. He took time to meet with local farmers, posing for photographs with local children and babies in between tours of hydroelectric facilities.[12]

Alemán wanted to impart the message that his trip was not merely to Washington, but rather to the United States as a whole.[13] This commitment led him to insist on traveling into the country's interior. He chose Kansas City, near Truman's hometown of Independence. It was in Kansas City that Truman first entered politics, making his career in the political machine of Tom Pendergast. On his brief stop, the new president accepted an honorary degree from the University of Kansas City's school of law, which he chose over offers from numerous other universities, among them Harvard, Johns Hopkins, the University of Pennsylvania, and the University of California (he also accepted one from Columbia University while in New York). Truman, noting that his attendance as head of state would be in violation of protocol, could not attend the ceremony.[14]

For both leaders, the trips represented historic firsts. No Mexican president had ever come to the United States on an official state visit. The only previous exchange of visits between sitting presidents occurred when Porfirio Díaz and William Howard Taft met along the Chihuahua-Texas border, in Ciudad Juárez and El Paso, in 1909. Roosevelt had met with Ávila Camacho in Monterrey during World War II, but Truman was the first to tour the capital. Even as the Truman administration aimed the majority of its foreign-policy efforts at areas other than Latin American affairs (for example, the Marshall Plan to rebuild war-torn Europe, the Truman Doctrine to ensure Soviet containment, the creation of the North Atlantic Treaty Organization [NATO], and the recognition of Israel as a sovereign state), it nonetheless embraced its special relationship with Mexico.

Although both trips were regarded as highly successful, they were not entirely absent of problems. During the ceremony at the Estadio Nacional held for Truman, one woman and another young girl were reportedly crushed to death when caught in the chaos of the crowd. Five children also apparently went missing and as many as fifty were hospitalized with injuries.[15] The accident, though noted in the US news, went largely ignored by the Mexican press.

On the US side, the process of arranging Alemán's trip to Kansas City hit an unfortunate snare when one of the president's advisers, Salomón de la Selva (the brother of Alemán's personal secretary, Rogerio de la Selva), chided University of Kansas City president Clarence Decker for the informality of the invitation that he, along with Kansas City mayor William E. Kemp and the Kansas City Chamber of Commerce, had extended to Alemán.[16] Decker's original invitation had offered Alemán a chance to see the heartland, to visit farms, and to increase goodwill between the two countries.[17] A subsequent letter indicated his desire for Alemán to give his university's commencement address.[18] The casual nature of what was otherwise a cordial letter offended de la Selva, who scolded Decker for his "preposterous" document (he appeared particularly incensed at the suggestion that Decker would arrange for an unnamed chaperone to conduct Alemán to Missouri). De la Selva implied that the letter threatened the entire trip and made him regret his earlier eagerness to go to Kansas City, since he had become the butt of jokes among the senior staff. He implored Decker to start over entirely, ending his correspondence by patronizingly asking if his instructions were absolutely clear.[19]

After nearly derailing the trip, their correspondence gradually became more cordial, beginning with an apology from Decker.[20] De la Selva even extended an invitation to Decker from the rector of the UNAM, ahead of Truman's visit to Mexico City, to receive an honorary degree. He also informed Decker that the foreign minister, Jaime Torres Bodet, would nominate him for the prestigious Order of the Aztec Eagle, the highest honor the Mexican government awards to foreigners (Decker never received the accolade).[21] Gradually the two hashed out the details of an acceptable compromise, reducing the original plan for a major event to a short, three-hour ceremony.[22] Mexican dignitaries, including governors Eduardo Vasconcelos of Oaxaca and Adolfo Ruiz Cortines of Veracruz,[23] did not attend as originally anticipated. Governor Phil Donnelly of Missouri came, but his counterpart from Kansas, Governor Frank Carlson, could not because of travel conflicts.[24] An old friend of Alemán's, the wealthy Lebanese immigrant and businessman Neguib Simón Jalife, who had initially offered to pay the 200,000 pesos (about US$41,700[25]) necessary to bring the 100-piece Jalapa Symphony Orchestra, the country's best, withdrew his proposal.[26] Despite their productive and generally polite correspondence, disagreements persisted: Decker expressed his frustration with the lack of publicity from the Mexican Embassy,[27] while he and de la Selva argued about the presence of the Kansas City Chamber of Commerce. While de la Selva insisted that the organization should not be invited, since its members were anti-Truman Republicans and would thus contribute to an inhospitable climate for Alemán,[28] Decker believed that despite their conservative leanings, they in fact were Truman supporters.[29]

With arrangements made for a modest ceremony, cordiality prevailed, and Alemán arrived by train in Kansas City. This was due, de la Selva explained, to the fact that he feared flying and avoided it whenever possible. He did not deliver the commencement address, but instead received a handful of dignitaries in a small ceremony. At the event, Decker presented Alemán with twenty-four signed original lithographs of scenes from Missouri and the rest of the Midwest by renowned artist Thomas Hart Benton, a Kansas City native.[30] Afterward, Decker and Alemán exchanged pleasant letters of thanks and congratulation for the success of the event.[31] The difficulties in arranging Alemán's visit to Kansas City, which arose over seemingly trivial matters, provide an important lesson on the nature of cultural diplomacy. While diplomacy tends to be described in grand terms—as intricate, strategic, and ceremonial—in practice it is often the result of less impressive forces, something far more mundane, tedious, and, at least in this case, even petty. But these mundane affairs produced something tangible. What had begun as a series of diplomatic blunders ended as a successful afternoon event that allowed Alemán to look beyond the confining environment of Washington's diplomatic circles.

The public optimism and ceremonial nature of both visits hid much of the stress caused by unforeseen circumstances such as the series of diplomatic mishaps that nearly derailed the Kansas City visit. The mainstream press in both countries, along with newsreels documenting the trips, emphasized the positive elements of Truman's visit, of which there were plenty. Still, not everyone offered such effusive praise. *El Popular*, Vicente Lombardo Toledano's pro-labor paper, cautioned readers against falling for Truman's good-natured gestures. Behind them, he warned, lay the same imperialist drive to target weak, semi-colonial countries, including Mexico, that the United States had demonstrated in so many instances before.[32] A cartoon by Martín Antoyo V. echoed this sentiment: Truman grins affably, while his spiraling glasses hypnotize those gullible enough to fall for his charms.[33]

This and many other cartoons captured much of the suspicion and cynicism surrounding the visit. Several of them pointed to the facelift given to the Mexican capital prior to Truman's visit. The cartoonist Arias Bernal produced several. In one, a portly woman dunks a young girl, labeled "Ciudad de México (Mexico City)," in a washbasin. Meanwhile, two working-class men in the background chat, one whispering to the other, "She's washing her face for the visit."[34] In another, a beautiful young woman pouts her lips as she applies makeup. A portrait of Truman sits atop her table, and the caption reads, "I'm washing my face for Harry, because if I don't . . ."[35] The caption aptly conveyed the high stakes of his visit. A cartoonist with only the signature Gallo produced one image that juxtaposed what he labeled poetry and vernacular; on the former side sits a welcome sign and an official portrait of Truman; on the latter, a winking maid sweeps an unidentified but clearly undesirable thing under the rug.[36] Another depicts Truman flying over Mexico City in the Sacred Cow. A sign warning of hoof-and-mouth disease (a recent epidemic afflicting thousand of cows along the border) has been taken down, replaced by one offering him a hearty "Wellcome [sic] to Mexico."[37]

These instances of what is visible and what is hidden, captured in satirical cartoons and evident in surviving documentation about diplomatic gaffes and trampled spectators, serve as a metaphor for the difference between the grand gestures of symbolic diplomacy and the much more difficult negotiations that took place behind closed doors. Indeed, both presidents admitted to encountering disagreements, though both turned coy when asked about the specifics of those disagreements, instead emphasizing that they would work them out as good neighbors.[38] Consequently, the visits produced positive results. For every negative cartoon published, a positive one reinforced the gains the two leaders had made. *El Universal* ran sketches of the various events of Truman's stay, such as his visit to Chapultepec Castle and the spectacle at the National Stadium.[39] *Excelsior* printed another with Alemán dressed as a western cowboy and Truman as Mexico's equivalent, the charro,[40] demonstrating their mutual embrace of the other's culture as well as the similarities between the two nations' traditions.

Since large diplomatic exchanges often mask the more intricate, behind-the-scenes negotiations inherent in international relations, gauging their long-term accomplishments is difficult. Nevertheless, the evidence of these two summits permits several conclusions. First, both countries invested a tremendous amount of capital and energy in making the visits a success, suggesting a mutual priority. Second, for both, the visit represented a historic first, meaning that the two countries did not undertake the missions merely to comply with a standing precedent of a courtesy visit. Third, the mutual exchange set the tone for relations between the two countries throughout and beyond Alemán's term. The fact that they occurred precisely at the moment of transition between World War II and the onset of the Cold War was no coincidence. Moreover, they produced a number of measurable accomplishments, including agreements on the direction of the migratory-labor and international-credit arrangements. The symbolic benefits sought by both sides proved more important. Truman's visit produced a feeling of goodwill toward the affable American president and, by extension, to the Good Neighbor Policy implemented by his predecessor. Alemán's trip allowed the US public to see a Mexican president making an effort to improve diplomatic relations through direct engagement with national leaders and ordinary citizens of the United States.

Oil!

The 1938 expropriation of foreign oil interests was a boon for President Cárdenas and a victory for revolutionaries who had fought since 1910 to assert their nation's economic autonomy. In this sweeping act, Cárdenas resolved an ongoing labor dispute and made a profound statement of his country's determination to control its natural resources. Yet even though the expropriation represented one of the supreme achievements of the revolution, it also became a source of frustration for subsequent administrations. Petróleos Mexicanos, or PEMEX, the public corporation responsible for all oil exploration, drilling, refining, and sale in the country and abroad, quickly became a bloated, wasteful burden.

As the process of import substitution industrialization steadily necessitated more and more export earnings to offset the influx of expensive imported capital goods, PEMEX should have been in a position to provide those earnings. Instead, it became a drain on the federal treasury. On the positive side, supplying industry with petroleum through PEMEX became the nation's single most important form of fomenting domestic industry through protectionism.[41] For the new generation of leaders under Alemán, the expropriation's fallout presented considerable challenges to their efforts to adapt to post–World War II realities. Ultimately, the Alemán administration, represented by PEMEX chief Antonio Bermúdez, had to strike a balance on twin fronts: maintain the public, nationalist character of PEMEX while also encouraging foreign investment, and generate sufficient export earnings while also subsidizing industry with oil.[42] Achieving this diverse set of objectives produced a good deal of conflict but also necessitated significant cooperation.

Alemán felt significant pressure on both sides of the oil debate. On the one hand, the expropriation represented one of the keystones of the revolution. On the other, PEMEX's financial woes burdened his administration from the outset. New opportunities for foreign credit opened up after 1945, but to access it, Alemán had little choice but to acquiesce to certain demands made by the US government to open various sectors of the oil industry to private investment from abroad. Thus, he made a series of structural adjustments to PEMEX that allowed him to overcome the most daunting obstacle to his administration's efforts to secure foreign credit. Once the PEMEX obstacle was removed, foreign credit flowed toward a wide range of projects, especially in infrastructure designed to support the administration's industrialization and commercial agricultural programs.

At the outset of his term, Alemán's government outlined a proposal to use foreign loans to pursue a number of important development projects, including making PEMEX a solvent public agency. The status of the PEMEX loan was bound together with a host of other development projects. The US government also had an interest in creating in Mexico a stable oil supply, especially with the recent emergence of political turmoil in Iran,[43] and displayed its eagerness to invest in its publically owned and managed petroleum system. Ultimately, Alemán secured over $200 million of loaned capital from the US Treasury's Export-Import Bank (usually abbreviated as Eximbank) over the course of his term.[44] Yet in spite of the two nations' mutual interest in oil development and long-term credit arrangements, the road to acquiring that credit was neither certain nor smooth.

State Department and Eximbank officials were prepared to support an extension of capital for petroleum refining and transportation projects, but both expressed reluctance to provide money for the exploration, development, and production of new sources of oil.[45] They had manifold objections. First, State Department officials considered private capital the most efficient manager of petroleum resources. Secretary of State George C. Marshall pointed to PEMEX's own financial woes as evidence of this in 1947. Second, they expressed concern that if new exploration and development continued to exclude private investors, especially foreign firms, then there was little incentive for Eximbank to award more loans. In this case, the economic benefit would be limited to Eximbank's interest earnings and would open little in the way of US private interests. Third, they saw the potential for such an arrangement to set a corrosive precedent. According to their logic, if one oil-rich country could nationalize its petroleum industry, expel foreign interests, and then borrow substantial sums of capital from the US government to develop its public oil industry, then there would be little to stop others in the region, such as Brazil or Venezuela, from doing the same.[46] As late as 1949 Secretary of State Dean Acheson expressed this concern to one of Truman's aides, John Steelman.[47] From 1949 to 1950 these concerns, coupled with disagreements between officials in the executive branch and several prominent congressmen, held up negotiations for a massive extension of credit from Washington.

While Alemán's government had little trouble obtaining the relatively modest quantity of $50 million in credit in 1947, this figure fell well short of his administration's original six-year plan, based on a proposed influx of $240 million of foreign loans.[48] The 1947 credit went some distance toward that goal, and his administration was further bolstered by close to $80 million coming from the International Bank for Reconstruction and Development designated for the construction of hydroelectric and steam electric stations to generate and distribute electricity.[49] In spite of these gains, by the halfway point of his sexenio, Alemán was well off the mark of his initial objective. Thus, the two governments entered into negotiations in 1949 for a second loan, one that would be substantially larger. The precise size of the loan proposed by both sides ranged widely and changed periodically, but the State Department's disagreement with the Alemán government's plan to devote significant portions of the loan to the oil-exploration and oil-production activities of PEMEX ultimately brought the final sum down significantly. The State Department's position from 1947 to 1950 was marked by striking continuity: both Secretary of State George C. Marshall in 1947 and his successor Dean Acheson in 1949–1950 expressed similar convictions and exerted substantial influence on Eximbank.

Negotiations for the loan were suspended on two occasions from late 1949 to early 1950, both at the behest of the Mexican government.[50] Ambassador Antonio Espinosa de los Monteros formally withdrew his country's requests on these occasions after it became clear to Alemán that progress on the oil loan would require major compromise. Various internal and external factors, many beyond his control, made matters more complex. A rumor floated through the US Embassy in Mexico City that only two figures supported the oil loan within the Alemán administration—PEMEX director Antonio Bermúdez and treasury minister Ramón Beteta—and that they supported it only for opportunistic reasons.[51] George Elsey, an administrative assistant to Truman, noted that Bermúdez never stopped angling for a loan specifically for oil, even after Alemán abandoned the unproductive effort.[52] It is not clear whether or not these rumors had any validity, but they suggest a strong possibility of a lack of unity within Alemán's administration.

The same can be said for the US government. A State Department memorandum noted the problems with the US position within the negotiation process, identifying four related issues. First, some within the Treasury Department, which held authority over Eximbank, thought that the State Department was meddling inappropriately in a treasury affair. Second, the overemphasis on PEMEX's status as a public corporation was inconsistent with prior policy, given that the US government had loaned Mexico

$17 million for its nationalized railway system with successful repayment. Third, the fact that the United States could give money for European reconstruction without the chance of repayment but could not provide a reasonably secure loan to Mexico also was inconsistent. Fourth, if the United States withdrew from the process, the Soviet Union might jump at the opportunity to provide its own loan, thus threatening US interests in the region. The communist threat seemed especially realistic since China had already established a steamship route to Mexico.[53]

The loan also found champions in other figures within the US government. Interior secretary Oscar Chapman implied that due to mutual interests, perhaps the two countries might work out an oil-for-steel arrangement (one that apparently never took off, making the public statement by such a high-ranking official perplexing).[54] Congressmen Robert Crosser and Charles Wolverton, each of whom served at different points as chair of the House Committee on Interstate and Foreign Commerce (Crosser as ranking Democrat and Wolverton as his Republican counterpart), both expressed a desire for the loan negotiations to proceed.[55] Crosser had initially called on the State Department to take on a more circumscribed role in the process.[56] Later, Wolverton's eagerness to finalize the loan negotiations caused some problems, especially when Commerce secretary Charles Sawyer, on an official visit to Mexico City in 1949, had to sidestep questions about Wolverton's vigorous public promotion of a loan.[57] Even though they occasionally clashed with White House, State Department, and Eximbank strategies (which appear to have been in virtual lockstep), the enthusiastic support from Crosser and Wolverton probably did more benefit than injury to the process, considering the publicity that these high-ranking members of Congress drew.

The State Department also used the negotiations as an opportunity to petition Alemán's government to address grievances from US private interests. The most controversial case revolved around a decade-old claim made by the Sabalo Transportation Company. The firm, registered in Mexico but principally controlled by three US investors—Sam Katz, George H. Morris, and George Butler, the latter two of the Bank of New York—had been contracted by PEMEX's predecessor agency, Petromex, to conduct drilling operations in the Poza Rica region of Veracruz just prior to expropriation. Once the contracted operations began, Petromex failed to secure proper authorization from the Ministry of National Economy, thus delaying commencement of Sabalo's work beyond the 1938 expropriation decree. Following the expropriation, Sabalo received compensation of an amount that its executives considered to be a substantial underestimation of its value.[58]

The company demanded $4.5 million plus interest to end its suit. After being rejected by the Cárdenas government and subsequently ignored for many years, the Mexican Supreme Court eventually ruled against Sabalo's claims. With the resumption of oil negotiations in 1949, the State Department again took up the issue, articulating its official position that $4 million represented a sufficient quantity to satisfy the company and remove any impediment to bilateral relations. The director of the US Central Intelligence Agency, Allen Dulles, warned Bermúdez that the case could hold up negotiations on oil. He asserted that he could use his influence with Assistant Secretary of State Edward G. Miller, along with his brother, Senator John Foster Dulles (both of whom were members of the powerful Sullivan and Cromwell law firm) and his friend, Secretary of State Dean Acheson, to push for a resolution.[59]

Miller's presence in the negotiations sparked controversy. Prior to his appointment in 1949 by Acheson as assistant secretary of state for Inter-American Affairs, he had been an attorney at Sullivan and Cromwell. At the time, Sabalo had retained the firm, with Miller acting as counsel on the case. Several figures, including Congressman Wolverton, viewed his influence in ongoing negotiations with Sabalo as a conflict of interest.[60] Acheson disagreed. In response to Wolverton's claims, he claimed in a letter to Representative John Kee, chair of the House Foreign Affairs Committee, that Miller had been properly vetted and had withdrawn all professional and financial ties to the firm. Undersecretary of State James Webb, in order to assure both governments and the press of Miller's impartiality, acted as the State Department's official representative in the negotiation process.[61] This allowed the negotiations to proceed without objection from Alemán's government over the personal or financial interests of State Department personnel.

The negotiations for the loan had finally succeeded by October of 1950. Mexico had rescinded its petition for a direct loan, along with its subsequent withdrawal from ongoing talks over the issue, replacing it with a request for a line of credit.[62] The plan worked: the Alemán administration received a revolving credit line extending to $150 million that would be allocated on a project-by-project basis, as opposed to receiving a lump-sum loan.[63] This allowed the United States to refuse funding for PEMEX projects it found objectionable, and it allowed the Mexican government to make any legal or operational adjustments in the event that it needed the money for those petroleum projects. Truman personally congratulated Alemán for achieving a massive extension of credit from Eximbank,[64] and Ambassador Espinosa de los Monteros lobbied the US government to avoid the term "oil loan" and to replace it with "line of credit" in Eximbank's press reports. This constituted an effort to emphasize that much of the credit was aimed at other constructive areas representing major advances in Mexico's national development, including agriculture, irrigation, hydroelectric power, highways, and railroads, and to avoid embarrassing Alemán.[65] In a press statement, the Eximbank noted that the $150 million credit line was an extension of the $50 million already loaned in 1947, and that it was made on the basis of the prompt and full payments made on existing obligations by the Alemán government.

The difficult oil-loan negotiations undertaken during Alemán's term exemplified the opportunities and challenges that both countries faced in the immediate post–World War II context. The US State Department was actively involved in the negotiations, and its officials, including two secretaries of state, considered the economic interests of US-based private firms a priority. The presence of State Department officials in the discussions, especially in the Sabalo case, generated accusations of impropriety from treasury employees, the press, and members of congress. Their concerns echoed the basic premise of later scholars who would argue that one of the central functions of US diplomatic practice has been to advance an agenda of economic imperialism.[66] Nevertheless, the negotiations revealed that far from existing in a state of dependency vis-à-vis its northern neighbor, Alemán and his representatives asserted their country's interests in a forceful and persuasive manner. Although they conceded ground on numerous points, ultimately they succeeded in getting what they needed out of the arrangement. In the process, both countries faced not only areas of conflict with one another but also internal disagreements about how to proceed. In Mexico's case, both White House and US Embassy officials pointed to discord within Alemán's administration. On the US side, Treasury and State Department officials jockeyed for authority in the proceedings, the former as the agency charged with fiscal policy, the latter as the guarantor of US interests abroad. In sum, the proceedings over the oil issue functioned as a microcosm of the early postwar period, as the United States used economic diplomacy to affirm its leading position in hemispheric affairs, and as the largest Latin American republics sought to reconfigure their relationship with the United States to greater advantage.

The Bracero Agreement: Postwar Continuity of a Wartime Program

The Bracero Program, first signed in 1942 as a bilateral arrangement to send Mexicans to the United States to serve as temporary replacement field laborers, had originally been intended as a measure that would end after World War II. Therefore, the successive extensions of the program until 1964, beginning with agreements that Alemán and Truman made in 1947, came as a surprise to many. The transformation of the Bracero Program into a long-term arrangement reflected broader patterns in bilateral relations that occurred between World War II and the early Cold War period. Both sides harbored particular motivations for extending the program, and both presidents faced domestic pressures from groups representing both sides of the issue. Government officials and academic researchers in Mexico, including prominent anthropologist Manuel Gamio, persuaded Alemán that the program would afford their country numerous benefits. According to the program's supporters, Bracero workers could go to the United States to learn proper work habits and to become familiar with the types of machinery being utilized in ISI and green-revolution initiatives. While gaining these vocational skills, they argued, workers would also adopt proper habits of hygiene, savings, and household management.[67] The result of these temporary labor exchanges would be more productive citizens who obtained financial and personal benefits and who, in turn, would benefit a growing and modernizing nation.

The program also allowed the PRI to establish and maintain strong bonds of loyalty from municipal officials, ejido leaders, union bosses, and low-level government functionaries, who could derive financial benefit from their participation in the program. Moreover, it could ensure the support of working-class constituents, who continued to be the program's most ardent supporters even long after the US Congress unilaterally terminated it in 1964. In this respect, the Bracero Program constituted part of a broader effort to create an expansive, patronage-based ruling party.[68] Thus, even as some decried the program's violations of basic human dignity,[69] Alemán saw its modernizing potential while simultaneously recognizing that it could yield substantial political dividends.

Truman encountered an entirely different set of considerations. Following the war, he faced the task of choosing his side in the pitched battle between farmers, who cited their considerable financial woes to justify their employment of migrant workers, and organized labor, whose representatives considered the Bracero Program both an insult and a threat to US workers.[70] Politicians with constituencies or backers supporting one or the other side also tried to get Truman to see their point of view. Prompted by Ambassador Messersmith and others, the White House took the twin positions that the Bracero Program could help hard-hit farmers weather the unpredictable postwar economy and could help promote a positive understanding of the United States in Mexico. Thus, in their minds the program fit within the scope of the Good Neighbor Policy. The argument from its US supporters was simple: by bringing laborers north, and by safeguarding them against racial discrimination, human abuses, and unfair pay through new legal protections that were non-existent during the war, Mexicans would be less inclined toward communism at a time when anti-American sentiment was on the rise in other parts of Latin America.[71]

The Bracero arrangement endured long after the war. Officials created several major revisions to the rules that governed the legal entry of temporary workers into the United States. Both governments harbored suspicions about the feasibility of a fair and beneficial postwar guest-labor arrangement. Several unexpected influxes of illegal immigration provoked concern among US officials. In one dispatch, US Ambassador Walter Thurston warned that the El Paso border crossing might need to be shut down due to an overabundance of incoming laborers, a concern reiterated by Senator Clinton Anderson of New Mexico.[72] Similar frustrations over unchecked illegal immigration fueled political debate among politicians, labor leaders, and farmers. In 1948 Metro-Goldwyn-Mayer studios even produced a film, called "Border Incident," that criticized government tolerance of large influxes of laborers who had not entered the country in accordance with the legal protocols of the Bracero Program.[73]

The US government's attempts to ensure that Mexican workers would receive acceptable wages also provoked considerable debate. A 1949 law demanding that employees earn forty cents per hour met with scorn from Texas Governor Allan Shivers, who balked that the decision should be a state's right.[74] By contrast, the editors of the *Brownsville Herald* argued that a rise in Bracero living standards would mean a rise in the living standard for everyone, since they participated in the economy as consumers while in the country. They also decried what they regarded as the false stereotype of the lazy Mexican, implying that opponents of wage guarantees used it as a smokescreen to hide their desire to avoid paying migrants the prevailing wage. The paper claimed that if their work ever flagged, it was due to their food options being worse than the "fish-and-grits diet of the deep South Negro."[75]

The concerns over illegal immigration, unfair labor competition, and wage parity compelled Truman to launch an initiative to study the question of labor. The effort began with the formation of the President's Committee on Migratory Labor in June of 1950, an idea that got mixed support within the federal government. The Departments of State, Labor, and Agriculture all supported the concept. The State Department took the position that the committee would allow the administration to consider total exclusion of migrant labor, which its officials regarded as a positive step, since they considered the Bracero arrangement a national embarrassment. Labor Department officials bolstered the argument, noting that whatever decision the administration ultimately pursued, the committee could absorb some of the scorn from the side whose interests lost. Officials at the Agriculture Department not only concurred with State that exclusion should be considered, but also figured that the formation of a committee could rally public and congressional support behind the idea. The Justice Department, on the other hand, objected to the proposal, arguing that thrusting what should be the administration's responsibility onto a committee could ultimately backfire on Truman, especially if the committee's plans were not economically beneficial.[76]

The political calculations behind the committee's formation reveal a deep concern among administration officials and advisers over its potential consequences. One internal memorandum, for instance, pointed out that if the committee were to uncover examples of negligence in immigration enforcement, it could cause embarrassment for the White House.[77] Yet despite such risks, Truman formed the committee, whose members included several noted professors along with the archbishop of San Antonio. What resulted from the committee's proceedings was a series of recommendations to alter the International Executive Agreement regarding migratory labor, which the two governments first signed in 1942 after Mexico declared war on the Axis. The recommendations called for more reliance on domestic labor, legislation explicitly forbidding employment of illegal immigrants, improved worker housing, the upholding of a minimum wage, improvements in job standards and worker rights, and more oversight in labor management and contracting. The US Farm Placement Service, a division of the Labor Department's Employment Service, would act as labor contractor and mediator in contracting disputes.[78] The US Congress also voted in favor of establishing reception centers along the border to allow for labor contracting under fairer conditions.[79] The successful implementation of these recommendations convinced the Mexican government to support the program's extension.

The committee's recommendations generated the support of the Mexican government and of organized labor in the United States, the biggest domestic obstacle to a migratory-labor agreement. William Green, president of the powerful American Federation of Labor (AFL), wrote to Truman to express his favorable assessment of the committee. James G. Patton, president of the National Farmers Union, also endorsed the committee's findings.[80] Labor leaders were especially optimistic about a commitment to providing migrant workers a prevailing wage, since a narrowing of the wage gap might persuade farmers to employ domestic laborers instead of their foreign counterparts. Truman and Alemán exchanged a series of letters over the issue throughout 1951. Truman noted his desire to cut off illegal immigration and to reduce the number of incoming laborers. The problem with too many foreign laborers, he argued, was that it drove down wages and thus depressed living conditions across the board. After pleas from Truman, Alemán agreed to support the plan for six months.[81] Approximately a year later, Truman and Alemán agreed that all immediate problems had been solved, and Truman announced his plan to request more congressional appropriations for the Farm Placement Service.[82]

Alemán only assented to an extended agreement after being assured that workers would receive equitable and humane treatment. Concern for worker mistreatment—a justifiable concern in light of the evidence of abuses—became the central preoccupation of Alemán's administration in the migratory-labor negotiations. For instance, US Undersecretary of Labor Michael Galvin, who visited Mexico in October of 1951 on a goodwill mission, faced questions about an alleged incident in which Bracero workers were fed canned meat clearly designated for animals. Galvin responded that this was a local and isolated problem and not a symptom of the failure of the newly constructed Labor Reception Centers. By attempting to deflect blame from the federal government, he tacitly acknowledged that the allegation of the incident's occurrence was true. He elaborated that a local Eagle Pass judge, Robert Bibbs, who had been contracted to supply food for the center, had purchased the food from someone named Stafford (first name unknown), also from the town, who managed a food plant called the Unión Ganadera de Coahuila on the other side of the border. Evidently, he had also sold similar products as food for patients in an Eagle Pass hospital.

Galvin spun the situation to demonstrate US officials' concern with the plight of migrant laborers. He issued an assurance that all contracts with Judge Gibbs had been canceled. He also noted a similar incident in Piedras Negras in which US authorities confiscated a shipment labeled dog food, which a supplier had sent to evade certain taxes levied on human food.[83] The issue put a temporary damper on an otherwise cordial trip that included meetings with Nuevo León governor Dr. Ignacio Morones Prieto, labor minister Manuel Ramírez Vázquez, and interior minister Adolfo Ruiz Cortines.[84] In his meetings and press conferences, he stressed his government's commitment to fair treatment. He cited the example of a new recruiting center under construction at El Centro, California, where Bracero workers would enjoy barracks designed to offer comfortable housing to one thousand men, along with a kitchen to feed half of them at any time, ample windows, and the highest standards of sanitation and comfort.[85]

Alemán and Truman arrived at a series of understandings that improved the Bracero Program and made it politically and economically tenable on both sides. Their mutual embrace of a peacetime Bracero Program, originally a temporary policy to supply replacement labor during the war, enabled an agreement that managed to satisfy competing interests: in Mexico, the debate centered on whether the program represented a setback to the progress workers had made in the revolution or whether it provided an opportunity to make a working class better suited to new domestic industrialization plans. In the United States, farmers facing a contraction in food demand and labor unions fearing an economy unable to absorb the postwar influx of workers, especially in a moment of high inflation, squared off on the issue of migratory labor. Through the course of their nearly concurrent terms, the two presidents and members of their administrations made the program mutually acceptable. Although the program continued to spark controversy until it finally buckled in 1964 under the pressure of union and religious opposition in the United States, the Bracero negotiations and subsequent bi-national accords epitomized a period of cooperation and compromise between the two countries.

Protectionism, Free Trade, and State-Led Development

Alemán identified a major drive toward industrialization as one of his administration's priorities immediately upon taking office. Building on the economic and diplomatic gains of World War II, his administration initiated an industrialization program that was unprecedented in its scope. This economic agenda, much like the shift in US-Mexican relations, simultaneously reflected major changes in international circumstances and the priorities of his generation. By the 1940s the major nations of Latin America had embraced the economic strategy of import substitution industrialization (ISI), adopting protectionist policies to make their economies more self-sufficient and diversified. The geopolitical circumstances of the postwar period made industrialization efforts even more attractive, since the United States could bolster its commitment to hemispheric solidarity and defense through direct loans to Latin American nations. Moreover, even as ISI required protectionist measures that violated the US preference for free trade, the opening of consumer markets in Latin America promised new markets for foreign investment and the sale of goods.

The industrialization program of Alemán's government thus reflected a region-wide trend, but its specific forms reflected the generational tendencies of the Alemán-era leadership. Alemán and other members of his administration, including treasury minister Ramón Beteta, based part of their planning on the success of the Tennessee Valley Authority (TVA), a massive, government-funded project to increase energy production in the United States. Indeed, many of Alemán's largest projects, especially the Papaloapan and Morelos hydroelectric dams, were inspired by his visits to the Chickamagua and Wilson Dams of the TVA.[86] More importantly, the TVA, an extension of the New Deal legislation, symbolized the possibilities of publically funded development within a largely capitalist framework. Indeed, the Keynesian-inspired policies of the United States in the 1930s, which used government investment to spur employment, stimulate consumption, and build infrastructure, seem to have made an impression on Alemán, who marveled at the TVA as a development model.[87]

The US government supported Mexico's drive to industrialize through direct loans from the Eximbank, provided that it was done on what officials considered a sound basis with a minimum of potentially destructive protectionism. Several prominent officials gave their own assessments of their southern neighbor's efforts at economic development. In most cases, they asserted that the United States, as the center of a significantly altered postwar global economy, had a vested interest in the promotion of free trade. Commerce secretary Charles Sawyer, in a speech to the American Society of Travel Agents during a 1949 visit to Mexico City, noted that trade between the two countries had exploded, but that it was also highly imbalanced. According to him, in 1938 the United States exported goods worth $62 million to Mexico and imported the equivalent of $49 million. By 1948, the United States sold goods worth $520 million and took in $247 million. In his speech he pointed to his government's wish to keep tariffs low to allow trade in both directions to flow unhindered by protectionist barriers, and to encourage more importation of Mexican products by the United States.[88] He noted that an increase in tourism, coupled with an effort to direct strategic materials to the United States, would help correct the trade imbalance. Nevertheless, he also cautioned that his country would seek strategic materials where they could be acquired at the cheapest price, hinting that any extensions of special wartime buy-up arrangements (during World War II, the US government bought Mexican goods at fixed price and quantity quotas as a form of rent-seeking behavior designed to keep the Axis from establishing its own economic links to the region) between the two countries were out of the question.[89] No doubt this signaled a shift in priority on the part of the US government away from Latin America and toward both the Asian and European markets, a dismissive turn that many Latin Americans found galling in light of the region's service to the United States before and during World War II.[90]

Sawyer's visit, while of course not as lavish as Truman's, included its share of fanfare. His trip included a large banquet, a private meeting with Alemán, a dinner hosted by interior minister Adolfo Ruiz Cortines, a trip to the pyramids of Teotihuacán, and a fishing trip on Alemán's private yacht in Acapulco.[91] While in Mexico, he also visited Distribuidora Mexicana, S. A., the furniture and office-equipment factory of Antonio Ruiz Galindo, Alemán's first minister of economy. Sawyer reported his positive impression of the facility: not only was it a modern, productive factory, but it also contained excellent worker amenities, including lockers, showers, gymnasiums, a swimming pool, a spacious cafeteria, and special buses to and from work.[92] Ruiz Galindo, whose primary investments were in residential and commercial furniture, had earned a reputation prior to his appointment in Alemán's cabinet as a leader in paternalistic owner-worker relations. Therefore, the fact that his factory was selected to showcase the nation's industrial progress made sense.

The visit's only hitch came when one of Sawyer's assistants at the Commerce Department expressed concern over a proposed overnight stay in the home of Rómulo O'Farrill Jr. The unnamed official remarked that while reception at the home of Rómulo O'Farrill Sr., a media mogul and close friend and associate of Alemán, would be acceptable, a stay with his son would not be commensurate with the prestige of the secretary of commerce.[93] A memorandum that circulated through the Commerce Department reported that O'Farrill was married to a daughter of Maximino Ávila Camacho, which had slightly and temporarily decreased the prestige of their otherwise illustrious name.[94] This minor disagreement appears not to have hindered Sawyer's trip in any respect, since a later Commerce Department memo said that the secretary had an enjoyable stay at the younger O'Farrill's home, where the Sawyers even taught Mrs. O'Farrill to play canasta.[95]

Sawyer's trip, and especially his public remarks, received wide exposure in the press. Charles R. Burrows, the first secretary of the US Embassy in Mexico City, noted in correspondence to the State Department that the visit generated particular attention because, while normally US officials only spoke about ways to sell their country's goods abroad, Sawyer emphasized the importance of increasing Mexico's sales to the United States.[96] Thus, Sawyer's assurance that his government would like to see more imports from Mexico met with enthusiasm, a sentiment bolstered by his assertion that the US population's love of Mexican art, culture, and life would facilitate the process.[97] In his view, the public's desire to travel there and the US business community's desire to buy goods would go far in correcting the trade imbalance. Addressing the recent devaluation of the peso by the Alemán administration, Sawyer expressed confidence that this would further remedy the imbalanced trade between the two nations.[98] While Alemán had initially wanted to move the peso-to-dollar ratio from 4.85:1 to 8:1, US officials proposed 10:1. After successive counter offers (8.33:1 from Mexico, 9:1 from US), the two governments settled on 8.65:1, suggesting US confidence in Mexico's economic potential.[99] Finally, Sawyer emphasized the point that under no circumstance would the US devalue its dollar, as the British government had recently done to the pound sterling.[100] Indeed, this topic reappeared several times during his visit, since a move to devalue the dollar would reverse the benefits of the peso devaluation, adding extra economic strain without correcting the trade imbalance.

Numerous other US officials mentioned their positions on the matters of free trade and domestic protectionism. Guy Ray, the head of the State

Department's Mexican Affairs Division, noted to Truman's presidential secretary, Charles Ross, that the United States fully supported Mexico's industrialization efforts, provided that the industry did not require what he called "exaggerated protection."[101] Echoing this same general perspective, the US Embassy's economic counselor, Merlin L. Bohan, noted in a speech to the Rotary Club of Mexico City that temporary protection was fine, whereas "excessive" protection would ultimately lead to negative consequences. The economy would flourish, he argued, only when a measured level of protection was applied to sound industry, rather than to the production of low-quality articles, and only when it did not contribute to especially inflated prices. He outlined a series of prescriptions for Mexico's economic development, including a recommendation to minimize government intervention in the economy over time.

Despite his stated preference for minimal government presence in economic affairs, he also acknowledged that a situation of total free trade was impossible at the present stage of economic development in both economies. He further asserted that nobody in the United States wished to encourage a "mercantilist" philosophy, thus indirectly addressing criticism of the uneven and dependent relationship that Mexico had traditionally experienced with his country. He instead argued that his government supported the buildup of machinery for power plants, cement plants, steel mills, textile mills, pulp and paper mills, chemical plants, and food-processing factories, among others. Nevertheless, he also encouraged the Alemán government to concern itself with the health of what he opaquely called the separate external and internal economies (presumably meaning the export sector and its counterpart aimed at internal consumption), reinforcing comments made by Secretary Sawyer on his visit.[102] In hindsight, the comment proved to be astute, considering that the overemphasis on government-supported industrialization eventually led to a crippling debt and balance-of-payments crisis throughout Latin America.

The Alemán administration's economic policies drew not only attention from abroad, but also criticism at home. Treasury secretary Ramón Beteta faced a harsh reproach in 1951 from Gustavo R. Velasco, the head of the Mexican Bankers Association, at its annual meeting in Guadalajara. In his introductory speech, Velasco criticized the government's meddling in economic affairs, calling it "unconstitutional, uneconomic, and unproductive" and claiming that it contributed to widespread inflation.[103] Presumably he was making a specific reference to the recent devaluation of the peso, though his critiques most likely applied to the administration's general ISI-oriented policies, given that protectionist policies for domestic industry often drive prices upward. Beteta retorted that the administration's policies were, contrary to Velasco's accusations, sound according to the evidence: national income had risen, taxes remained low, inflation was in check, and currency outflow had halted. He further asserted that a series of price controls ensured that the nation's poorest sectors would not fall victim to price fluctuations, pre-empting criticism that Alemán's administration had not done enough for the poor.[104]

Beteta made similar explanations about the devaluation three years earlier, noting that it was a onetime measure to stop depletion of currency reserves.[105] At the end of the previous year, the US Treasury had authorized a transfer of $10 million to Mexico's Treasury for the cost of 48.5 million pesos in order to shore up its foreign reserves, prompting Beteta to issue some assurance to treasury secretary John Snyder that it would not become a pattern.[106] Snyder, who attended the 1951 meeting in Guadalajara, praised the administration's successes in securing foreign credit and promoting economic development.

The drive toward a protectionist-based development strategy that relied on foreign investment, coupled with periodic crises that necessitated currency devaluation, produced debate and concern at home and abroad. Yet despite the significant disagreements that Alemán's economic agenda provoked, he succeeded in striking a balance between pursuing an inward-looking program of economic nationalism, exemplified by ISI, and participating in a free trade–based global economy. The balance contained inherent contradictions and necessitated compromises, but it allowed his government to pursue an industrial-development program while satisfying the investment requirements of the US government. Just before leaving office, Alemán hosted the fifty-four member countries of the Bretton Woods Accords at the annual meeting of the IMF and World Bank, its central banking institutions. Snyder complimented Alemán on his efforts, noting in a personal letter the success of the Mexico City summit.[107] The meeting symbolized the Alemán administration's achievements in defining bilateral economic relations that endured for the next three decades.

Conclusion

Alemán presided over a formative period in US-Mexican relations. Free from the wartime constraints that limited the options of his predecessor, he made both symbolic diplomatic overtures and substantive policy changes that drew the two countries closer together. The Truman administration responded favorably. The foreign-relations strategies that Alemán pursued were the outcome of a matrix of contextual factors, including domestic political pressures combined with opportunities to gain credit and capital from the United States. Those opportunities often came with demands, ones that Alemán met in order to see his agenda bear fruit. At the same time, the realignment of bilateral relations reflected the ethos of a ruling generation whose members envisioned their country as a modern industrial power. A closer relationship with the United States served as one of the means to that end.

Alemán deftly manipulated the circumstances of the early Cold War period to his advantage. Even as the United States emerged as a global superpower, its position of economic and political hegemony in Latin America was tenuous. US officials relied on the maintenance of a hemispheric, inter-American alliance as part of the Truman Doctrine of communist containment, providing Alemán some bargaining power as he negotiated agreements on migratory labor, oil loans, and numerous other bi-national issues. Consequently, Alemán could carry out an ambitious domestic agenda while simultaneously building stronger relations with the United States. Other issues that had little relevance to his administration's political designs provided Alemán an opportunity to demonstrate his commitment to positive relations with the United States. For example, the 1946 outbreak of hoof-and-mouth disease, a consequence of the importation of Brazilian Zebu bulls, required that both governments issue a swift and comprehensive response. The result was a process, lasting roughly the duration of Alemán's term, in which scientists and officials from both countries carried out a two-stage response, first with a mass slaughter of cattle in Mexico that might potentially be destined for the United States, then with a vaccination campaign that succeeded in eradicating the disease. The cooperation demonstrated by both sides earned Alemán's government praise from the scientific and political communities in the United States,[108] which could only have helped his efforts to achieve positive bilateral relations. Through this and other efforts at collaboration, he and Truman resolved many of the lingering issues in the relationship between the two countries.

The two leaders, despite their progress in diplomatic and economic relations, did not succeed in resolving all of the issues that confronted their two countries. The case of Chamizal, a small spit of land created by a change of course along the Rio Grande that occurred after nineteenth-century territorial surveys had determined the exact coordinates of the border, stands as one example. Despite Truman's contention that a largely uninhabited piece of land totaling around one square mile could not possibly mean that much to either country,[109] the dispute was not resolved until Presidents Lyndon Johnson and Adolfo López Mateos negotiated an agreement in 1963. The Alemán and Truman governments reached a similar impasse on the issue of civil aviation. Mexico demanded a monopoly on certain routes, stoking the ire of US officials who demanded free competition. The demand galled their Mexican counterparts, who regarded it as hypocrisy, given the subsidies that US carriers received. Extended negotiations did not work until 1957, when the two governments reached a mutually satisfactory civil-aviation agreement.[110]

These issues, unresolved when Alemán left office in 1952, point to the complex and evolving nature of bilateral relations between the two countries. While Alemán's administration did not succeed in correcting all of the challenges it faced, and while subsequent administrations faced a myriad of other challenges, Alemán and Truman nonetheless set the pace for relations between Mexico and the United States for years to come. The domestic agenda Alemán pursued, especially ISI coupled with green-revolution and other commercial agriculture initiatives, relied on the supply of capital investment from the US government, along with private foreign investment. This basic platform defined internal-development policy, and consequently foreign policy related to the United States, through the 1970s. Thus, the domestic-policy and foreign-relations approaches utilized by Alemán were mutually reinforcing and together defined much of the legacy of his generation.

CHAPTER FIVE

Away from Alemanismo

THE *DEDAZO* STANDS AS ONE OF THE MOST PERSISTENT MYTHS OF THE PRI's long tenure at the helm of national politics. The selection of presidents every six years has largely been attributed to this phenomenon, which evokes an image of the president pointing his "big finger" at his chosen successor (or tapping him on the shoulder, depending on the source). Until recently, the dedazo, one of the most recognizable features of Mexico's twentieth-century political culture, has represented the only viable explanation of the presidential selection process during the years of single-party rule. Part of this tendency to reduce such a monumental decision to such a simple metaphor derives from the secretive political culture of the PRI era. Leaders tended to make decisions behind closed doors, without notifying or seeking the consultation of the electorate. The dedazo myth also reflects the common presidentialist interpretation of the PRI years, which has exaggerated the president's ability to make the decision unilaterally. In either case, it fails to explain the complexity of the presidential selection process within the party and ignores altogether the presence of a political opposition.

Discussions of the presidential succession have minimized the importance of intra-party debate. While the party's leading figures maintained the same aura of consensus during the lead-up to the 1952 election that they always had, the behind-the-scenes negotiations over the selection process proved more contentious. Influential members of the party, known collectively as the Revolutionary Family, had competing ideas about who would be best suited to occupy the country's highest office. At least some of those concerns sprung from presidential ambition; others proved more principled. Former military officers, who had fought a revolution only to watch their political influence diminish, expressed their dissatisfaction with the civilian-dominated establishment. Others had grown disgusted with the extent of corruption at the highest levels of the administration, and those who did not share in the benefits of Alemanismo longed for a return to the redistributive social policies of the 1930s. The candidacy of Miguel Henríquez Guzmán, a venerable revolutionary general and old cardenista hand, provided an outlet for those who shared these frustrations. It appears, moreover, that a segment of the party, with Cárdenas as their leader, played a significant role in pushing Alemán to choose a candidate outside of his personal circle.

Others lodged their grievances with Alemanismo by supporting smaller opposition parties. On the left, the Popular Party (PP) advocated a Marxist path for Mexico, critiquing Alemán's relations with the United States in a language of anti-imperialism and calling for a renewed commitment to working-class interests as the country continued to industrialize. Former CTM chief Vicente Lombardo Toledano, who had first established the party in 1947 as a movement to steer the official party in a new direction, shifted his focus to full-scale opposition in the early 1950s and stood as his party's candidate in 1952. On the right, the National Action Party (PAN), founded in 1939 by former Banco de México director and UNAM rector Manuel Gómez Morín, clarified its identity as an opposition political party, rather than as a lay Catholic movement on the margins of politics. The two parties attempted to attack the PRI's political hegemony from two opposing ideological poles, while the PRI occupied a far larger share of the political spectrum through its corporate sectors. Thus, neither the PP nor the PAN, despite being headed by two of the country's leading intellectuals (both of whom also had long-standing associations with Alemán), succeeded in gaining much traction in the 1952 election. Adolfo Ruiz Cortines, the official candidate, thus won with little trouble. His colorless personality and reputation as a relatively unambitious candidate offered the perfect antidote to the excesses associated with Alemán, even as he promised a continuation of the majority of Alemán's policies. His win helped to cement Alemán's legacy for the immediate future by confirming that the party, which was consolidated into its lasting form during his sexenio, faced little immediate competition.

Alemán's Choices

The process of selecting a presidential candidate to succeed Alemán provoked controversy within the ruling party. The first point of contention sprung from a short-lived effort to reelect Alemán. Various individuals offered theories to explain the origin of this push for reelection. The US Embassy concluded that the plan was officially launched from outside the Alemán administration, but that most likely several officials from his administration actively tried to persuade the president to run for another term.[1] Alemán's son, Miguel Alemán Velasco, provided another explanation: that the idea came from Rogerio de la Selva, his father's longtime presidential secretary. According to Alemán Velasco, de la Selva did not want his father to run for another six-year term, but rather to prolong his term for a shorter (though undefined) length of time, thus avoiding constitutional limitations on reelection.[2] Former administration officials and personal friends commented that Alemán never wanted reelection, and never said or did anything publicly to perpetuate talk of the possibility of staying in office.[3]

These versions all de-emphasize the place that Alemán had in promoting his own reelection. Lombardo Toledano offered a contrasting explanation, claiming that the idea came directly from the president. In a 1965 interview, he recounted a conversation with Alemán about the issue. According to Lombardo Toledano, it was US President Harry Truman who gave Alemán the reelection bug by telling him that a third world war was just around the corner. In the interest of stability in the face of an emergency, Alemán reasoned, Mexico would benefit more from continuity of leadership than from a distracting and costly electoral cycle and the disruption of establishing a new administration. Lombardo Toledano assured the president that this was absurd and that Truman was merely trying to stir such fear to promote US interests. The conversation, according to Lombardo Toledano, contributed to the deterioration of their relationship. The two agreed to revisit the issue several months after the initial discussion. At the subsequent meeting, Alemán admitted he was wrong, but Lombardo Toledano claimed that the two men's personal relationship never mended. Lombardo Toledano admitted that while Alemán always had the dignity to receive him, he did not always do so cordially. At one point, the president declared the former voice of Mexican labor his personal enemy.[4]

Whether the idea for reelection originated outside his administration or within it, Alemán certainly appears to have harnessed the speculation to his advantage. Ernesto Uruchurtu, the minister of the interior at the time of election, argued that the reelection talk allowed Alemán to maintain political control until the end of his term, reducing the lame-duck period of sharply diminished influence that characterizes the last phase of most presidencies.[5] It also allowed him to forestall the inevitable onset of futurismos, the name given to attempts by potential candidates to gain visibility, gather information, and vie for support within the party. The reelection buzz thus neutralized the ambitions of maverick presidential hopefuls and provided a useful distraction, giving Alemán an opportunity to maneuver within the party to get his way with the 1952 selection. Yet despite the boon that the reelection spectacle provided him, it appears that Alemán was nonetheless boxed in by various forces within the party.

Rumors abounded regarding Alemán's personal preference for a successor. Even decades later, Alemán's former colleagues harbored their own theories about who had actually been Alemán's personal preference. Many suggested Fernando Casas Alemán (no familial relation), the Mexico City mayor who had also served as interim governor of Veracruz when Alemán left in 1939 and who had accumulated considerable influence over unions within the city. There is no doubt that his ambitions were pointed in that direction, although that ambition appears to have hindered him ultimately. Others suggested that early in his administration, Alemán had his eye on longtime friend and business colleague Gabriel Ramos Millán, who served as head of the National Corn Commission from 1947 until his death in a plane crash two years later.[6] Still others looked to treasury minister Ramón Beteta, one of Alemán's most trusted economic advisers and one of the first technocratic leaders in the political system. And of course there was talk of Ruiz Cortines, the honest but colorless former governor of Veracruz and interior minister.

The list of names was long: Héctor Pérez Martínez (Alemán's first interior minister and former governor of Campeche), Raúl López Sánchez (governor of Coahuila and later navy secretary), and Nazario Ortiz Garza (Alemán's agriculture minister and former Coahuila governor) were all mentioned.[7] Even Antonio Carrillo Flores, a trusted economic adviser to Alemán as his director of Nacional Financiera and Beteta's successor as treasury minister under Ruiz Cortines, claimed that Alemán once told him he could be president if he so desired. His reply to Alemán was that he was a technocrat, not a politician. He further protested that even though he knew influential people (ranging from the Rockefellers to the head of the IMF), he did not know the right people—the state governors, the union bosses—to win the presidency.[8]

One commonly accepted theory is that Casas Alemán was Alemán's top choice, but that his public image as being too corrupt and too confident that he would be chosen made him unacceptable to the public, to other figures within the party, and eventually to Alemán.[9] Casas Alemán had apparently secured the informal support of the CNOP, the party corporation representing the growing and increasingly influential urban middle sectors, while Ruiz Cortines had captured the CTM's approval. One theory regarding Casas Alemán was that Alemán considered him to have been most amenable to accepting the presidency in exchange for Alemán acting as a kind of shadow president who called the shots from behind the scenes.[10] Domestic intelligence memoranda and foreign correspondence both reported that Cárdenas and Ávila Camacho, in part out of fear of such an outcome, had leaned on Alemán to go with Ruiz Cortines. It thus appears that Ruiz Cortines represented something of a compromise candidate between different interests within the Revolutionary Family.

One of the most pressing concerns with Ruiz Cortines had nothing to do with his abilities or loyalty, but rather with his health.[11] Known to some as the "viejito" (the old man) or the "calavera" (skullface), his health was rumored to be quite poor, something aggravated by his heavy smoking. His gray complexion and phlegmatic personality only fueled speculation that he might die in office.[12] Alemán's daughter perhaps described him best as "gloomy."[13] These traits, predictably trumped up by those opposed to his nomination, contrasted sharply with Alemán's athletic appearance and youthful vigor. In some ways, Ruiz Cortines's rise to the top is remarkable, given the combination of administrative talent and personal loyalties among the Alemanistas. In either case, the fact that Ruiz Cortines was not an Alemanista insider further suggests that forces beyond Alemán had a hand in his selection.

Discord in the Revolutionary Family

Within the party, the left, personified in Cárdenas, held considerable sway in electoral procedures. In a moment when the alemanista leadership had drawn national politics to the right, Cárdenas stood out as a political lightning rod. He nonetheless remained a revered figure for many and maintained a visible presence both in domestic and international politics. He supported the American Continental Congress for Peace in 1949[14] and was one of several prominent delegates to sign the Stockholm Appeal, issued by the World Peace Council the following year (Cárdenas did not formally represent the Alemán administration, which sent no delegates).[15] His presence in national politics, where he exercised the greatest behind-the-scenes influence, proved controversial and prompted US Embassy secretary Charles R. Burrows to comment that the PRI was anything but the big, happy revolutionary family it purported to be.[16] Indeed, Cárdenas, as well as Ávila Camacho, drew a good deal of concern not only from the US government, but also from the Mexican intelligence community.

The Alemán administration benefited from the dramatically expanded intelligence services, organized under both the preexisting General Directorate of Political and Social Investigation (DGIPS), which formed part of the Ministry of the Interior, as well as the new Federal Security Directorate (DFS), established in 1947, which answered directly to the president. Recent research has demonstrated that government officials utilized these increasingly professionalized services for political purposes, especially by gathering information to smear opposition candidates.[17] National Security files also indicate that beyond the intelligence community's interest in the activities of leftists outside of the PRI, it also tracked party stalwarts, including Cárdenas and Ávila Camacho. In addition to what the reports say about the role of the intelligence services in solidifying the PRI's dominance over its opposition, their content reveals a fragmentary but telling picture of what went on within the official party as the 1952 presidential selection approached. More specifically, the newly released national security files, coupled with US diplomatic correspondence and interviews of political insiders, point to substantial disagreement within the Revolutionary Family.

Germán Parra, a former undersecretary of economy who served as an informant to the US Embassy, accused the Alemán administration of conducting surveillance on anyone deemed suspicious, including not only himself, but also Cárdenas and Ávila Camacho.[18] Reports filed at the DFS by one of its agents, Arturo Schick G., tracked the activity of Cárdenas with a surprising degree of precision.[19] His report was one of several from 1948 onward that expressed suspicions about Cárdenas's plans for Alemán. While Schick alleged a conspiracy between Cárdenas and Lombardo Toledano to topple the president, others suggested a joint effort by Cárdenas and Ávila Camacho to launch a coup d'état.[20] Still others proposed that Cárdenas would lead a coalition of former military officials to overthrow the president.[21] These sorts of rumors reflected a paranoid Cold War mentality and contained a high measure of exaggeration, especially since Cárdenas at no point gave any indication in public statements that he would support a candidate from outside the party.

At the same time, these rumors should not be dismissed as meaningless. Taken together, they form a persuasive explanation of the extent to which individuals within the PRI, such as Cárdenas and Ávila Camacho, as well as other "old-guard" revolutionaries, influenced Alemán's selection of a presidential successor, a process typically described as the president's alone. Reports filed at both the DFS and the US Embassy were rife with the suggestion that Henríquez was the favorite of Cárdenas for the PRI's nomination.[22] Several also suggested that Cárdenas had given sincere consideration to supporting Henríquez, regardless of whether he was the official candidate or not,[23] and several memoranda went so far as to suggest that Cárdenas and Alemán had hammered out a deal as early as 1946 that Henríquez would be the candidate.[24] While a specific revelation of how Alemán arrived at the decision to promote Ruiz Cortines is unlikely to occur, it is nonetheless apparent that he was reluctant to pick Ruiz Cortines over someone from his inner circle. Indeed, various sources all tell a similar story: that Cárdenas, concerned about cronyism and social policy, had preferred Henríquez, and when it became clear that Alemán would not give Henríquez the nod, Cárdenas helped to convince Alemán to seek a compromise in the form of Ruiz Cortines. That bargain did not, however, stop Henríquez from running.

The Henríquez Threat

The 1952 general election, unlike the previous one in 1946, saw the most formidable challenge to the official candidate come from within the military establishment. Miguel Henríquez Guzmán had been an officer in the revolution and later a zone commander under Cárdenas. Through his career he had demonstrated a mix of charisma, loyalty, military talent, and ambition. He led the military response to the uprising of Saturnino Cedillo in San Luis Potosí in 1938, and in 1940 he was sent to Monterrey by Cárdenas to neutralize the political ascendancy of Juan Andreu Almazán (the principal opposition candidate that year), even though he shared much in common with the general. Both had become wealthy through their military contacts; Henríquez had been particularly fortunate in meeting US businessmen while serving in the North.[25]

Henríquez had flirted with the idea of a run in 1946, a year after forming the Federation of Parties of the Mexican People (FPPM). He ultimately declined, leaving room for the contest between Alemán and his primary opponent, Ezequiel Padilla. Yet by the second half of Alemán's term, he, like Cárdenas and various others from either the left or from the military establishment, had grown frustrated with Alemán's performance in office. He thus began his futurismos early, to the extent that by 1951 he had been expelled from the PRI for his indiscipline. This led to a full-fledged opposition campaign. Without the help of Cárdenas or Ávila Camacho, who both stuck with the party they had helped to consolidate, Henríquez could not hope to offer a serious threat to Ruiz Cortines. Ultimately, the FPPM garnered just shy of 16 percent of the popular vote, a sizeable number for an opposition candidate but nonetheless a very distant second-place finish.

This did not mean that the PRI and its leaders dismissed the opposition out of hand. Rather, the party's president, Gen. Rafael Sánchez Taboada, made significant efforts to discredit Henríquez, whom he regarded as a violent, even murderous person who had little to offer the increasingly evolved political system. He also pointed to Henríquez's lucrative contracts, especially in road and rail construction, hinting at corruption as evidence of his lack of suitability for the presidency. Rhetorical attacks of this sort were not confined to the party leadership; administration officials also jumped into the fray. In one heated exchange, Henríquez attacked the Alemán administration, fuming to Beteta that the government was responsible for too much unfinished construction. Beteta simply retorted that Henríquez, who along with his brother controlled a sizeable interest in two large construction firms, had grown rich off of contracts that the government had awarded him.[26] He was right. Henríquez, in a similar fashion to Almazán, had achieved considerable wealth by securing construction contracts, which allowed him (again like Almazán) to build a base of political support from rail workers under his watch.

Such exchanges represented the ugly side of the campaign cycle. Party president Sánchez Taboada received criticism for his self-aggrandizement and pompous behavior in the process of smearing the official candidate's opponent. Henríquez responded in equally harsh terms, calling into question Ruiz Cortines's revolutionary service during the invasion of Veracruz by US Marines in 1914, alleging that he helped the other side.[27] One piece of *henriquista* propaganda, distributed by railway workers who supported the general, accused Ruiz Cortines of trafficking in cocaine during the Veracruz invasion.[28] Even Gen. Francisco Múgica, once considered to be Cárdenas's top choice to follow him as president, joked that Ruiz Cortines could not harm him, since he had already attacked him once (and lost) when he had joined with the US forces in Veracruz.[29] Ruiz Cortines, who had served as an officer stationed in Veracruz during the invasion, provided documented evidence of his military loyalties during the revolution. In the final count, the move to question Ruiz Cortines's revolutionary credentials by offering up unsubstantiated claims that he was a traitor probably backfired.

It bears repeating that Henríquez, while a military man and a candidate supported by numerous individuals within the military establishment, did not represent the military formally, nor did his campaign reflect a consensus among the officer class. Thus, the contest between Ruiz Cortines and Henríquez did not fall into the recognizable situation in twentieth-century Latin America of a military at odds with a predominantly civilian government. In fact, Henríquez carried himself much as any other civilian candidate would, just as the revolutionary generals who had occupied the presidency—including Obregón, Calles, Cárdenas, and Ávila Camacho—had done before. What the Henríquez campaign did represent, however, was a general statement of dissatisfaction among the older generation of military officers, a reaction as much to Alemán's decisions as to the reduction of the military's influence in national politics. In rejecting Alemanismo, Henríquez effectively made Cardenismo his message. Yet his campaign was not the only word from the left.

Vicente Lombardo Toledano, The Partido Popular, and the Left

The left had a lot to complain about with Alemán. His administration's troubling record of hostility toward organized labor and lack of concern for the rural poor provided an unending source of frustration. It was not the generally pro-business orientation of the administration that most offended those on the left. After all, rapid import-substituting industrialization was common across the region, so they could not readily point to Alemán's pro-industry approach as especially unique. Moreover, ISI was designed to reduce foreign dependency, create new employment, and widen overall prosperity. The problem with Alemán, as many saw it, was the exaggerated nature of his administration's particular version of this process. Rather than seeking balance, Alemán and his allies chose excess.

During Alemán's sexenio, the relationship between the government and organized labor underwent a dramatic realignment. The process, essentially a drawn-out campaign to discipline labor into a subordinate position, began just before Alemán's inauguration in 1946, when oil workers went on strike, against the wishes of the CTM leadership. Once he became president, Alemán sent his PEMEX chief, Antonio Bermúdez, to negotiate a deal with the striking workers. When they pushed back, Alemán resorted to sending in troops to break the strike. From there, the oil workers joined forces with the railway workers' union, led by Luis Gómez Z., a onetime candidate to head the CTM who had lost a power struggle with its eventual chief, Fidel Velázquez. The telephone, mining, and cement workers, along with telegraph operators, streetcar drivers, and electricians, left the CTM to join the oil and rail unions, forming the United Confederation of Workers (CUT).

The fallout changed the course of relations between government and labor for the remainder of the century. The sudden exodus of such a large segment of the CTM's membership threatened its political potency, prompting Velázquez to take a harder line with members who appeared to have similar inklings of independence or who sympathized with communism. This shift in attitude forced Lombardo Toledano out of the organization once and for all. The generally accepted version of the story is that he was expelled, although Lombardo Toledano would later claim that he left voluntarily in order to fulfill his duties to the Workers Confederation of Latin America (CTAL).[30] Either way, it paved the way for the crackdown on independent labor mobilization known as the charrazo (see the introduction), or really the succession of charrazos that each had a similar effect, between 1948 and 1950. It also led him to found the Alliance for Workers and Peasants of Mexico, something he said would create a bulwark against Alemán's meddling in organized labor, which they openly called counterrevolutionary.[31]

The intervention into the oil workers' strike in 1946 foretold how Alemán would react to future labor unrest. The peso devaluation in mid-1948 provided the motive for precisely that form of unrest. The policy, designed to correct the nation's balance of payments, had the effect of making goods more expensive by reducing the purchasing power of the currency. In reaction to the devaluation announcement, the CUT-affiliated rail workers had struck. Their leader, who had succeeded Gómez Z. earlier that year, was Jesús Díaz de León, known as "El Charro" because of his tendency to wear the costume of the folkloric Mexican cowboy to union functions.[32] Díaz de León, in a risky but shrewd move, launched a kind of internal coup against the railway union leaders who either remained close to Gómez Z. or who were partial to communism. He was aided by the police: Gómez Z., after being accused by Díaz de León of misappropriating CTM funds to the benefit of the CUT, was thrown in jail. Without his presence or the help of his allies, the CUT fell apart. With Alemán's knowledge and support, El Charro took the reins of the rail workers' union and moved it back into the CTM, effectively dissolving the CUT. Alemán had won.

The 1948 showdown in the railway union presaged similar conflicts among oil workers in 1949 and mining workers in 1950. By 1951 the oil workers, the first to have withdrawn, were left standing alone, and consequently were reabsorbed into the CTM. The administration's willingness to use force, and its success in installing loyal party hard-liners in the charro mold, effectively ended any lingering hope for independent organized labor. One last attempt at forming an independent union, to be called the General Union of the Workers and Peasants of Mexico (UGOCM), was dead on arrival.

By 1948 Lombardo Toledano had been pushed away from the Confederation of Mexican Workers (CTM). Fidel Velázquez, the cryptic man who had originally replaced Lombardo Toledano as president of the CTM during the Ávila Camacho years and who ruled the CTM until 1997, now headed a fully subordinated labor sector. Under him stood a new group of loyalists who gained a reputation for their harsh discipline. One of Velázquez's first acts following Lombardo Toldano's departure was to disallow CTM members from joining any political party other than the PRI. The great tragedy in all this, at least as far as Lombardo Toledano and his allies were concerned, was that he had supported Alemán in the 1946 election, figuring that full-scale support of the official candidate, who was guaranteed to win anyway, would do more for the CTM than would supporting an opposition candidate. Lombardo Toledano thus attached himself to Alemán's campaign, advocating a pact between workers and industry.[33] In his mind, industry would bring the greatest result, so long as workers' interests were adequately served. According to the Marxist doctrine to which Lombardo Toledano had long subscribed, the shift to industrial capitalism represented a necessary and therefore welcome step on the pathway to socialism.[34] Considering the expectations Lombardo Toledano had for Alemán, the course of national politics after 1946 must have provoked nothing short of despair for him.

Years later Lombardo Toledano decried what the CTM had become as a result of the charrazo: a sad organization that had once been a vital national institution. To express his frustration over the pettiness and opportunism of the CTM's new leadership, he quoted a popular Spanish phrase: "There are individuals who prefer to be the rat's head rather than the lion's ass."[35] Lombardo Toledano remained on as head of the CTAL, but the charrazo made him a pariah within his own country's politics. It was this shift in the political winds from 1948 to 1950 that resulted in the transformation of the nascent Popular Party into a small but sincere movement that opposed the PRI.

Lombardo Toledano first created the PP in 1947, just as his place within the CTM hierarchy had begun to look shaky. Making a point that he admired much about the Alemán administration, Lombardo Toledano noted that he had initially intended his new party to critique the regime, rather than to oppose it or condemn its actions.[36] As he described it, the purpose of the party was to contribute to the nation's democratic institutions and civic life.[37] To that end, he formed the Workers University to promote cultural and educational advances for the working class.[38] For the Workers University, he enlisted the support of Alemán's predecessor, Manuel Ávila Camacho.[39] The PP thus came into existence as a pro-government effort designed to nudge the official party in a new direction, one which Lombardo Toledano described in ideological terms as anti-imperialist and rooted in the Mexican revolution.[40] He was careful not to cast his party in terms that might alarm authorities bent on stamping out communism, since the Mexican Communist Party (PCM) had its registration revoked in 1946 and its members had been persecuted by the Alemán administration.

In creating the PP, Lombardo Toledano was joined by numerous well-known and celebrated personalities, including the muralists Diego Rivera and David Alfaro Siqueiros, along with prominent intellectuals Narciso Bassols, Alejandro Gómez Arias, Andrés Henestrosa, and Salvador Novo.[41] Several from this circle, including Bassols, Gómez Arias, and Henestrosa, had long-standing personal, academic, or professional associations with Alemán that extended to his school days in the 1920s. These individuals and their political allies, including immigrants, embassy officials, and other foreign-born residents from Germany, Poland, Czechoslovakia, Italy, and Spain,[42] had become increasingly attracted to communism.[43] The debilitation of the Mexican Communist Party very likely led them to the PP. This support from such a diverse segment of the intellectual community fortified the PP in its earliest days, but also made it an obvious target for administration officials concerned with stamping out communism.

The events of 1948 changed the orientation of the PP. As Lombardo Toledano later recounted, the PP's tilt away from being a pro-government party and toward full-scale opposition was prompted not only by the breakdown in labor relations that resulted in his departure from the CTM, but also by outrage over the effects of the 1948 peso devaluation. Not only did the reduction in the peso's relative value further impoverish the already struggling working majority, but it also represented a capitulation to the demands of the IMF. This, in Lombardo Toledano's mind, was not only bad economic policy in the short run; it also violated the anti-imperialist mandate of the 1910 revolution.[44] Thus, by 1949, the PP was fielding candidates (it is said to have won the Sonoran governorship, but its candidate was blocked from taking power[45]). In 1952, Lombardo Toledano, against his initial inclination, ran for president as an opposition candidate.

Lombardo Toledano, in a fashion typical of politicians seeking to craft a messianic image of themselves, insisted after the fact that he was pushed into running in the 1952 election by a desperate population.[46] At the PP's 1952 convention, it was decided that supporting the most visible opposition candidate, Gen. Miguel Henríquez Guzmán, was unthinkable. Despite his overtures to the left and his credibility as a true revolutionary seasoned in combat, his reputation with workers was abysmal. Lombardo Toledano claimed, for instance, that he had worked with Henríquez and his brother on an irrigation project in the southern part of the country, and that at one point the two had burned a whole workers' settlement. And there was no way that the PP could support the ruling party's official nominee, Adolfo Ruiz Cortines, after what the Alemán administration had done to the working class.[47] Thus, the burden (as he was careful to frame it) fell to Lombardo Toledano. In his recollections, he was proud of the campaign he ran. The Communist Party, which had initially supported Henríquez Guzmán, threw its support to the PP. His was the only campaign to have held a massive rally in Mexico City, something even the official candidate could not claim. Above all, he was struck by how much money the humble classes had given to support the effort.[48] Yet despite the popular enthusiasm from the poorest segments of society, Lombardo Toledano's party received a paltry 2 percent of the vote in the official count. Although the vote-earning potential of the PP was probably reduced substantially by the late alliance made between the PP and the FPPM, the statistic provides a telling measure of the place of the left in Mexico's modernizing authoritarian system. The fact that the parties of Lombardo Toledano and Henríquez Guzmán together amounted to less than 20 percent of the vote confirms that the PRI had succeeded in neutralizing the left, purging communism, and co-opting the working classes into the CTM.

Throughout the process, the administration, acting through the DFS (the government's largest and most powerful intelligence-gathering agency), kept close tabs on Lombardo Toledano and his allies, especially since many remained members of the Communist Party. The regime, despite Lombardo Toledano's attempt at conciliatory rhetoric, regarded the PP and its leadership as threatening. PRI president Rafael Sánchez Taboada, whom Lombardo Toledano described as a "leper" and a "lunatic,"[49] was especially vitriolic in his anti-PP rhetoric. In a moment of candor inconsistent with the normally tight-lipped party leadership, Sánchez Taboada called the ejido–based collective approach to agriculture a failure and an example of communism and suggested that the government should open ejidos to privatization at the same time that the PRI purged its ranks of communists.[50] The zealous statement, intended to promote Alemán's policies favoring commercial agriculture, would have been a grievous misstep even a few years earlier, since it criticized one of the pillars of cardenista revolutionary reform. Yet Sánchez Taboada's remarks were perfectly in step with Alemanismo and with the general sentiment of anti-communism that Mexican leaders had no choice but to embrace if they were to expect support from the United States in the early Cold War years. As the PRI increasingly slid into this Cold War discourse, voices like Lombardo Toledano's became washed out.

The PAN as an Emerging Political Force

The PAN was scarcely a decade old at the time of the 1952 election. Manuel Gómez Morín, one of the "Seven Sages" of Mexico's Generation of 1915, announced the party's formation in 1939 and immediately set out to define its philosophical basis and its place within the nation's political system. Gómez Morín drew personal inspiration from a number of sources, something that reflected the poly-intellectualism and aversion to dogma among his intellectual generation. Among many others, these influences included the anti-positivist philosophies of Henri Bergson and José Ortega y Gassett, the corporatism of Charles Maurras, and the modernizing dictatorship of Gen. Miguel Primo de Rivera in Spain, especially the civilian right represented by his chief technocrat and finance minister, José Calvo Sotelo.[51] The importance of these inspirations notwithstanding, the PAN in reality was less a reflection of Gómez Morín's intellectual character and more a reaction to the Cárdenas regime.

In the view of Gómez Morín and the small circle of intellectuals, professionals, and businessmen who formed the earliest membership of the PAN, the administration of Lázaro Cárdenas posed a grave danger to Mexican society. By the late 1930s Cardenismo had alienated the middle classes, the landed elite, the few captains of industry then in Mexico, and the devoutly Catholic.[52] The PAN was thus created as an institutional forum for those who felt they had no voice in the revolutionary party's second form, the Party of the Mexican Revolution (PRM). Nevertheless, opposition to Cardenismo could not sustain the party for long, nor did Gómez Morín's diverse intellectual interests add up to any kind of doctrine. The project of finding an ideology for the PAN thus fell to the person regarded as the party's co-founder, Efraín González Luna.

A prominent lawyer and political thinker from Guadalajara, González Luna drew the PAN into the orbit of Catholic Social Teaching, a body of thought that stemmed from the *Rerum Novarum* encyclical issued by Pope Leo XIII in 1891. The document addressed the plight of the working class and became the theoretical foundation of Christian Democracy. While the PAN did not formally identify itself as a Christian Democratic party until 1998, it nonetheless shared Christian Democracy's pursuit of a "third way" between individualist capitalism and egalitarian communism from the outset. This third-way ideology rested on the idea of an organic society in which entrenched social institutions would function in harmony to advance the common good, even if they were inherently unequal. The PAN saw Mexico's salvation springing from various sources: the university, which would produce generations of technical experts to lead its society; the free municipality and a functional legislature, which had both, in their minds, become a fiction; the Catholic Church, with its deep historical rooting in the country; and above all the family, as the most fundamental organism of society.[53]

The PAN rejected the liberal tendencies that had first appeared in Mexico in the mid-nineteenth century and had been consolidated with the revolution. The secular and anti-clerical liberalism adopted by the revolutionaries, in the minds of the early PANistas, was at odds with Mexico's long-standing Roman Catholicism. Moreover, they argued that the liberal celebration of the individual lent itself to an abusive form of capitalism. Gómez Morín was also deeply critical of the government's centralization, which he saw as out of step with the goals of the revolution and as relegating the family to secondary importance as a social institution.[54] He also rejected the party's adoption of a corporatist structure organized around social classes, since that merely invited class antagonism.[55] In its place, he conceived of a different kind of corporatism, organized around the nation's historically rooted social institutions, that would allow Mexico to realize its potential by embracing rather than suppressing its organic society.

Gómez Morín and González Luna faced a number of obstacles in their efforts to build a genuine opposition party. First, the party increasingly came to be associated with Catholicism during the 1940s and 1950s, owing largely to the fact that Gómez Morín's initial collaborators had been Catholic militants from their student days. This identity gave it a kind of exclusivity and singularity of purpose at odds with Gómez Morín's initial vision.[56] The PAN was further challenged by having to compete with the National Synarchist Union (usually called the Sinarquistas), a Falangist organization composed primarily of militant Roman Catholic peasants, for support from Mexico's base of Catholic conservatives. The problem gradually diminished, as the Sinarquistas came under attack by the Ávila Camacho administration for their pro-Axis stance and staunch opposition to the ruling party. Competition between the two groups gave way to a brief alliance in 1946, the year the Sinarquistas organized the Popular Force Party (PFP), but by 1949 the organization had ceded most Catholic-inspired political activity to the PAN after the Alemán administration banned the extreme-right PFP the prior year.[57]

Gómez Morín had also envisioned the PAN as the representative of private enterprise and an educated technical elite. This proposition made sense in the waning years of Cardenismo, but by the early 1940s, more and more of the university-educated middle class entered the public bureaucracy through the official party's popular sector, the CNOP. This process accelerated dramatically after 1946. Moreover, import-substituting industrialization policies created a powerful entrepreneurial class that was intrinsically linked to the PRI. For these dual reasons—because the PAN was so closely linked to Roman Catholicism as a cause and because it lost the race to become the "party of the lawyers," as Gómez Morín had envisioned it—the party suffered something of an identity crisis in its first two decades.[58]

In spite of these difficulties, the PAN made several advances during the Alemán years. Most significantly, in 1946 the party won its first seats in the Chamber of Deputies, the lower house of the legislature. The PAN had floated candidates in far more races than the four seats it eventually received, and thus alleged fraud when the results were announced. Gómez Morín and González Luna, representing their respective home states of Chihuahua and Jalisco, had run and lost. The following year, the PAN picked up a handful of mayoral victories in small municipal elections. Notwithstanding the small number of deputies elected and the general impotency of the legislature at the time, the election of candidates was a move toward electoral competitiveness that would only become recognizable decades later. The success was short-lived: in 1949, during the next cycle of elections, the PAN lost its seats. In the meantime, one of the original four deputies, Aquiles Elourdoy, had been expelled from the party for protesting a public Catholic demonstration that he claimed had violated the law. The party, now squarely in the orbit of Roman Catholicism, had purged one of its four congressional representatives for blasphemy.[59]

The PAN found as much wrong with Alemanismo in these years as it had with Cardenismo at its founding in 1939. Speaking in the 1960s about Alemán's administration, Gómez Morín noted that it had been absurd to focus so intensively in the 1940s on industrialization when more than half of the nation's population lived in rural areas. He conceded that while Mexico should not necessarily be a predominantly agrarian nation, given its small percentage of arable land and the many geographical challenges it faced, its agriculture could nonetheless be far more productive than it actually was. He noted, moreover, that Alemán's industrialization scheme simply did not make sense, since at the time there was no consumer market to support it or sufficient raw materials to feed it.[60]

Gómez Morín also maintained that his party did not represent a form of "Her Majesty's loyal opposition," despite various scholars' claims to the contrary. Instead, he protested, it was simply an opposition party that was in the minority at that moment.[61] Either way, its move to offer a presidential candidate in 1952 pushed it further into the realm of political opposition than it had previously gone. The candidacy of Efraín González Luna in 1952 represented a major step in the PAN's transition toward becoming a competitive opposition party. At its nominating convention, the membership of the still inchoate party had encouraged Gómez Morín, a more forceful and recognizable national figure than his counterpart from Guadalajara, to run. He declined, leaving the intellectually bright but rhetorically uninspiring González Luna as the only plausible choice.[62] The PAN, with a relatively small membership and insufficient resources, ran a lackluster campaign, revealing its immaturity as a political force. It is clear that the PAN had little in common with its later self, which would represent large segments of the business elite, particularly in Monterrey, Guanajuato, and other strongholds in the north. For the time being, it functioned as the institutional voice of lay Catholics, and it suffered because the PRI had succeeded in becoming the nation's professionalized, technocratic party. In the end, González Luna captured 7.8 percent of the popular vote in the official count.

Failure of the Opposition and Dominance of the PRI

By early 1952 it was clear that if the opposition to the PRI had any chance at winning, then it would only happen through some form of unification of the candidacies. This prompted Henríquez and Lombardo Toledano to form a kind of political pact. Cándido Aguilar, the onetime patron of Alemán in Veracruz who had eventually fallen at odds with the president, also joined them. Aguilar had led a small electoral movement earlier that year through the Revolutionary Party (PR), but he failed to gain official recognition or much traction.[63] González Luna, representing a right-leaning party supported by dissatisfied Catholics and segments of the business community not linked to the PRI, did not participate. This hasty unification of the three left-leaning candidates was interrupted by a July riot in Mexico City, followed by the uncovering of a stockpile of arms and an alleged plot in Veracruz, somewhat tenuously linked to Aguilar, to launch an armed resistance to the official candidacy. Faced with the alternative of a lengthy arrest, Aguilar agreed to be absorbed into the Ruiz Cortines campaign, while the credibility of Henríquez crumbled.[64] Even if Henríquez had been the behind-the-scenes favorite of Cárdenas and Ávila Camacho, any show of public support for the beleaguered opposition candidacy from either of the former presidents would have had negative consequences for the political system and their public images. At this late point, only days before the election, the loosely organized pact between three weak candidacies had dissolved, and the PAN had run an uninspired campaign. These factors, combined with the PRI leadership's constant barrage of anti-henriquista propaganda (especially from the arrogant Sánchez Taboada), paved the way for Ruiz Cortines.

The increasingly efficient electoral machine that would ensure Ruiz Cortines's ascent to office was further oiled by the 1951 Federal Elections Law, which gave oversight and administrative responsibility for electoral procedure to the Ministry of the Interior, and thus effectively to the PRI. Despite protests from leading opposition figures, including PAN president Gómez Morín, that the law represented anything but a democratic reform, it came into existence with little public outrage. Opposition to the new law, like the opposition candidacies in general, thus did little to dent the PRI's domination of the 1952 election. The PAN's frustration with the PRI's electoral tampering was nothing new. As early as the midterm election of 1949, the PAN had seen its hopes of a meaningful response to its allegations of electoral fraud dashed when the Supreme Court dismissed a case regarding the issue. The PAN leadership had little choice but to accept the ruling, at least in the short term, seeing no opportunity for redress from the impotent judicial system or from the electoral oversight bureaucracy, which was staffed entirely by members of the PRI.[65] The changes in electoral laws and the wrangling over election procedure exemplify the PRI's growing stranglehold over the nation's electoral mechanisms. In the end, Ruiz Cortines won by over two million votes, capturing nearly three quarters of the popular vote and completely eclipsing the other candidates.

The Playboy President and Skullface

Alemán and Ruiz Cortines maintained cordial public relations and outwardly supported one another in public settings. In this regard their interactions and public statements about one another were consistent with protocol in the Revolutionary Family that had stood since Ávila Camacho's National Unity campaign. Ávila Camacho had launched the initiative upon coming to power as a way to ease the tensions caused by the ideologically polarizing administration of his predecessor. Its most striking symbolic component was a public ceremony in which former president Plutarco Elías Calles appeared alongside Lázaro Cárdenas, the man who had sent him into exile. National Unity, which existed on the surface as a way to promote a general atmosphere of consensus as Mexico entered World War II, had a larger purpose: to keep the various ideological differences, policy debates, and personal squabbles within the party in balance, and also out of the public eye. Thus, the public would see a Revolutionary Family that operated in harmony. The effort bolstered the creation of a corporatist party that had the appearance of being mass-based but that was in fact highly disciplined. If the party had the veneer of absolute consensus at the top, then it could devote its full attention to neutralizing potential conflicts among or within the different class-based sectors.

This outward display of unity was crucial to the party's self-projection. Yet Ruiz Cortines deviated just slightly from it, and in doing so he created a pattern replicated by nearly all of his successors. The incoming president's anti-corruption campaign targeted the previous administration's notorious record of cronyism and graft. The campaign was more of a rhetorical exercise than a hard-nosed attempt to snuff out corruption. The Ruiz Cortines administration took no legal action against former Alemán administration officials, nor did it enact any major legal or bureaucratic reforms, with one exception: the new president made incoming public officials submit a statement of financial disclosure at the beginning and end of their terms in government.[66] While Ruiz Cortines did not point the finger at anyone in particular and particularly avoided mentioning Alemán, it was clear that he sought the public's trust by smearing his predecessor's reputation.[67] Without knowing it, he had created a new protocol. From that point forward, anti-corruption campaigns became a ritual adopted by nearly all presidents at the beginning of their sexenios.[68] This meant that the ritual also became more predictable over time and eventually became meaningless, since the political system under the PRI continued to be known for encouraging corruption. At the time, however, the anti-corruption effort helped to solidify Ruiz Cortines's image as an honest public servant who would correct the excesses of the Alemán years.

It is important to emphasize that corruption is a tricky concept. In practical terms, it is difficult to define and even harder to measure, not least because its exact meaning changes depending on context. Consequently, it loses analytical potency when used as a catchall term by scholars or as a rhetorical weapon by those seeking political gain. Scholars have long grappled with the nearly unending list of behaviors that might qualify as corruption, and with their causes. Corruption can be interpreted, for instance, as the rational action of individuals seeking to maximize opportunities. Others might see it as having a life force all its own, as something that leads people to become corrupt through participation in a particular system. Most observers, whether explicitly or implicitly, apply some form of moral judgment, condemning the greed and self-interest of those who purport to represent the public good. Still others, including analysts of the Alemán years and other moments in Mexican history, have correlated political corruption with moments of significant economic growth and specific forms of development.[69]

Regardless of how expansive the term might be, Alemán and his political and business associates behaved in a way that most people intuitively recognize as corrupt. In particular, their style of crony capitalism has lingered in the collective memory and influenced scholarly appraisal of their politics. Yet for all the abundant recognition of the Alemán generation's legendary corruption, there is startlingly scarce documentation proving it, a lamentable testament to their skill in covering their tracks. The most notable method of hiding ill-gotten gain, the prestanombre, or front man, made it possible for private citizens to hide the investments of political figures with whom they did business while appearing to carry out the transactions in plain sight. For the most part, the prestanombre has made proving corruption in the Alemán generation an impossible mission for scholars. Yet in spite of the absence of absolute proof, there can be little doubt that Alemán and his closest associates strayed from collective standards of public morality. Thus, in their context and according to that measure, they were corrupt. Moreover, the fact that Alemanismo symbolized corruption is no less crucial, since it contributed to a gradual erosion of public confidence in the political system over time. There are multiple reasons Alemán and corruption became virtually synonymous, but the Ruiz Cortines anti-corruption campaign bears some responsibility for the correlation, both because it was unprecedented in its moment and because it initiated a tradition in which the PRI acknowledged (however dismissively) corruption in order to neutralize further dissent over the topic.

To Alemán, Ruiz Cortines's anti-corruption campaign was a stab in the back. It is not surprising that Alemán would be furious over such statements, not least because they were made by his chosen successor. After all, the prevailing consensus was that Ruiz Cortines's ascent to the presidency had more to do with Alemán than with his own abilities or achievements. Of course, Alemán was far too astute to say anything negative about his successor on the record,[70] especially since direct retaliation on his part would only draw further public attention to the issue of corruption. Instead, Alemán maintained the appearance of cordiality in public and otherwise focused on adding to the positive side of his legacy, especially through his efforts to promote tourism. Behind closed doors, on the other hand, he proved far more candid, particularly with those from his inner circle whom he trusted, in sharing his views of Ruiz Cortines.

According to Antonio Carrillo Flores, Alemán's overall impression of Ruiz Cortines was that he lacked optimism and tended to be overly austere.[71] The comment suggests more than a simple personal disagreement between the two presidents. Rather, it seems that they possessed fundamentally different personalities, and that their respective traits—Alemán's grandiosity contrasted with Ruiz Cortines's cautious nature—affected their political decision-making. In one meeting with Fernando Román Lugo, a friend of Alemán from their school days and early career in Veracruz, the former president raged that his successor had betrayed his trust, then swore they would not be discussing Ruiz Cortines ever again.[72] Andrés Serra Rojas, Alemán's minister of labor and another former fellow classmate, plainly stated that Alemán regretted his selection of Ruiz Cortines. The topic of Ruiz Cortines evidently had become a sore spot for Alemán, who pleaded with his former cabinet minister not to ask him about his successor, whom he found to be ungrateful.[73]

Ruiz Cortines had complaints of his own. Beyond his criticism of the Alemán administration's legacy of corruption, he also complained about Alemán's economic policies, noting that despite its success in achieving impressive growth, the alemanista economic model also produced severe inequality and inflation.[74] It appears, moreover, that he resented the fact that Alemán's policies depleted the treasury's currency reserves and left too many spending commitments unresolved, a situation that led to the 1954 peso devaluation.[75] Ruiz Cortines fumed to one longtime Alemán associate that he was doing away with Alemán's overambitious plans altogether.[76]

The devaluation issue proved to be a sticking point for the two presidents and other members of their administrations. In some ways, Ruiz Cortines had good reason to complain. Carrillo Flores, for instance, claimed that the construction of the University City (CU), at the cost of a 200-million-peso debt (about US$41.7 million[77]) to the Banco de México, contributed to the sluggish economy Ruiz Cortines faced, and ultimately helped to spur the devaluation of the peso in 1954. Carillo Flores nonetheless echoed other economic analysts in identifying other factors, such as the US recession and the immediate effects of the Korean War, that also contributed to Mexico's economic downturn.[78] Either way, the admission by Carillo Flores, a loyal alemanista technocrat, that Alemán's economic program yielded negative results is especially telling.

Yet where Carillo Flores accepted some blame for the 1954 devaluation on behalf of the Alemán administration, Beteta deflected it. Comparing the 1948 devaluation while he was head of the treasury with its counterpart in 1954, Beteta argued that the Alemán administration's effort was more systematic. According to him, the administration floated the currency to ascertain its true value, then devalued accordingly, thus replenishing the Banco de México's depleted reserves. In contrast, the 1954 devaluation was abrupt and unexpected, prompting questions about both its necessity and the specific relative value that officials had decided the peso was worth. Thus, Beteta insisted, it proved to be a disaster, with the central bank actually losing money.[79] Beteta was responding, in part, to criticisms that he had left the Ruiz Cortines administration with a depleted treasury, and thus his comments come off as defensive. Whether Beteta's interpretation is correct or not, the devaluation produced hardship for the poor, as it raised prices on basic goods, something that in turn put pressure on the Ruiz Cortines administration.[80]

Despite these economic challenges, and despite his critiques of his predecessor's handling of the economy, Ruiz Cortines for the most part continued Alemán's economic platform. In fact, he actually amplified his predecessor's tendency to replace social spending with expenditure on economic and infrastructural development (although he worked harder to contain inflation without sacrificing growth). In the process, he became, according to historian James Wilkie, "more *alemanista* than Alemán."[81] Thus, while he may not have shared Alemán's grand ambition, he nonetheless carried forward Mexico's move away from cardenista-inspired social policy. And despite his frustrations, Ruiz Cortines appears to have harbored a grudging respect for Alemán. In one conversation, he admitted that Alemán could resolve in five minutes what would take him three months.[82]

The choice of Ruiz Cortines, according to former Baja California Governor Braulio Maldonado, was met with a tepid response within the administration.[83] Some even reacted with open hostility.[84] Gilberto Limón, Alemán's defense minister and one of only two military officers in his cabinet, described Ruiz Cortines as bland and dominated by his wife.[85] No one was more incensed over the selection of Ruiz Cortines than Ramón Beteta, Alemán's treasury minister and one of the most talented policymakers and economic thinkers of his generation.[86] In an interview conducted in the 1960s, Beteta shared his thoughts on Ruiz Cortines, which had not softened much with time.

According to Beteta, Ruiz Cortines had launched the anti-corruption campaign, and had made disparaging comments about Alemán's economic policies, out of desperation. Beteta's accusation was that while Ruiz Cortines was intelligent enough, he was hardly brilliant. Since he had not had the stellar political career of others from the Alemán administration, and since he was not part of the university generation that occupied much of Alemán's cabinet, he had developed something of an inferiority complex. Moreover, since the Mexican presidency was subordinate to no one, Ruiz Cortines had to reverse public perceptions that he had a weak personality. While he could not impart an image of being cultured or particularly ambitious, he could at least come across as honorable. There was a more practical consideration, as well. During the campaign, he would face the inevitable barrage of questions: Why had some peasants not gotten their ejidos? Why had some villages not received electricity? Alemán provided a perfect scapegoat.[87]

Beteta's criticism of Ruiz Cortines was both sincere and self-serving. His disdain for Alemán's successor is unmistakable. His contrast of the two administrations captures his view precisely:

> The government of Lic. Alemán created a euphoria, created a security, created a state of excitement that encouraged people to invest their money, to work, to take risks, to start new enterprises. This is what it did for the country. And then came the era of Ruiz Cortines, which . . . was a disaster . . . . The biggest problem with Ruiz Cortines was that he ended that sense of security that was created in the previous administration.[88]

From this and other statements, it becomes clear that Beteta's estimation of Ruiz Cortines aligned with Alemán's. He quibbled on the topic of corruption, noting that in a moment of significant construction, as the Alemán years had been, there were bound to be a lot of contracts that made people wealthy, but that this represented something altogether different from embezzlement or other corrupt practices. He similarly refuted the idea that it was all a ploy to make Alemán's friends rich, and he considered the idea that Alemán was one of the world's wealthiest individuals the stuff of legend; according to him, people had said the same about Porfirio Díaz and Plutarco Elías Calles, both of whom died with modest fortunes. He did, however, say that there were plenty of activities, such as government functionaries investing in potentially lucrative property based on insider knowledge of future development plans, that blurred the line between the illegal and the unethical.[89] Beteta's on-record comments echoed what Alemán had reportedly said in private: that accusations of corruption and economic mismanagement by Ruiz Cortines were merely attempts to deflect criticism from his own feckless administration.

Conclusion

The electoral contest of 1952 provides a snapshot of the political system at that moment as well as a glimpse of what it would become in subsequent decades. If 1946 was the year in which the second-generation civilian establishment replaced the original revolutionaries at the top, then 1952 was the last time that the old generation made its presence felt. Even though the PRI's candidate trounced Henríquez in the general election, the former general's campaign and significant electoral following confirm that Alemanismo did not sit well with a large segment of the population. The presence of Henríquez Guzmán confirmed that the revolutionary generation's heyday had passed, and that the modernizing, authoritarian system was there to stay. But it also exposed that system's flaws.

The opposition candidacies of Lombardo Toledano and González Luna offer similar lessons. The PP commanded a statistically negligible share of the vote and ultimately proved to be an ephemeral party, while the PAN, still struggling to define its identity, was decades away from being a serious electoral contender. On the surface, both appear to be easily dismissed, but that would be an erroneous assumption. The two candidates and their parties were attacking the PRI from opposite extremes of the political spectrum at a moment in which the official party successfully occupied the majority of the center. As the century wore on, its control over the center could not hold, and things fell apart. Therefore, analysis of the opposition parties, however weak they might have been in 1952, tells us as much about the PRI at its authoritarian nadir as it does about the concerns of the political opposition.

Under Alemán, the single-party dominant political system cohered into the form it would retain for the rest of the century. Yet while it retained its form, it gradually lost its sense of legitimacy and ability to derive consent from the population. If at the moment of the 1952 election one were to look at the political system in panorama, one would see a commanding party in control of a responsive government guiding a rapidly growing economy. The system's authoritarian tendencies were balanced by a commitment to pursuing co-optation and using incentives rather than resorting to sheer force, and its unequal pattern of economic development was offset by the belief that everyone would eventually share in the abundance of growth.

But the model of the PRI clarified and consolidated by Alemán had inherent paradoxes. On the one hand, the political system was at its strongest, yet its anti-democratic qualities gradually eroded its authority. Similarly, both the economy in general and the economic role of the federal government were at their most robust; starting in the Alemán years, the combination of domestic industry, foreign investment, and state protectionism produced a level of growth heralded as a miracle. Yet as the decades wore on, mounting debt and an imbalance of payments brought crisis, while the bloated size of the federal bureaucracy, the very thing responsible for such rapid growth, became the economy's Achilles heel.[90] This ambivalent scenario, and Alemán's similarly ambivalent record, drew the parameters of the 1952 election. The electoral contest, at the PRI's mid-century zenith, defined Alemán's legacy and foretold both the strengths and weaknesses of the political system over the remainder of the century.

CONCLUSION

Of Myths and Miracles

"MIGUEL ALEMÁN BELIEVED IN REVOLUTION. NOT IN 'THE REVOLUTION' in quotation marks or with any of the usual adjectives, but in revolution. He never betrayed that."[1] These words, penned by the writer Arturo García Formenti, who attended law school with Alemán, convey a familiar sentimentality, a way of seeing the past with rose-colored glasses. But with them, he captured a vital and often-overlooked element of his generation: these men had deep, personal connections to the 1910 revolution. Even though they were too young to participate in combat, most were born in time to witness some part of its violence. Many, including Alemán, came from families that had suffered immensely for the revolutionary cause. Thus, the fact that Alemán and his colleagues so decisively turned their attention away from completing the unfinished business of the revolution presents something of a paradox.

Logically, an analysis of these men should yield the conclusion that no matter the constraints they faced, nor the temptations they encountered, they would have maintained some commitment to fulfilling the revolution's unrealized potential. Yet they directed their priorities elsewhere, in many cases to the detriment of those who built their expectations around the movement's lofty promises to alleviate poverty and inequality, protect workers and peasants, maintain domestic control of national resources, and promote a revolutionary nationalist culture. Many of those promises had been enshrined in the landmark 1917 Constitution, a fact that did little to foil Alemán's plans. While Alemán's predecessors in the 1920s and 1930s had laid the groundwork for the pattern of state-supported capitalist development that would flourish beginning in the 1940s, they nonetheless remained committed to addressing the material issues facing the poor majority. By contrast, Alemán set that agenda aside to make way for a new path of national development that benefited wealthy industrialists, foreign investors, and the urban middle sectors. The purpose of this study has been to determine why that was the case.

Analysis of the Alemán administration demonstrates that a combination of structural and personal factors lay behind the permanent rightward turn that Mexico took in the years immediately following World War II. Neither factor predominated over the other, nor did the two exist independently of one another. To attribute these changes to the forces of context alone would be to deny Alemán and his colleagues any personal agency, and to relieve them of any responsibility for the shortcomings of their policies. On the other hand, to attribute the changes that took hold in this period to the personal preferences of Alemán and his collaborators would be to ignore the considerable pressures they faced and thus to interpret their actions ahistorically. Monocausal explanations tending to either extreme fail to capture the motivations of the Alemán generation.

In structural terms, the alemanista agenda was shaped and constrained by the dynamics of the emerging Cold War. The administration's efforts to embrace US capital, empower domestic business, encourage rapid industrialization, restrict labor militancy, and purge communist influence all formed part of a larger strategy to adjust to this new global and hemispheric political environment. In varying degrees, leaders in the other major Latin American countries reacted in similar ways to these shifting geopolitical circumstances.[2] Yet Mexico's experience proved to be unique in its scope and forms, and Alemán and his ministers had a number of alternatives at their fingertips. This presents a second, related paradox: how could a nation that had such an explosive and transformational revolution at the beginning of the century end up with one of the most politically conservative political establishments in the region by mid-century? Again, the answer is to be found in the combination of a long process of socialization, which made these leaders' priorities incompatible with those of the revolutionary generation, and new political exigencies, which required immediate and practical responses.

To critics at the time, and to the majority of scholars ever since, the ends that Alemán and his colleagues sought did not justify the excessive means they used to reach them. The administration imposed hostile, corrupt, and often violent government loyalists on the CTM's affiliate unions, while the amendments made to Article 27 of the constitution empowered wealthy landholders and foreign interests while slowing the momentum of land reform to a virtual standstill. Both efforts came across, at least to the many workers and peasants they affected, as punitive measures. Moreover, the administration's diplomatic overtures to the United States, while to some degree a necessity in the moment, seemed like obsequious gestures aimed at luring foreign capital. In the view of critics like Lombardo Toledano, Alemán sold out the revolution's anti-imperialist accomplishments for easy money.

Other initiatives hit more optimistic notes, and even Alemán's most ardent critics have had no choice but to acknowledge his administration's enviable record of accomplishments. The list is long: urban housing, suburban development, hydroelectricity, irrigation, highways, airports, tourism, universities. Many of these large state projects, when coupled with protectionist economic policies, augured the multiple decades of stunning economic growth that were to come. Taken together, these initiatives gave Alemanismo its juridical, institutional, physical, and aesthetic forms, representing constituent parts of an ambitious vision of national development. It is no secret that these men derived unprecedented financial perquisites along the way. Nevertheless, acknowledgment of their sincerity in crafting a vision of national development should not be interpreted as an apology for their misdeeds. The two issues are in fact separate, and neither their legacy of corruption nor the high social and financial costs of their policies change the fact that their political efforts constituted a genuine effort to push their country toward becoming an industrial leader with a predominantly urbanized population and a powerful middle class.

The members of the Alemán generation acquired this collective vision of national development through a quarter century of collective social experience, and this gradual process gave Alemanismo its personal stamp. From their earliest prep school contact through their rise up the political ranks, the civilians who took office in 1946, with Alemán as their personal standard-bearer, developed a distinct set of values, a ruthless sense of pragmatism, and a keen self-awareness of their political destiny. The National Preparatory School and National University served as the seedbeds of this generation's formation. In Mexico City these newly acquainted students encountered a range of social and intellectual influences, along with early exposure to the cold realities of what a life in politics would entail. Examination of their scholastic experience reveals that their tendency toward policies that benefited the urban middle sectors represented, at least in part, an extension of their experiences as students in the capital. School friendship formed the basis of Alemán's political network, and the schools became primary locations of political recruitment. Yet to regard the personal relationships between these young men in the 1920s only in terms of the development of their political clique obscures the fact that they became friends and remained friends because they shared common experiences and because they, like most students, had fun together.

Over the following decade, they encountered unprecedented opportunities for financial and political advancement. Through the 1930s the consolidation of the political system occurred simultaneously alongside the solidification of their political generation. The new party, with its inchoate bureaucracy and evolving institutional structure, allowed them to move upward with far more security than their predecessors could enjoy. They faced none of the danger of choosing the wrong side—the risk that ultimately took Alemán's father's life. For this new generation, the route to power was far more assured, and the professional careers of Alemán and the members of his school cohort provided a level of prosperity that for many of them was entirely unfamiliar. By the time they reached the pinnacle of national power, they were insinuated into the inner workings of the system, and thus had considerable skill in manipulating them to their advantage. This again set them apart from their military predecessors, who had been saddled with the task of creating that system in a political vacuum.

Alemanismo thus represented the collision of two forces: the application of a political approach incubated over decades, and the adaptation of that approach to the circumstances of the time. By the end of Alemán's term in office, his administration's policies had left a complex legacy. The framework for a self-sufficient, industry-driven economy, one centered in prosperous cities, fed by productive agriculture, and funded by robust exports, had taken shape. The costs of growing inequality, mounting debt, and depleted currency reserves appeared immediately, but seemed only to be the inevitable but temporary setbacks common to rapid industrialization schemes. Ultimately, however, they proved to be permanent systemic weaknesses that necessitated economic restructuring and threatened the political legitimacy of the official party. Alemanismo thus produced varied results with unequal benefits and costs for different social groups.

Alemán, of course, cannot collect the credit, nor suffer the blame, for all political developments from the mid-1940s onward. From Plutarco Elías Calles, he inherited a strong, de facto official revolutionary party; from Lázaro Cárdenas, a corporatist structure to make it functional and inclusive, but also authoritarian; from Manuel Ávila Camacho, a move toward state-driven industry, a thaw in relations with the United States, and a military that yielded to civilian authority. These inherited legacies notwithstanding, the rise and tenure of this generation represents a major turning point in the nation's political history. Alemán and the members of his administration became the first generation of professionally trained political leaders within the single-party dominant system. With skill and flexibility of options, they crafted an approach to political and economic leadership that lasted into the early 1980s, when the PRI began to move in a more technocratic and neoliberal direction.

From 1946 onward, the PRI became increasingly anti-democratic, functioning less as an avenue for popular political participation and more as an instrument of political control for the president. While leaders occasionally resorted to means of repression to assert political authority, as was the case in the 1958–1959 railway worker strikes and the student movement a decade later, these occurrences were rare. Instead, authorities tended to seek other mechanisms to secure loyalty and facilitate the political process. Thus, the pattern of co-optation, fraud, graft, cronyism, nepotism, bribery, and patronage that came to define the years of the PRI resulted in a relatively non-violent and paternalistic form of authoritarianism, especially when compared to the military regimes elsewhere in Latin America. Such informal means became the screws that held the system together and the grease that made it move. All of the twentieth-century presidents confronted corruption in their own ways, some with more success than others, but Alemán's administration earned the reputation for being the most willing to employ these tactics, and the most skillful at turning them to the administration's advantage.

The Alemán administration's legacy of corruption is perhaps the most familiar memory that most Mexicans, and most scholars looking into Mexico from the outside, carry in their minds. Yet it was not the only one, nor even necessarily the most important. In reality, the long process of political consolidation that played out in the wake of the 1910 revolution reached its final phase under Alemán, as governors and union leaders conceded authority to the president and as civilian politicians and technocrats permanently came to occupy the highest echelons of government. These processes created a political apparatus that, while not without considerable flaws, had unique and admirable qualities that endured for several decades—stability, strong economic performance, imperviousness to military intervention, and an aversion to the routine use of state violence.

This raises a third and final paradox: could the alemanista approach, which in its time ranked as among the most conservative in Latin America and to many appeared to be an outright betrayal of the revolution, have spared Mexico from some of the harshest brutalities of the Cold War? On this matter, Alemán's focus on the middle class turned out to be prescient. During the 1960s and 1970s, at the height of Cold War hysteria, the region's middle classes grew to become some of the most vocal and influential proponents of the violent, US-supported coups d'états and military dictatorships that overtook virtually the entire region. Middle-class citizens came to view political intervention by the armed forces as the only viable solution to their fears of communism and their collective perception that left-leaning populists posed a threat to their interests. Mexico's success in avoiding this outcome can be partially attributed to the middle-class focus and pro-business (especially US business) attitude of the Alemán administration. If Alemán failed the nation's poor majority as president, then his obsessive dedication to the interests of the middle classes paid considerable dividends, as Mexico weathered the storm of Cold War military intervention that swept across Latin America during the 1960s, 1970s, and 1980s. Indeed, the two factors that most influenced military interventionism in the region—middle-class dissatisfaction and US government suspicion—were concerns addressed by Alemán in the 1940s and 1950s.

The effort to contain the military's influence also worked to the nation's long-term advantage in avoiding direct military intervention in national politics. While that effort began well before Alemán arrived on the national scene, his ascent to the presidency, not least because of its timing at the outset of the Cold War, played a vital role in curbing the military's potential political tendencies. Cold War-era militarism became especially pronounced following the 1959 Cuban revolution, which had stoked fears of communist infiltration of the region both domestically and among foreign officials, especially in the United States. From that point onward, anti-democratic coups d'états supported by the US government, repressive military dictatorships notorious for their use of torture, and politically motivated armed forces that cast their anti-communism in messianic tones, all became common features of the region. In defiance of this pattern, Mexico enjoyed seamless continuity of civilian rule, even if that gain came at the cost of an increasingly undemocratic and conservative single-party establishment.

Mexico's national experience in the decades following Alemán's term allows for balanced reflection on the legacies of his generation and administration. And in those decades, one can see the contrasting experiences that defined the nation's development and that make the task of summarizing his legacy a difficult one. In the years following World War II, the single-party dominant system stabilized into a highly successful authoritarian model, one that relied on paternalism rather than resorting to brutality most of the time. The tradeoff was the erosion of whatever democratic tendencies remained up to that point. In economic terms, the administration set off a period of unbridled growth, but again the benefit came at a price. In the short run, Alemán's immediate successor, Adolfo Ruiz Cortines, had no choice but to champion a more austere approach to counteract his predecessor's excesses, something that rarely breeds popularity. In the long run, the import substitution model broke down altogether, leaving Mexico with little to show for its three-decade economic miracle.

Above all Alemanismo symbolized a new direction for Mexico, as it shed its revolutionary identity and emerged on the world stage as a modernizing nation. For those who stood to gain, the experience of the 1940s and 1950s squared with the enthusiasm heard in official rhetoric. For those who stood to lose, it was as though the revolution had passed them by and disappeared forever. If Alemán and his coterie were the revolution's fortunate sons, then these unfortunate masses became its forgotten children. All of these outcomes remind us that the impact of Alemanismo is most clearly seen not through economic indicators or policy directives, but through the experiences of those who emerged in better or worse shape as a result of the transformative changes that these leaders brought to mid-twentieth-century Mexico.

EPILOGUE

Alemán After Alemanismo

MIGUEL ALEMÁN, AT FORTY-NINE, WAS YOUNG ENOUGH WHEN HE LEFT the presidency in 1952 to pursue an active career over the next three decades. In keeping with precedent, he exercised minimal public influence in Mexico's electoral affairs and the PRI's internal politics. Nonetheless, he used his status as an experienced statesman to promote a tourism industry that had boomed during his presidency, spending the remainder of his life as head of the National Tourism Council (CONATUR), a governmental department that his administration had created. Alemán certainly was not the first of the twentieth-century presidents to have had an important role after his presidency. Lázaro Cárdenas, for instance, served as Manuel Ávila Camacho's defense minister following his declaration of war on the Axis, although his presence was most likely used to drum up support for war participation from a reticent public. Even some of the weaker presidents, namely Abelardo Rodríguez and Emilio Portes Gil, who governed during the so-called Maximato period in which former president Plutarco Elías Calles exercised considerable influence from behind the scenes, went on to have influential and productive political careers after the presidency. Rodríguez continued to function as a political kingmaker in Sonora, while Portes Gil occupied a number of diplomatic and cabinet posts before becoming president of the PNR.

Alemán was not the first president to experience financial gain after office, but he was the first since the 1910 revolution to use his political successes and connections as a pathway to extreme wealth and to establish himself as a permanent fixture within the business community.[1] His glamorous lifestyle set him apart from his immediate predecessors and successors, who maintained a dignified but bourgeois public image. Whether he was entertaining

US presidents at his Acapulco estate, dining with British royalty, yachting with Frank Sinatra, or indulging in the finest accommodations of Paris or Venice with his mistress and entourage, Alemán's persona after he left the presidency was every bit as distinct as his leadership style as president. The former president, as tourism booster, debonair socialite, prominent businessman, and eventually elder statesman, remained an important political presence for decades, and his post-presidential career shaped his legacy in important ways.

As his country's foremost promoter of tourism, Alemán devoted his greatest attention to Europe, where he established several offices to encourage visitors to cross the Atlantic. In 1977 the International Edition of the Official Tourism Gazette, headquartered in Madrid, named him its Personality of the Year.[2] Alemán frequently shuttled to South America, the United States, and Europe, often to meet with prominent figures of the tourism industry. In his numerous foreign travels he displayed consummate cultural sensitivity and curiosity, the products of his many years as a statesman, his personal enthusiasm for touring new places, and his desire to represent his country favorably. He demanded that anyone accompanying him exhibit the same level of awareness.

On one trip to Taiwan, after a member of his entourage rudely attempted to order a *tehuacán* (evidently a Mexican drink) from his Chinese hosts, Alemán chided, "When you're in China, you're not in Mexico."[3] In another example, Alemán lectured his longtime friend Carlos Soto Maynez on the virtue of propriety. "Remember," he warned, "that you're not Perón and I'm not Evita,"[4] a stern suggestion that they act with prudence and modesty as guests in the same building that contained Perón's own apartment just down the hall. Alemán often traveled with Soto Maynez, the brother of former Chihuahua governor Oscar Soto Maynez, with whom he had lived while in school in the 1920s. In many cases, his mistress of twenty years, Lenora, accompanied him. The pair frequently met up with the industrialist Bruno Pagliai and his wife, Hollywood star Merle Oberon, in Europe and South America.[5]

Beyond the self-evident benefits of luxury and glamour, Alemán's worldly travels allowed him to rub shoulders with celebrities and powerbrokers. This, in turn, served the dual purposes of promoting his country's attributes in various parts of the world and expanding his personal investments abroad. In a 1963 letter to Ramón Beteta, who followed his term as Alemán's treasury minister by becoming the general director of the publication *Novedades* (the newsmagazine headed by another longtime Alemán associate, Rómulo O'Farrill), the former president emphasized that he wanted to give the well-known journalist Howard Kingsbury Smith, who would be covering the Week of Salutation to Mexico, a grand welcome from the CONATUR delegation at the event.[6]

Beteta, one of Alemán's closest advisers and a rumored presidential possibility in 1952, appears to have served as a connection point between the media and Alemán's tourism interests. In another letter from 1963, Denis I. Duveen of the Duveen Soap Corporation sent Beteta's nephew, Ignacio, a letter saying that a division of his company, Fuller Brush Magazine, wanted to do a series on deep-sea angling. He planned the issue to feature Mexico, the Florida Keys, and the Bahamas, but he wanted to devote the most attention to Pacific fishing in Mexico, owing to his successful outings in Acapulco and Puerto Vallarta. Beteta immediately took up the promotional opportunity with Alemán to agree on what sum to invest.[7] Others targeted Beteta as a direct conduit to Alemán. Williams Haynes, the owner of the Hotel Prince in Mexico City, for example, approached the former cabinet minister about getting access to Alemán so he could interview him for his upcoming book, *Motor in Mexico—And Have Fun*, to be published by Doubleday.[8] These myriad dealings suggest a strong connection between Beteta at *Novedades* and Alemán at CONATUR. Given Alemán's long-standing connections to the *Novedades* ownership, the connection comes as little surprise.

Alemán's professional dealings often involved a stay at his mansion in Acapulco, where he hosted everyone from foreign dignitaries to domestic politicians to world-famous entertainers. Trips to visit Alemán at his beach home usually also included a cruise aboard his yacht, the *Sotavento*. He and Cárdenas reportedly discussed Henriquismo and the presidential succession aboard the vessel during the lead-up to the 1952 election.[9] Over the years numerous celebrities visited Alemán in Acapulco. A radiogram from December 1952 from incoming US vice president and future president Richard Nixon thanked Alemán for taking him and his wife, Pat, aboard the yacht.[10] At other times well into the 1970s, dignitaries ranging from the Duke of Edinburgh, Prince Phillip (the queen's consort);[11] Princess Alexandra (her sister);[12] former US president Lyndon Johnson and his wife, Lady Bird;[13] former US secretary of state Henry Kissinger;[14] US congressman James Roosevelt, the eldest son of Franklin Roosevelt;[15] and singer Frank Sinatra, among others, all visited the gem of Alemán's tourism development efforts. This style of personal diplomacy, especially toward those who might influence his country's prestige on the world stage, did not begin after his presidency. Rather, his efforts after 1952 formed an extension of a style that he honed while in office. During his presidency, Alemán had a long-standing reputation for hospitality toward foreign investors.[16] For example, Conrad Hilton, the patriarch of the family dynasty built on the eponymous hotel chain, wrote Alemán in 1953 to thank him for a meeting at Los Pinos, the presidential palace, to help get the Hotel Continental in Mexico City and the Hilton resort in Acapulco off the ground.[17]

Alemán did not reserve his leisure time only to entertain foreigners. He also maintained a vast network of personal friendships that overlapped with his business and political interests. In many cases, these friends, along with Lenora, accompanied him as a kind of entourage on foreign trips. Among the places they visited were Rio de Janeiro, Buenos Aires, Paris, and Venice. She even accompanied him on what would normally be reserved for men: a bear-hunting trip. Along with Jorge Pasquel (the country's pioneering baseball commissioner and a close business associate of Alemán) and Carlos Soto Maynez, they slept in sleeping bags in terribly cold cabins, where Alemán managed to burn the bedding after overheating the fireplace.[18]

The business and personal relationships he maintained after his presidency suggest significant overlap between his administration's policies and his personal financial interests. His relationship with Bruno Pagliai, a naturalized Italian immigrant who took a chance on Mexico after failing to make a satisfactory fortune in the United States, typified his interactions with the business community. Pagliai first entered elite social ranks after joining the famous Jockey Club. His association with the Alemán and Ávila Camacho networks began when Ávila Camacho's wife, Soledad Orozco, hired him at the capital's elite equestrian Racetrack of the Americas, which gave his career an immediate boost. With Alemán's help, he created a steel-tube-manufacturing company in Veracruz called TAMSA (Steel Tubes of Mexico) in 1952, and the company grew to be the country's fourth largest steel producer. He later expanded into other forms of metallurgical production, always centered in Alemán's home state of Veracruz, forming associations with the US-based aluminum conglomerate ALCOA, as well as Hughes Tools and Taylor Forge. He also spearheaded the creation of an investment society with the West German corporation Siemens, the Wall Street firm Allen and Col, and the Belgian company Sybetra. Finally, he and Alemán invested in the Editorial Novaro, which produced crime mystery novels and comic books. The Ministry of Treasury estimated that he earned between 50 million and 60 million pesos annually (between US$4 million and US$4.8 million at the time[19]).[20]

Alemán and Pagliai remained close friends long after his presidency. Pagliai and Oberon housed many of the foreign dignitaries who came to visit Acapulco, including Prince Philip. Princess Alexandra also visited their house during a separate visit. When Lyndon Johnson visited in 1971, Pagliai played golf and dined with the former US president, along with Alemán and Antonio Ortiz Mena, the two-term treasury minister under the Adolfo López Mateos and Gustavo Díaz Ordaz administrations.[21] Pagliai also donated money to the charity activities of Alemán's wife, First Lady Beatriz Velasco de Alemán, who used his and others' funds to start a school breakfast program.[22] The relationship between Alemán and Pagliai exemplified the kind of symbiosis between the former president's business interests, those of his closest associates, and his political inner circle. His relationship with leading figures of both print and television media, especially newspaper tycoon Rómulo O'Farrill and television mogul Emilio Azcárraga, further underscored this relationship.[23] Indeed, his administration was the first in the nation to establish a television transmission and, in subsequent years, both Alemán and his son, Miguel Alemán Velasco, became important shareholders in the dominant network Televisa.

Alemán gained a reputation for his commitment to protecting the friends who populated his inner circle, and in return he demanded loyalty (Antonio Carrillo Flores claims to have once told him that he would shoot himself over an accusation of corruption within Nacional Financiera[24]). During and especially after his presidency, Alemán attracted criticism for his ability to make money as a result of these associations. He tended overwhelmingly to stay silent on the matter, except in private company, where he expressed frustration over accusations of corruption pointed at him. From his perspective, the personal fortune he amassed never presented any moral dilemmas, nor did he see any incongruity between a life of public service and the accumulation of wealth. On various occasions, he made similar points to his friends, and he fulminated against *Fortune* magazine's unsubstantiated claim that he was one of the world's richest men.[25]

Near the end of his life, he confided to one friend that he considered the current group of PRI technocrats, including Miguel de la Madrid (president from 1982 to 1988), to be morally bankrupt. As he saw it, his own gradual accumulation of wealth over six decades contrasted with the greedy get-rich-quick schemes of the newer politicians.[26] He reacted coldly to another colleague, Alfonso Noriega, when they got onto the same subject. Alemán asked him whether he thought he had earned his money honorably. Noriega responded by joking, "The only person who makes money honorably is the one who doesn't make any at all," a comment that provided Alemán no amusement whatsoever.[27] Alemán also devoted a share of his fortune to philanthropic efforts, including a sizeable donation to the Mexican Academy of Language. Though he spoke candidly and frequently about his desire to establish a foundation to fund various social, economic, and cultural projects,[28] he never followed through with the plan. Alejandro Carrillo Castro, the current director of the posthumously founded Miguel Alemán Foundation, speculates that he did not want to promote a cult of personality that might result from such a venture.[29]

Despite considerable success in business and formal training in law, Alemán's closest friends and colleagues almost unanimously described him as born for politics, a field for which he had more natural intuition than he did for the legal system or the financial world.[30] Thus, it comes as little surprise that his interest in the workings of the government and the official party persisted beyond his presidency. He claimed to one friend that he considered himself to have been the most influential voice not only in Cárdenas's choice of Ávila Camacho as his successor, but also Ruiz Cortines's selection of López Mateos. The influence he claimed to have exercised in the selection of three presidents appears to have been a source of consid erable pride for Alemán, though he openly acknowledged that his influence waned thereafter.[31]

In public, Alemán expressed unwavering support for PRI presidents, upholding a long-standing protocol within the Revolutionary Family. Behind closed doors he occasionally became more candid about what he saw as their undesirable qualities and decisions. He regarded José López Portillo's expropriation of all bank assets as less of a nationalization and more of what he termed a "statisization,"[32] suggesting that the move, far from benefiting the nation and its citizens, stood to benefit a much narrower political elite and bolster the power of the state. He displayed this level of candor only when confident that there was no risk of exposure to the press. As the first president to represent the PRI, Alemán set a precedent for post-presidential decorum. Disagreements, however inevitable or bitter they might become, were to be expressed outside of public view. This certainly fueled part of his discontent with Ruiz Cortines, who established another precedent, that of sitting presidents smearing the preceding administration's records in the areas of economic management and toleration of corruption, to generate political capital.[33]

Alemán continued his travels until his last years. The death of Beatriz in 1981 did not slow the pace of his life much, but it did leave him a more introspective and somber man. Her death came as the result of an aneurysm in the cavity of her left eye, which she had lost some months before. Her health had deteriorated considerably in those last years, and her forced sedentary lifestyle put added pressure on her heart. With her passing, a grieving Alemán lamented that he had shamed her.[34] As his son later explained, despite his father's known excesses with women, his love for Beatriz never waned,[35] and her death took a toll on his well-being.

From that point forward, Alemán, known as an athletic, healthy man, a sparse eater and a light drinker,[36] gradually lost his vigor. Over the next two years, he continued to travel both for his own pleasure and to promote tourism, even as his health began to flag. He visited no fewer than seven medical specialists in the United States, including ones in Boston, Houston, and New York. In the midst of his treatments, he still found the energy to attend the 1982 World Cup in Spain. Nevertheless, this frenetic lifestyle eventually subsided, and he gradually began to move less and to lose his appetite. His doctors in the United States informed him that he had, in addition to prostate cancer, an ailment that left water in his lungs, a condition possibly linked to asbestos exposure. Alemán speculated that it might have been the roof of Los Pinos, the presidential residence. He died of a heart attack in 1983.[37]

Upon his death, his children (Miguel Alemán Velasco, Beatriz Alemán de Girón, and Jorge Alemán Velasco), along with a handful of associates, established the Miguel Alemán Foundation to perpetuate his personal legacy through philanthropic and research initiatives. The foundation, funded largely by Alemán's own fortune coupled with contributions from close friends and associates, continues to promote a number of domestic priorities. Its primary areas of focus are rural-development projects, health programs, environmental-protection efforts, and tourism investment.[38] Through these myriad functions, the foundation ensures substantial investment in a number of areas that demand planning and funding, especially in a period in which ongoing austerity measures have shifted the onus away from government and toward the private and non-governmental sectors. The philanthropic institution that bears Alemán's name ensures that the former president remains an important presence in the political and social evolution of a nation he helped to shape so dramatically.

Appendix

Members of the Alemán Generation

The table below contains a partial list of the members of the scholastic generation of the 1920s who later came to occupy prominent public positions, particularly during the Alemán years. It does not include all members of Miguel Alemán's administration, nor all the members of his personal and professional circles throughout his career, such as his later business associates. Instead, it connects the associations these young men made in the 1920s as students with public service later in life. For a discussion of the social lives of some of these young men in their school years, see the introduction. The table includes the positions held by these men, and it notes early connections of particular interest, such as collaboration in certain activities as students or as early-career professionals. Sources for this information are noted at the end of the table.

Table 1. The Alemán Generation

Name	**Prominent Positions**	**School and Early Professional Connections**
Oscar Soto Maynes	Gov. of Chihuahua, 1950–1955	H Group; Eureka paper; Polaco Group; close friend and roommate of Alemán in school
Horacio Terán Zozaya	Gov. of Tamaulipas, 1951–1957	School companion of Alemán
Miguel Alemán	Pres., 1946–1952; min. of interior, 1940–1945; gov. of Veracruz, 1936–1939	H Group; Eureka paper; Polaco group

Table 1 (*continued*)

Name	**Prominent Positions**	**School and Early Professional Connections**
Rogerio de la Selva	Personal secretary of Alemán as gov. of Veracruz, min. of government, and pres., 1936–1952	Polaco Group; participant in 1929 Vasconcelos presidential campaign; friend of Alemán and member of his cohort since law school
Alfonso García González	Gov. of Baja California del Norte, 1947–1953; dir. gen. of tourism, 1959–1961	Close personal friend of Alemán, who was at his bedside at time of death
Raúl López Sánchez	Gov. of Coahuila, 1948–1951; sen. from Coahulia, 1946–1948; fed. deputy of Coahulia, 1943–1946; sec. of navy, 1952	H Group; Polaco group; friend of Alemán, Salvador Novo, and others in school
Mario Sousa Gordillo	Head of dept. of Agrarian Affairs, 1946–11952	
Carlos Novoa	Dir. gen. of Banco de México	
Salvador Novo	Theater dir. at Instituto Nacional de Bellas Artes	
Fernando Casas Alemán	Mayor of Mexico City, 1946–1952	Polaco group; knew Alemán in school; later legal associate
Manuel Gual Vidal	Min. of public education, 1946–1952	Professor of Alemán in law school
Manuel R. Palacios	Dir. gen. of National Railroads	Eureka paper; participant in 1929 Vasconcelos presidential campaign
Héctor Pérez Martínez	Min. of government, 1946–1948	Knew Alemán and was friends with Salvador Novo in school
Ernesto P. Uruchurtu	Min. of interior, 1948 and 1951–1952; mayor of Mexico City, 1952–1966	Attended law school with Alemán, Antonio Carrillo Flores, Andrés Serra Rojas, and Alfonso Noriega
Eduardo Bustamante	Sub-min. of finance, 1946–1949	Friend of Alemán, Manuel Gual Vidal, Jaime Torres Bodet, Antonio Carrillo Flores, and others since law school

Antonio Carrillo Flores	Dir. of Nacional Financiera, 1946–1952; min. of finance, 1952–1958; amb. to USA, 1958–1964; min. of foreign relations, 1964–1970; amb. to USSR, 1980–1981	Friend of Alemán, Ernesto Uruchurtu, Antonio Ortiz Mena, Andrés Serra Rojas, Manuel Ramírez Vázquez and others since law school
Angel Carvajal	Supreme Court justice, 1958–1972; min. of government, 1952–1958; gov. of Veracruz, 1948–1950	Friend of Alemán, Antonio Carrillo Flores, and others since law school; participant in 1929 Vasconcelos presidential campaign
Raúl Rojina Villegas	Fed. judge, professor, and lawyer, 1930s–1970s	
José Rivera Pérez Campos	Sen. of Guanajuato, 1970–1976	
Antonio Ortiz Mena	Pres., Inter-Am. Dev. Bank, 1971–1988; min. of finance, 1958–1970	Eureka paper; knew Alemán and others in school
Braulio Maldonado	Fed. deputy of Baja California del Norte, 1952–1953; gov. of BCN, 1953–1959	Knew Alemán in school and participated with him and others in 1927 presidential campaign
Andrés Serra Rojas	Sen. of Chiapas, 1964–1950; min. of labor, 1946–1948; fed. deputy of Chiapas, 1943–1946	Friend of Alemán, Antonio Carrillo Flores, and others in preparatory and law school
Antonio Dovalí Jaime	Dir. gen. of PEMEX, 1970–1976; dir. of construction at Chihuahua-Pacific Railroad, 1952–1958; sub-min. of public works, 1949–1952	Friend of Alemán and numerous others at university
Antonio Martínez Báez	Fed. deputy of Michoacan, 1970–1973; min. of industry and commerce, 1948–1952	Law student with Ramón Beteta (Alemán's min. of finance); prominent lawyer and professor of law
J. Jesús Castorena	Provisional gov. of Guanajuato, 1947–1948	Law student with Antonio Martínez Báez (above); prominent labor lawyer
Bernardo Iturriaga A.	Sub-min. of finance	

Table 1 (*continued*)

Name	**Prominent Positions**	**School and Early Professional Connections**
Agustín García López	Min. of public works, 1946–1952	Knew Alemán in school as law professor
Julio Serrano Castro	Sen. of Chiapas, 1949–1958; subdirector of PEMEX, 1946–1950; sub-min. of labor, 1946	Knew Alemán in school
Adolfo Orive Alba	Min. of hydraulic resources, 1947–1952	Close friend of Alemán and Antonio Dovalí Jaime in school (not law school; was an engineering student)
Carlos Franco Sodi	Attorney gen. of Mexico, 1952–1956; attorney gen. of Fed. District and Fed. Territories, 1946–1952	Friend of Alemán in school
Gabriel Ramos Millán	Fed. deputy of Oaxaca, 1943–1946; sen. of Oaxaca, 1946–1947; dir. of National Corn Commission, 1947–1949	H Group; Eureka paper; Polaco group; close friend and colleague of Alemán from school onward; died in plane crash in 1949
Manuel Ramírez Vázquez	Min. of labor, 1948–1952; sub-min. of labor, 1946–1948	Polaco group; friend of Alemán, Antonio Carrillo Flores, and others in school
Mariano Ramírez Vázquez	Supreme Court justice	Friend of Salvador Novo from school; brother of Manuel (above)
Adolfo Zamora	Dir. gen. of National Urban Mortgage Bank of Public Works, 1947–1953	Eureka paper; friend of Antonio Ortiz Mena in school
Alfonso Romandia Ferreira	Dir. gen. of Financiera Industrial Azucarera (Sugar Industry Finance Corporation), 1946–1953	Friend of Alemán since law school
José Castro Estrada	Sub-min. of agriculture (for forest resources), 1952	Friend of Alemán, Antonio Carrillo Flores, Andrés Serra Rojas, and others of the 1929 graduating year in law school
Manuel Sánchez Cuen	Dir. gen. of National Mortgage Bank, 1952–1958; sub-min. of industry and commerce, 1948–1952	Attended law school with Alemán, Antonio Carrillo Flores, Alfonso Noriega, and others

Alfonso Noriega	Sec. gen., then acting dir. of UNAM; dir. of Nat. Law School, 1943–1945	H Group; friend or colleague of Alemán, Ernesto Uruchurtu, Antonio Carrillo Flores, Manuel Ramírez Vázquez, Antonio Ortiz Mena, and Andrés Serra Rojas in law school
Raúl Noriega (Ondovilla)	Fed. deputy of Fed. District, 1967–1970; oficial mayor (third-ranking official) of min. of finance, 1951–1958	Friend of Alemán in law school
Ezequiel Burguete Farrera	Numerous mid-level positions in law, judiciary, and executive branch of government	Knew Antonio Carrillo Flores in law school
Alfonso Guzmán Neyra	Supreme Court justice, 1965–1969, 1952–1958	Student leader in 1929 autonomy movement
Luis Felipe Canudas Orezza	Asst. attorney gen. of Mexico, 1949–1951, 1944–1949	
Antonio Armendáriz	Dir. gen. of Bank of Foreign Commerce, 1965–1970; amb. to Great Britain, 1960–1965; sub-min. of finance, 1952–1958	Knew Antonio Carrillo Flores, Andrés Serra Rojas, Antonio Ortiz Mena, and others in law school; participant in 1929 Vasconcelos presidential campaign
Luciano Huerta Sánchez	Gov. of Tlaxcala, 1970–1976; sen. from Tlaxcala, 1964–1970	Knew Antonio Carrillo Flores and Antonio Armendáriz at university (not law school; was a medical student and later physician)
Salomon González Blanco	Substitute gov. of Chiapas, 1978–1980; min. of labor, 1958–1964; sub-min. of labor, 1953–1957	Friend of Antonio Carrillo Flores and Manuel Ramírez Vázquez in law school
Alberto González Blanco	Numerous judicial and executive positions	Brother of Salomon (above)
Mariano Azuela	Sen. of Jalisco, 1958–1960; Supreme Court justice, 1960–1971, 1951–1957	Son of famous revolutionary novelist Mariano Azuela; participant in 1929 Vasconcelos presidential campaign
Salvador Azuela		Brother of Mariano (above)

Table 1 (*continued*)

Name	**Prominent Positions**	**School and Early Professional Connections**
Leopoldo Chávez	Sub-min. of public education	
César Garizurieta (Ehrenzweig)	Fed. deputy of Veracruz, 1949–1952, 1940–1943	
Enrique Torres Sánchez	Gov. of Durango, 1950–1956	Student with Alemán, Mariano Azuela, Eduardo Bustamante, and others in law school
Adolfo López Mateos	Pres., 1958–1964; min. of labor, 1952–1958; sen. of Mexico State, 1946–1952	Participant in 1929 Vasconcelos presidential campaign
David Romero Castañeda	Fed. deputy of Mexico State, 1946–1949	H Group; Eureka paper; Polaco group
Efraín Brito Rosado	Sen. of Yucatán, 1946–1952; fed. deputy of Yucatán, 1940–1943	Participant in 1929 Vasconcelos presidential campaign and university autonomy strikes; friend of Alemán and Adolfo López Mateos as students
Andrés Henestrosa	Fed. deputy of Oaxaca, 1964–1967, 1958–1961	Participant in 1929 Vasconcelos presidential campaign and university autonomy strikes with Adolfo López Mateos; well-known author of short stories and expert in literature
Jaime Torres Bodet	Min. of education, 1958–1964, 1943–1946; dir. gen. of UNESCO, 1948–1952; min. of foreign affairs, 1946–1951	Classmate of Salvador Novo; founder of Atheneum of Youth in 1918; major figure in intellectual life of Mexico
Ramón Beteta	Min. of finance, 1946–1952	Only Alemán cabinet member to have prior cabinet experience (was sub-min. of foreign relations under Lázaro Cárdenas, 1936–1940, and sub-min. of finance under Manuel Avila Camacho, 1940–1945)
Ernesto Aguilar Álvarez	Supreme Court justice, 1966–1977	Polaco Group

Fernando Román Lugo	Attorney gen. of Fed. District and Fed. Territories, 1958–1964; subsec. of government, 1953–1958	Polaco Group
Enrique Parra Hernández		Polaco Group
Manuel Heredia		Polaco Group
José Pérez y Pérez		H Group
Marco Antonio Muñoz		Polaco Group

SOURCES

Miguel Alemán Valdés, *Remembranzas y testimonios*. Mexico City: Grijalbo, 1987.

Roderic Ai Camp, *Mexican Political Biographies, 1935–1981*. 2nd ed. Tucson: University of Arizona Press, 1982.

———. "La campaña presidencial de 1929 y el liderazgo político en México," *Historia Mexicana* 27, no. 2 (Oct.-Dec., 1977): 231–259.

———. "Education and Political Recruitment in Mexico: The Alemán Generation," *Journal of Interamerican Studies and World Affairs* 18, no. 3 (Aug., 1976): 295–321.

Various files, Archivo de la Biblioteca Mexicana de la Fundación Miguel Alemán, AC.

Notes

Introduction

1. Smith, *Labyrinths of Power*, 23; Camp, "Education and Political Recruitment," 295–98.
2. Lieuwen, *Mexican Military*, 143–46.
3. Camp has argued that this educational preparation, in addition to contributing to their collective socialization and aiding in political recruitment, made them the first technocratic generation in the single-party system. While their high level of education, career-long public service, and authoritarian tendencies made them similar to later technocrats in Mexico and across Latin America, the model most readily identified with technocrats involves leaders trained in macroeconomic planning (for example, the so-called Chicago Boys, the University of Chicago–trained disciples of Milton Friedman, who advised Chilean dictator Gen. Augusto Pinochet to adopt neoliberal economic policies); Camp, *Metamorphosis of Leadership*, 156, 164; Camp, "The Revolution's Second Generation," 468–79.
4. Brandenburg, *Making of Modern Mexico*; Cline, *Mexico: Revolution to Evolution*, 157–59; Wilkie, *Mexican Revolution*; Torres, *Historia de la Revolución*; Medina, *Historia de la Revolución Mexicana.*
5. Morris, *Corruption and Politics*, 71; Hansen, *Politics of Mexican Development*, 83–88.
6. Niblo, *Mexico in the 1940s*, 183–188.
7. Cosío Villegas, "Crisis de México," 29–51. On de la Selva's warning, see Joseph and Henderson, *Mexico Reader*, 470.
8. Pérez Montfort, "La ciudad de Mexico en los noticieros filmicos," 219–37.
9. *La Ley de Herodes*, DVD, Estrada, 1999.
10. Montes de Oca, "The State and the Peasants," 53; Villarreal, "Policy of Import-Substituting Industrialization," 67.
11. The debate over the characteristics of Cardenismo (i.e., authoritarian vs. popular or democratic; radical or progressive vs. conservative or reactionary) is vast, has taken several turns, and continues to engage scholars. For a brief synthesis

of the general trends (e.g., populist, revisionist, post-revisionist) in the historiography of the Cárdenas period, see Knight, "Cardenismo," 73–107; for a recent synthesis, see Porter, "Apogee of the Revolution," 453–67.

12. Sherman, "Mexican 'Miracle,'" 575–620.
13. Miguel Alemán, quoted in "Mexico: Good Friend," *Time*, Apr. 28, 1947.
14. Biography as a historical methodology has experienced something of a resurgence in recent years. The *American Historical Review* devoted an issue to a discussion of this topic. See Nasaw et al., "Roundtable: Historians and Biography."
15. The concept of political generations has been utilized by other scholars in various contexts. For some comparative examples, see the following: Bailes, *Technology and Society under Lenin and Stalin*; Yahuda, "Political Generations in China," 793–805; Searing, "Comparative Study of Elite Socialization," 471–500; Beissinger, "Generations in Soviet Politics," 288–314; Samuels, "Political Generations and Political Development," 1–8.
16. José Ortega y Gasset, *Nuestro tiempo*, 15.
17. Gillingham and Smith, "Introduction," *Dictablanda*, 1–43.
18. The thesis of Mexico's "apolitical military" stems from the work of Edwin Lieuwen. With few exceptions, the basic contours of civil-military-relations historiography has taken his assertion of Mexico's exception as a given; see Lieuwen, *Mexican Military*, 129, 143–46. Recent scholarship has asserted persuasively that the military's political character was not eliminated entirely by 1940, as the previous assumption had suggested. Nevertheless, it ceased to pose any threat to the stability of the national government after the 1930s; see Rath, *Myths of Demilitarization*.
19. Walker, *Waking from the Dream*, 45–72.
20. For an explanation of corporatism under the PRI, see Cockcroft, *Mexico's Revolution*, 70–74; the literature on populism is vast; for a sense of its place in Latin American history, see Conniff, "Introduction," *Populism in Latin America*, 1–21. The two leaders in Mexico generally recognized as populists were Lázaro Cárdenas (president, 1934–1940) and Luis Echeverría (1970–1976); see Knight, "Populism and Neo-Populism," 223–48; and Kiddle and Muñoz, "Men of the People," 2–7.
21. The literature on Mexico's dirty war has undergone a recent expansion. See Aviña, *Specters of Revolution*, and the collected chapters in Calderón and Cedillo, *Challenging Authoritarianism in Mexico*; for worker crackdowns, see Alegre, *Railroad Radicals*.
22. The recent availability of declassified sources from both the General Directorate of Political and Social Investigation and the Federal Security Directorate have led to a surge in new research. See Aguayo Quezada, *Charola*; Navarro, *Political Intelligence and Modern Mexico*. Tanalís Padilla and Louise

Walker recently edited a special journal issue on the secret police archives as well: "Spy Reports."

23. As Susan Eckstein notes, the party had little independent power and was in most cases subservient to the president; see Eckstein, "The State and the Urban Poor," 24. I borrow the idea of the party as an instrument of control within a presidentialist system, as opposed to the idea that the party was an independent political actor, from personal conversations with Soledad Loaeza and from her unpublished work in progress on Manuel Ávila Camacho's failed electoral proposition. Presidential studies are dominant in the Mexican historiography. For examples of presidentialist treatments specifically of the Alemán years, see Torres, *Historia de la Revolución*; Medina, *Revolución Mexicana*; Martínez, "El modelo económico," 227–62; Medin, *Sexenio alemanista*.
24. Loaeza, *Partido Acción Nacional*, 11; Loaeza, *Llamado de las urnas*, 241.
25. While electoral fraud was not considered to be a major presence in the 1940s and 1950s, as the PRI retained its capacity to generate sufficient electoral support, the problem of fraud would increase over the course of the century.
26. Paxman and Fernández, *Tigre*; González de Bustamante, *'Muy Buenas Noches,'* xxii–xxiii.
27. Smith, *Labyrinths of Power*, 203, 214; Meyer, "Authoritarian State in Mexico," 16; Camp, *Entrepreneurs and Politics*, 22–23.
28. Paxman, "Espinosa Yglesias Becomes a Philanthropist."
29. Morris, *Corruption and Politics*, 65–82.
30. Villareal, "Policy of Import-Substituting Industrialization," 67–71.
31. Knight, *Mexican Revolution, Vol.* 2, 500–511.
32. Babb, *Managing Mexico*, 28; Bennett and Sharpe, "State as Banker and Entrepreneur," 165–74.
33. Martínez, "Modelo económico," 227–62.
34. Villareal, "Policy of Import-Substituting Industrialization," 81–83.
35. Kingstone, *Political Economy of Latin America*, 19–44.
36. Eckstein, "State and the Urban Poor," 23–24; Davis, *Urban Leviathan*, 102–3.
37. Roxborough, "Mexico," *Latin America Between World War II and the Cold War*, 190, 206.
38. Bernal Tavares, *Lombardo Toledano y Miguel Alemán*, 161–86.
39. The most recent source to examine this topic is López, *Crafting Mexico.* Several of the essays included in Vaughan and Lewis, *Eagle and the Virgin*, examine this cultural project through different lenses, including film, popular music, schools, and public art. Full-length monographs by its contributors explore these various sub-themes more thoroughly.
40. Scholars have emphasized that the behaviors and mindset of modern consumerism can be detected in the Porfiriato and the revolutionary period; however, there never existed such an embrace of consumerism among officials before

Alemán; see Moreno, *¡Yankee Don't go Home!*, 179; for Porfiriato, see Bunker, *Mexican Consumer Culture.*

41. Author Susan Gauss uses the broadly encompassing term industrialism, rather than the more narrowly economic idea of industrialization, to characterize the entire intellectual and policy project of building a protected industrial economy, an interventionist state, and a consumerist society as a pathway to modernization; see Gauss, *Made in Mexico*, 3–5.
42. The literature on hero cults in the Mexican revolution is substantial; see, for example, O'Malley, *Myth of the Revolution*, 4–7; various essays in Johnson, *Death, Dismemberment, and Memory*, also address the topic.
43. Benjamin, *La Revolución*, 14–33.
44. Krauze, *Biography of Power*, 526–29.
45. Cedillo, *Los Nazis en México*, 15, 35–58; Niblo, *Mexico in the 1940s*, 215–16.
46. Hershfield and Maciel, *Mexico's Cinema*, 33–36.
47. Tatum, "La Familia Burrón"; Wicke, "The Burrón Family."
48. K. Villareal, "Gladiolas for the Children of Sánchez."
49. *Los Olvidados*, DVD.
50. Lewis, *Children of Sánchez*; Lewis, *Five Families.*
51. Fuentes, *Death of Artemio Cruz*; Rulfo, *Pedro Paramo.* Rulfo's surrealist, dystopian, and experimental novel, though part of the same critical tradition as *Artemio Cruz*, made the failures of agrarian reform in the countryside its central target.
52. Zolov, *Refried Elvis*, 1–17.

Chapter One

1. Camp, "Education and Political Recruitment"; Gil et al., "Caso de Miguel Alemán."
2. Archivo de la Biblioteca Mexicana de la Fundación Miguel Alemán (hereafter FMA), Testimonio de Andrés Henestrosa, Box 6, Exp. 177, Sept. 12, 1985; Nettie Lee Benson Library, University of Texas at Austin (hereafter NLB), Salvador Aceves Parra, personal communication with Roderic Camp, Jan. 29, 1976.
3. FMA, Testimonio de David Romero Castañeda, Box 6, Exp. 175, Mar. 20, 1985; FMA, Testimonio de Luis Danton Rodríguez, Box 7, Exp. 203, June 4, 1986.
4. FMA, Testimonio de Antonio Carrillo Flores, Box 7, Exp. 182, June 10, 1985; NLB, Sealtiel Alatriste, interview with Roderic Camp, June 24, 1975; NLB, Antonio Armendáriz, interview with Roderic Camp.
5. FMA, Testimonio de David Romero Castañeda.
6. FMA, Testimonio de Andrés Henestrosa.
7. Camp, "Campaña presidencial de 1929."

8. FMA, Testimonio de Alfonso Noriega, Box 6, Exp. 179, Apr. 8, 1985; FMA, Testimonio de Marco Antonio Muñoz, Box 7, Exp. 199, Mar. 6, 1985.
9. FMA, Testimonio de Andrés Henestrosa.
10. Alemán served in both the Madero and Constitutionalist years in the armed phase of the revolution before rising to more prominent ranks in the 1920s. See Dulles, *Yesterday in Mexico*, 445.
11. FMA, Testimonio de Evangelina Mendoza, Box 7, Exp. 181, June 3, 1985.
12. Krauze, *Biography of Power*, 531–33.
13. FMA, Testimonio de Carlos Soto Maynez, Box 8, Exp. 213, May 17, 1985; FMA, Testimonio de David Romero Castañeda; FMA, Testimonio de Andrés Henestrosa.
14. FMA, Testimonio de Victoria Soto de Córdoba.
15. FMA, Testimonio de Carlos Soto Maynez.
16. FMA, Testimonio de Gilberto Limón, Box 18, Exp. 444, Mar. 12, 1985.
17. Martínez, *Border Boom Town*, 170.
18. FMA, Letter from Miguel Alemán González to Miguel Alemán Valdés, Box 20, Exp. 536, Feb. 7, 1920.
19. FMA, Letter from Miguel Alemán González to Miguel Alemán Valdés, Box 20, Exp. 536, June 15, 1925.
20. FMA, Report by Alfonso Chanona L., Pagador de la Segunda Division de Oriente, Box 20, Exp. 536, July 30, 1924
21. FMA, Letter from Miguel Alemán González to Miguel Alemán Valdés, Box 20, Exp. 536, Dec. 23, 1920.
22. FMA, Letter from Miguel Alemán González to Miguel Alemán Valdés, Box 20, Exp. 536, June 15, 1925.
23. FMA, Letter from Carlos M. Jiménez to Guillermo Schulz, Box 20, Exp. 536, Dec. 9, 1925; FMA, Letter from A. Campillo Seyde to Guillermo Schulz, Box 20, Exp. 536, n.d.
24. Dulles, *Yesterday in Mexico*, 442–45.
25. FMA, Confederación Nacional de Estudiantes Anti-Reeleccionistas Pro-Arnulfo R. Gómez, Box 23, Exp. 538, June 8, 1927.
26. FMA, Candidatura Pro-Gómez-Alemán, Box 23, Exp. 538, n.d.
27. FMA, Miguel Alemán González, "A la Nación," Box 23, Exp. 538, Mar., 1923.
28. FMA, Testimonio de David Romero Castañeda; FMA, Testimonio de Manuel R. Palacios; FMA, Testimonio de Marco Antonio Muñoz.
29. FMA, Testimonio de Rafael Moreno Henríquez, Box 8, Exp. 216, Apr. 18, 1985.
30. FMA, Testimonio de Evangelina Mendoza, Box 7, Exp. 181, June 3, 1985.
31. Alemán Valdés, *Remembranzas y testimonios*, 102.
32. FMA, Testimonio de Beatriz Alemán de Girón, Box 9, Exp. 242, Oct. 11, 1985.
33. Ibid.; FMA, Testimonio de Miguel Alemán Velasco, Box 9, Exp. 243, Mar. 29, 1985.

34. FMA, Testimonio de Antonio Carillo Flores; FMA, Testimonio de Carlos Soto Maynez; FMA, Testimonio de Arturo García Formenti, Box 14, Exp. 346, n.d.
35. Alemán Valdés, *Remembranzas y testimonios*, 152.
36. While the full list can be seen in the appendix, and while part of the list that follows is repeated in the text of the introduction, this is a more complete view of the generation. Beyond Alemán, this group included Antonio Carillo Flores (director of Nacional Financiera, the public-development corporation, in the Alemán years, then minister of finance, 1952–1958, Ambassador to the United States and the USSR, and minister of foreign affairs, 1964–1970), Antonio Ortiz Mena (minister of finance, 1958–1970), Andrés Serra Rojas (minister of labor, 1946–1948), Braulio Maldonado (governor of Baja California Norte, 1953–1959), Oscar Soto Maynez (governor of Chihuahua, 1950–1955), Ernesto Uruchurtu (minister of the interior, 1948 and 1951–1952, and mayor of Mexico City, 1952–1966), Adolfo López Mateos (president, 1958–1964), Rogerio de la Selva (personal secretary to Alemán as governor and president), Gabriel Ramos Millán (federal deputy then senator from Oaxaca, 1943–1947, and head of the National Corn Commission, 1947–1949), David Romero Castañeda (federal deputy from the State of Mexico, 1946–1949), Alfonso Noriega (the secretary general, then acting director of the UNAM, then director of the National Law School, 1943–1945), Manuel Ramírez Vázquez (minister of labor, 1948–1952), Efraín Brito Rosado (federal deputy, then senator from Veracruz, (1940–1943 and 1946–1952), Alejandro Gómez Arias (federal deputy, then senator from Yucatán, 1949–1958). Academic luminaries such as Andrés Henestrosa also formed part of the generation, and other notable academics, such as Jaime Torres Bodet (secretary of education, 1943–1946 and 1958–1964, secretary of foreign affairs, 1946–1951, and director-general of UNESCO, 1948–1952) and Ramón Beteta (secretary of finance, 1946–1952) came just before, and often gave classes at one or both schools. Torres Bodet had the distinction of being the only person to have served previously in a cabinet position (sub-ministerial positions excluded), and Beteta represented only one of several instructors of members of this generation who would later enter government ranks (noted anthropologist Alfonso Caso, for instance, became the first administrator of the *Instituto Nacional Indígena*, or INI, created in 1951).
37. Hale, *Transformation of Liberalism*, 25–26; Guerra, *Antiguo regimen a la Revolución*, vol. 1, 378–89, and vol. 2, 79–100.
38. Incógnito, "La tiranía honrada," *La Libertad*, Oct. 3, 1878, 2.
39. Hale, *Transformation of Liberalism*, 25–63.
40. For examples of these ideas, see the polemic between Francisco Cosmes and José María Vigil: Francisco Cosmes, "La constitución y el Sr. Vigil," *La Libertad*, Sept. 11, 1878, 2; Cosmes, "La constitución y el Sr. Vigil II," *La Libertad*, Sept. 18, 1878, 2; Sin autor, "*El Monitor* y la metafísica," *La Libertad*,

July 10, 1879, 2; see also Sin autor, "La voz de alerta," *La Libertad*, Sept. 15, 1878, 2; Sin autor, "Un pseudo-programa," *La Libertad*, Sept. 25, 1878, 2; Cosmes, "La constitución," 2; Cosmes, "Verdades," *La Libertad*, Sept. 4, 1878, 2.

41. FMA, Testimonio de Marco Antonio Muñoz.
42. Krauze, *Caudillos culturales*, 46–52.
43. Calderón Vega, *Siete sabios de México*, ix–xii.
44. Krauze, *Caudillos culturales*, 74.
45. Calderón Vega, *Siete sabios*, 20.
46. Krauze, *Caudillos culturales*, 222–28.
47. Bernal Tavares, *Lombardo Toledano y Miguel Alemán.*
48. FMA, Testimonio de Manuel R. Palacios.
49. NLB, Antonio Armendáriz, interview with Camp; NLB, Miguel Alemán, interview with Camp, Oct. 27, 1976; FMA, Testimonio de Andrés Henestrosa; FMA, Testimonio de Manuel R. Palacios; FMA, Testimonio de Fransisca Acosta Lagunes, Box 6, Exp. 180, June 18, 1985.
50. NLB, Miguel Alemán, interview with Camp.
51. Alemán Valdés, *Remembranzas y testimonios*, 53–80.
52. NLB, Cardiel Reyes, interview with Camp, n.d.
53. NLB, Francisco González de la Vega, interview with Camp, July 23, 1974.
54. FMA, Testimonio de Renato Leduc, Box 7, Exp. 185, July 11, 1985.
55. NLB, Sealtiel Alatriste, interview with Camp.
56. FMA, Testimonio de Andrés Henestrosa; FMA, Testimonio de Manuel R. Palacios.
57. Camp, "Education and Political Recruitment," 295–98.
58. FMA, Testimonio de Dr. Gómez (no listed first name) and Modesto Sánchez, Box 7, Exp. 198, Mar. 14, 1985; FMA, Testimonio de Manuel Ramírez Vázquez, Mar. 15, 1985.
59. FMA, Testimonio de Antonio Carillo Flores.
60. FMA, Testimonio de Manuel Ramirez Vázquez.
61. FMA, Testimonio de Dr. Gómez and Modesto Sánchez.
62. FMA, José Pérez y Pérez to Miguel Alemán, Box 20, Exp. 536; FMA, "Grupo H–1920," Box 20, Exp. 536.
63. Camp, *Metamorphosis of Leadership*, 159.
64. FMA, Testimonio de Manuel R. Palacios.
65. The two issues are housed at the archive of the *Fundación Miguel Alemán* with a duplicate of the first at the Nettie Lee Benson Library at the University of Texas.
66. *Eureka* 1:1, July 8, 1924.
67. *Libro de Oro conmemorativo.*
68. Diego Rivera, "Sobre la pintura," in *Eureka* 1:1, July 8, 1924.
69. "El Flirt," in *Eureka* 1:1, July 8, 1924.

70. The opening chapter to López, *Crafting Mexico*, 1–26, contains an excellent discussion of official and non-official efforts to create a national ethnic identity beginning in the 1920s.
71. "Por la Escuela Hogar 'Sor Juana Inés de la Cruz,'" in *Eureka* 1:1, July 8, 1924.
72. Moncrayon, "Al márgen de pelonas," in *Eureka* 1:3, Aug. 6, 1924.
73. Esperanza Zambrano, "La mujer que trabaja," in *Eureka* 1:1, July 8, 1924.
74. Albert Meural, "El Wildeismo," in *Eureka* 1:3, Aug. 6, 1924.
75. FMA, Testimonio de Luis Dantón Rodríguez; Alberto Terán, "La ideología de la juventud actual," in *Eureka* 1:3, Aug. 6, 1924.
76. Terán, "La ideología de la juventud."
77. Jean Charlot, "La pinturas de la E.N.P.," in *Eureka* 1:3, Aug. 6, 1924.
78. Rochfort, "The Sickle, the Serpent, and the Soil," 45.
79. FMA, Testimonio de Antonio Carrillo Flores.
80. NLB, Salvador Azuela, personal communication with Camp, July 10, 1974.
81. NLB, Sealtiel Alatriste, interview with Camp.
82. NLB, Julio Faesler, personal communication with Camp, n.d.
83. FMA, Testimonio de Henestrosa; NLB, Salvador Aceves Parra, personal communication with Camp, Jan. 29, 1976.
84. Several students had documentation suggesting financial trouble; for example, Archivo Histórico, Instituto de Investigaciones Sobre la Universidad y la Educación, Universidad Nacional Autónoma de México (hereafter IISUE), Expedientes de Estudiantes, 3766: Andrés Serra Rojas.
85. FMA, "Planilla que postula el Partido Rojo," Box 39, Exp. 730, May 21, 1924.
86. NLB, Salvador Aceves Parra, personal communication with Camp; FMA, Testimonio de Andrés Henestrosa.
87. FMA, Testimonio de Alfonso Noriega.
88. NLB, Manuel Ulloa Ortiz, personal communication with Camp, n.d.; FMA, Testimonio de Andrés Henestrosa; FMA, Testimonio de Manuel R. Palacios.
89. FMA, Testimonio de Mary Córdoba de Marín, Box 7, Exp. 184, July 11, 1985; FMA, Testimonio de Dr. Gómez and Modesto Gómez; FMA, Testimonio de Victoria Soto de Córdoba, Box 7, Exp. 202, July 8, 1985.
90. FMA, Testimonio de Andrés Henestrosa.
91. FMA, Testimonio de Alejandro Gómez Arias, Box 7, Exp. 201, Sept. 13, 1985.
92. FMA, Testimonio de Alfonso Noriega.
93. FMA, Testimonio de Manuel R. Palacios.
94. FMA, Testimonio de Renato Leduc.
95. Camp, "La campaña presidencial de 1929 y el liderazgo político en México," 231–59.
96. FMA, Testimonio de Andrés Henestroa; NLB, Ricardo Rivera Pérez, personal communication with Camp, Nov. 21, 1975.
97. FMA, Testimonio de David Romero Castañeda.
98. FMA, Testimonio de Manuel R. Palacios.

99. NLB, Efraín Brito, personal communication with Camp, n.d.
100. FMA, Testimonio de Alejandro Gómez Arias.
101. FMA, Testimonio de Alejandro Gómez Arias; NLB, Antonio Armendáriz, interview with Camp; NLB, Ricardo Rivera Pérez to Camp.
102. FMA, Testimonio de Manuel R. Palacios.
103. FMA, Testimonio de Andrés Henestrosa.
104. Camp, "La campaña presidencial de 1929 y el liderazgo político en México," 231–59.
105. FMA, Testimonio de Andrés Henestrosa; NLB, Antonio Armendáriz, interview with Camp.
106. FMA, Testimonio de Antonio Carillo Flores.
107. NLB, Manuel Ulloa Ortiz to Camp.

Chapter Two

1. Camp, "Education and Political Recruitment in Mexico," 306.
2. FMA, Miguel Alemán, "Accidentes del Trabajo," Tesis para la facultad de derechos y ciencias sociales, Box 47, Exp. 868.
3. FMA, Testimonio de Miguel Alemán Velasco, Box 9, Exp. 243, Mar. 29, 1985.
4. Alemán Valdés, *Remembranzas y testimonios*, 129.
5. FMA, Testimonio de David Romero Castañeda, Box 6, Exp. 175, Mar. 20, 1985.
6. Alemán Valdés, *Remembranzas y testimonios*, 130.
7. FMA, Testimonio de David Romero Castañeda.
8. FMA, Testimonio de Justo Fernánez, Box 8, Exp. 226, Apr. 4, 1986; FMA, Testimonio de Manuel Suárez, Box 9, Exp. 234, Oct. 9, 1985; FMA, Memorandum, Sociedad Mocambo S. A. de C. V., Box 39, Exp. 720, Apr. 5, 1938.
9. Alemán Valdés, *Remembranzas y testimonios*, 132.
10. FMA, Testimonio de Pedro Valdés and Gabina Damián Reyes de Valdés, Box 14, Exp. 347, n.d.
11. Ibid.
12. FMA, "Repartió Juguetes Ayer la Señora doña Tomasa Valdés Viuda de Alemán," Box 15, Exp. 369.
13. Alemán, *Remembranzas y testimonios*, 341–44; Mijares Sánchez, *Mexico*, 165–66. The Cárdenas administration, as an expression of support for the Republican forces in the Spanish Civil War, gave refuge to exiles.
14. FMA, Testimonio de Miguel Alemán Velasco; FMA, Testimonio de Pedro Valdés and Gabina Damián Reyes de Valdés.
15. FMA, Testimonio de Miguel Alemán Velasco.
16. Ibid.
17. FMA, Testimonio de Victoria Soto de Córdoba, Box 7, Exp. 202, July 8, 1985.
18. FMA, Testimonio de Alfonso Noriega, Box 6, Exp. 179, Apr. 8, 1985.

19. FMA, Testimonio de Evangelina Mendoza, Box 7, Exp. 181, June 3, 1985.
20. FMA, Testimonio de Beatriz Alemán de Girón.
21. Alemán Valdés, *Remembranzas y testimonios*, 113.
22. FMA, Testimonio de Beatriz Alemán de Girón.
23. FMA, Testimonio de Carmela Díaz de Vogel, Box 7, Exp. 196, July 18, 1985.
24. Alemán Valdés, *Remembranzas y testimonios*, 117.
25. FMA, Testimonio de Manuel Ramírez Vázquez; FMA, Testimonio de Andrés Henestrosa, Box 6, Exp. 177, Sept. 12, 1985.
26. FMA, Testimonio de David Romero Castañeda.
27. FMA, Testimonio de Alfonso Guzmán Neyra, Box 9, Exp. 240, Feb. 21, 1986.
28. FMA, Testimonio de Silvestre Aguilar, Box 9, Exp. 248, Apr. 23, 1985.
29. FMA, Testimonio de Luis Danton Rodríguez, Box 7, Exp. 203, June 4, 1986.
30. Ibid.
31. Santoyo, *Mano negra*, 146–49.
32. Mijares Sánchez, *Mexico*, 144–49, 180–82.
33. Santoyo, *Mano negra*, 149–54.
34. Archivo General del Estado de Veracruz (hereafter AGEV), Telegram from PNR National Executive Committee, Exp. 242/541/1, Comité Ejecutivo Nacional del Partido Nacional Revolucionario, July 9, 1936.
35. Archivo General de la Nación (hereafter AGN), Presidencias, Lázaro Cárdenas del Río (hereafter LCR), Letter from Juan Martínez Silva, Exp. 544.2/29, Elecciones, Gobernadores, June, 29, 1936; FMA, Testimonio de Fernando Román Lugo, Box 8, Exp. 209, May 29, 1985.
36. FMA, Testimonio de Ezequiel Coutiño, Box 6, Exp. 178, Nov. 25, 1985. *Jarocho* is the identifier most often used to refer to people from Veracruz.
37. FMA, Testimonio de Rafael Moreno Henríquez.
38. FMA, Testimonio de Ezequiel Coutiño; FMA, Testimonio de Silvestre Aguilar.
39. FMA, Testimonio de Alfonso Guzmán Neyra.
40. FMA, Testimonio de David Romero Castañeda.
41. Blázquez Domínguez, *Breve historia*, 194–95; FMA, Testimonio de Luis Dantón Rodríguez.
42. AGEV, Circular from Emilio Portes Gil, Exp. 242/541/1, Comité Ejecutivo Nacional del Partido Nacional Revolucionario Feb. 1, 1936.
43. Alemán Valdés, *Remembranzas y testimonios*, 151–54.
44. FMA, Testimonio de Luis Dantón Rodríguez; FMA, Testimonio de Justo Fernández; FMA, Testimonio de Andrés Henestrosa; FMA, Testimonio de Ezequiel Coutiño; FMA, Testimonio de Francisca Acosta Lagunes, Box 6, Exp. 180, June 18, 1985; FMA, Testimonio de Fernando Román Lugo.
45. FMA, Testimonio de Andrés Henestrosa; FMA, Testimonio de David Romero Castañeda.
46. FMA, Testimonio de Fernando Román Lugo.
47. Alemán Valdés, *Remembranzas y testimonios*, 153.

48. AGEV, Article by Amado J. Trejo, Exp. 242/547/0, Elecciones, Ley Electoral, y Poderes Federales, July 29, 1936.
49. Alemán Valdés, *Remembranzas y testimonios*, 151–54; FMA, Testimonio de Francisca Acosta Lagunes.
50. FMA, Testimonio de Emilio Coutiño; FMA, Testimonio de Andrés Henestrosa.
51. FMA, Testimonio de Manuel Ramírez Vázquez; FMA, Testimonio de David Romero Castañeda.
52. FMA, Testimonio de Marco Antonio Muñoz.
53. Ankerson, *Agrarian Warlord*, 149.
54. Beezley, "Role of State Governors," 10–12.
55. Fallaw, *Cárdenas Compromised*, 33–37, 69–74, 100–108.
56. On Yocupicio, see Bantjes, *Cardenismo, Sonora, and the Mexican Revolution*, 176–86.
57. Falcón, *Revolución y caciquismo*, 264–69; Ankerson, *Agrarian Warlord*, 149–51.
58. For the best explanation of how Cardenismo balanced these seemingly contradictory elements, see Knight, "Cardenismo," 73–107.
59. Blázquez Domínguez, *Breve Historia*, 194–95; Alemán, *Remembranzas y testimonios*, 155–60; FMA, Testimonio de Marco Antonio Muñoz.
60. FMA, Testimonio de Justo Fernández; FMA, Testimonio de Manuel Suárez. The pages of *El Dictamen*, one of the state's largest dailies, are replete with announcements of public-works inaugurations.
61. Mijares Sánchez, *Mexico*, 168–69.
62. AGEV, Letters from Alemán to Legislature, Exp. 253/012/2 Decreto No. 132, que concede al Ejecutivo facultades extraordinarias en todos los ramos, June 23, 1937, and June 30, 1937; AGEV, Letter from Legislature to Alemán, Exp. 253/012/14, Decreto No. 253, que concede al Ejecutivo facultades extraordinarias, Dec. 14, 1937.
63. AGEV, Ernesto Arnoux Siqueiros to Alemán, Exp. 00/13, Sec. Particular/Gobernador, June 18, 1937; AGEV, Alemán to Arnoux, Exp. 00/13, Sec. Particular/Gobernador, June 24, 1937.
64. Wood, *Revolution in the Street*, xv–xxi.
65. Mijares Sánchez, *Mexico*, 161–63, 175–76.
66. FMA, Testimonio de Luis Dantón Rodríguez.
67. FMA, Testimonio de Antonio Carrillo Flores, Box 7, Exp. 182, June 10, 1985.
68. Alemán Valdés, *Remembranzas y testimonios*, 170–73.
69. Both peso-to-dollar conversions calculated from data in Martínez, *Border Boom Town*, 170.
70. AGN, LCR, Ramón Murillo Vidales to Cárdenas, Exp. 543.1/28, Charges against Carlos Serrano, Aug. 7, 1939.
71. AGN, LCR, Unnamed citizen to Gobernación, Exp. 543.1/28, Charges against Carlos Serrano, Nov. 30, 1937.

72. AGN, LCR, G. Santos Gallardo, Subsec. of Gobernación to Alemán, Exp. 543.1/28, Charges against Carlos Serrano, July 20, 1938.
73. AGN, LCR, Adalberto Tejeda to Cárdenas, Exp. 543.1/28, Conflictos Políticos, Estados, June 27, 1939.
74. Martínez, *Border Boom Town*, 170.
75. AGN, LCR, Cap. Manuel Hernández to Cárdenas, Exp. 543.1/28, 25, Charges against Carlos Serrano, Aug. 25, 1937.
76. AGEV, "Manifiesto a la Nación," Exp. 476/164/1, Insurreción Cedillista en San Luis Potosí, May 23, 1938.
77. AGEV, Manifesto, Liga de Comunidades Agrarias y Sindicatos Campesinos del Estado de Veracruz, Exp. 476/164/1, Insurreción Cedillista en San Luis Potosí, May 24, 1938.
78. AGEV, Circular from Emilio Portes Gil, Exp. 242/541/1, Comité Ejecutivo Nacional del Partido Nacional Revolucionario, Feb. 1, 1936.
79. AGEV, Letter from Comité Municipal Femenino del PNR, Veracruz, Exp. 242/542/1, Comités Municipales del Partido Nacional Revolucionario, Jan. 14, 1936.
80. FMA, Testimonio de Rafael Moreno Henríquez; FMA, Testimonio de Fernando Román Lugo.
81. AGN, Presidencias, Lázaro Cárdenas del Río, Letter from Juan Martínez Silva, Exp. 544.2/29, Elecciones, Gobernadores, June 29, 1936.
82. FMA, Testimonio de Fernando Román Lugo; FMA, Testimonio de Luis Danton Rodríguez.
83. FMA, Testimonio de Justo Fernández.
84. FMA, Testimonio de Beatriz Alemán de Girón.
85. Personal conversation between author and Soledad Loaeza.
86. For an explanation of some of the governorships that fell during the Alemán years, see Moncada, *¡Cayeron!*, 183–228.
87. Navarro, *Political Intelligence*, 45–52.
88. Brandenburg, *Making of Modern Mexico*, 93; Navarro, *Political Intelligence*, 52.
89. Paz, *Strategy, Security, and Spies*, 61.
90. Jones, "'The War Has Brought Peace,'" 130.
91. Roxborough, "Mexico," 194–95.
92. Personal conversation between author and Soledad Loaeza.
93. Jones, "'The War has Brought Peace,'" 279–80.
94. Navarro, *Political Intelligence*, 11.
95. Jones, "'The War has Brought Peace,'" 62.
96. Brandenburg, 99.
97. Ibid.
98. Jones, "'The War has Brought Peace,'" 108–9.
99. Cedillo, *Nazis en México*, 60, 81–82.
100. Navarro, *Political Intelligence*, 139.

101. Ibid., 138–40; Cedillo, *Nazis en México*, 15, 35–58.
102. Jones, "'The War has Brought Peace,'" 280–81; Paz, *Strategy, Security, and Spies*, 171.
103. Paz, *Strategy, Security, and Spies*, 171.
104. Martínez, *Border Boom Town*, 170.
105. Ibid., 130n32; Niblo, *Mexico in the 1940s*, 162.
106. Martínez, *Border Boom Town*, 170.
107. Miguel López Azuara, "Hay semejanzas maravillosas González Guevara, buen compensador, Paradoja de las posiciones," *Proceso* 134, May 28, 1979.
108. Jones, "'The War has Brought Peace,'" 283.
109. Paz, *Strategy, Security, and Spies*, 237.
110. Ibid., 236–37.
111. Niblo, *Mexico in the 1940s*, 162–63.
112. Paz, *Strategy, Security, and Spies*, 240–41.
113. Jones, "'The War Has Brought Peace,'" 276–79.
114. Niblo, *Mexico in the 1940s*, 90, 164.
115. AGEV, Maximino Ávila Camacho to Miguel Alemán, Exp. 476/164/1, Insurreción Cedillista en San Luis Potosí, May 27, 1938.
116. AGEV, Juan Cerdán to Manuel Limón Maciel, Exp. 476/164/1, Insurreción Cedillista en San Luis Potosí, June 6, 1938.
117. Jones, "'The War Has Brought Peace,'" 273–76.
118. Ibid., 285–86; Paz, *Strategy, Security, and Spies*, 237–41.
119. Researchers can consult the proceedings of the roundtables in *Conferencias de mesa redonda*.
120. Martínez, "Modelo económico," 234–35.
121. Archivo Manuel Gómez Morín (hereafter MGM), Efraín González Luna to Manuel Gómez Morín, Vol. 579, Exp. 1862, Feb. 18, 1946.
122. MGM, Efraín Gonález Luna to Manuel Gómez Morín, Vol. 579, Exp. 1862, Feb. 14, 1946.
123. MGM, Efraín González Luna to Manuel Gómez Morín, Vol. 579, Exp. 1862, Feb. 18, 1946.
124. Martínez, *Border Boom Town*, 170.
125. MGM, Efraín Gonález Luna to Manuel Gómez Morín, Vol. 579, Exp. 1862, Feb. 21, 1946.
126. Blázquez Domínguez, *Breve historia de Veracruz*, 194–95.

Chapter Three

1. Disagreements over how to confront the booming sector of poor urban residents became one of the most contentious political processes in the 1950s and 1960s. A contest between the anti-growth, middle-class aligned mayor of

Mexico City, Ernesto Uruchurtu, who despised squatter settlements and opposed subway construction, and the pro-growth, pro-subway president Gustavo Díaz Ordaz, eventually led to the former's ouster in 1966; Davis, "Social Construction of Mexico City," 386–400.

2. For a comprehensive quantitative analysis of federal government expenditure, see Wilkie, *Mexican Revolution*, xxi–xxii, 38, 86, 129. Wilkie argues that Alemán was the first to make economic expenditure the top priority while de-emphasizing the social spending of Cárdenas.
3. Cárdenas, "Accelerated Industrialization," 176–77.
4. Kingstone, *Political Economy of Latin America*, 32.
5. Cárdenas, "Accelerated Industrialization," 182–85.
6. Cárdenas, "Great Depression and Industrialisation," 196.
7. Kingstone, *Political Economy of Latin America*, 28–31.
8. Bennett and Sharpe, "State as Banker and Entrepreneur," 176.
9. Ibid., 177–79.
10. Ibid., 179–80.
11. Brandenburg, *Making of Modern Mexico*, 105, 268.
12. Cockcroft, *Class Formation, Capital Accumulation, and the State*, 158.
13. The failure to create a progressive tax system that increased revenue, minimized popular opposition, maintained political legitimacy, and balanced state and federal needs is explained in Smith, "Building a State on the Cheap," 255–70.
14. Ramírez, "Mexico's Development," 46; Hansen, *Politics of Mexican Development*, 49–50, 83–84; Babb, *Managing Mexico*, 78.
15. Kingstone, *Political Economy of Latin America*, 38–39.
16. Ibid., 38–40.
17. Ibid., 43–44.
18. Ramírez, "Mexico's Development," 49–52.
19. Hansen, *Politics of Mexican Development*, 87–88.
20. Ibid., 34.
21. Cockcroft, *Class Formation, Capital Accumulation, and the State*, 210–12.
22. Smith, *Labyrinths of Power*, 203, 214; Meyer, "Historical Roots of the Authoritarian State," 16; Camp, *Entrepreneurs and Politics*, 22–23.
23. Brandenburg, *Making of Modern Mexico*, 102.
24. Cockcroft, *Class Formation, Capital Accumulation, and the State*, 152.
25. Cárdenas et al., "Introduction," *Economic History*, vol. 3, 22.
26. Cockcroft, *Class Formation, Capital Accumulation, and the State*, 187.
27. Brandenburg, *Making of Modern Mexico*, 106; Cockcroft, *Class Formation, Capital Accumulation, and the State*, 170–72; Cárdenas et al., "Introduction," *An Economic History*, vol. 3, 22.
28. Cockcroft, *Class Formation, Capital Accumulation, and the State*, 187.
29. Navarro, "Case of Eva Perón," 229–40.

30. Conniff, "Introduction," *Populism in Latin America*, 1–21; Knight, "Populism and Neo-Populism," 223–48; for an excellent synthesis of debates over how to define populism, see Kiddle and Muñoz, "Men of the People," 2–7.
31. Cockcroft, *Mexico's Revolution*, 70–74
32. Though populist regimes drew support from the working class, in part through pro-worker policies, Roxborough and Bethell note that popular mobilization was thwarted across the region between 1945 and 1948; from then on, working-class reform became a largely authoritarian effort in nearly all of the populist regimes in the region; Bethell and Roxborough, "Introduction: The Postwar Conjuncture," 1–32; Bethell and Roxborough, "Latin America Between the Second World War and the Cold War," 167–89.
33. Olsen, *Artifacts of Revolution*, xv–xvi, 171–98, 212.
34. Ibid., 199–201, 209–19.
35. Conniff, *Populism in Latin America*, 6–7.
36. Beezley and MacLaughlin, *Mexicans in Revolution*, 11; López, "The Cadaverous City," 121–44.
37. The best description of the material improvements to Mexico City during the Porfiriato (1876–1911) can be found in Federico Gamboa's naturalist novel *Santa*, first published in 1903. The novel contrasts the moral decay associated with prostitution against the visible progress of a city in its heyday.
38. Waters, "Remapping Identities," 221–42.
39. The most extensive information on Pani's life and work, especially the philosophical basis of the massive multifamiliares built under Alemán, can be found in the work of Graciela de Garay at the Instituto Mora. Her work includes written publications, oral interviews, and documentary film; see Garay, *Mario Pani*; Garay, *Mi multi es mi multi* (VHS); Garay, "¿Quién pone el orden el la vivienda moderna?," 13–68.
40. Vaughan, *Cultural Politics in Revolution*, 4–6.
41. Wilkie, *Mexican Revolution*, 163.
42. *Ciudad Universitaria*, 83–84.
43. Guillermo Aguilar and Guillermo Olvera, "Control de la expansión urbana," 96n6.
44. *Ciudad Universitaria*, 90–92.
45. Lorenzo Lazo, personal interview with the author, Feb. 1, 2011.
46. Davids, "Mythical Terrain," 1.
47. Lorenzo Lazo, personal interview.
48. Davids, "Mythical Terrain," 4–9.
49. Alemán Valdés, *Remembranzas y testimonios*, 320.
50. Krauze, *Biography of Power*, 587; Pensado, *Rebel Mexico*, 149.
51. Lorenzo Lazo, personal interview with author.
52. Taracena, *La vida en México bajo Miguel Alemán*, 348–49.
53. FMA, Testimonio de Antonio Carrillo Flores, Box 7, Exp. 182, June 10, 1985.

54. Davids, "Mythical Terrain," 1.
55. Krieger, "Body, Building, City, and Environment," 410.
56. Davids, "Mythical Terrain," 5.
57. Garay, *Mi multi es mi multi* (VHS).
58. Ibid.
59. Ibid.
60. Tatum, "La Familia Burrón"; Wicke, "Burrón Family."
61. Garay, *Mi multi es mi multi* (VHS).
62. Durán Reveles, "Presentación," 7.
63. Cortés Rocha, "Ciudad Satélite," 27–29.
64. Krieger, "Body, Building, City, and Environment," 410.
65. Cortés Rocha, "Ciudad Satélite," 29–31.
66. Scott, *Seeing Like a State*, 109, 120.
67. Ibid., 103–17.
68. Cortés Rocha, "Ciudad Satélite," 20–21.
69. Niblo and Niblo, "Acapulco in Dreams," 33–37.
70. Sackett, "Fun in Acapulco?," 167.
71. Niblo and Niblo, "Acapulco in Dreams," 38–43.
72. Ibid., 40–43.
73. Sackett, "Fun in Acapulco?," 170.
74. Ibid., 169–78.
75. Brandenburg, *Making of Modern Mexico*, 105–6.
76. Cockcroft, *Class Formation, Capital Accumulation, and the State*, 152–53.
77. Perkins, "Rockefeller Foundation in Mexico," 102–17.
78. Cotter, "Green Revolution," 224–40; Cockcroft, *Class Formation, Capital Accumulation, and the State*, 165.
79. Machado Jr., *Historical Survey of Foot-and-Mouth Disease*.
80. Pilcher, *Food and the Making of Mexican Identity*, 81–82, 92–93.
81. Cotter, "Green Revolution," 235–36.
82. Niblo, *Mexico in the 1940s*, 31.
83. Alemán Valdés, *Remembranzas y testimonios*, 283.
84. Cotter, *Troubled Harvest*, 179.
85. Cotter, "Green Revolution," 239–40.
86. Cárdenas et al., *Economic History*, vol. 3, 21; Cockcroft, *Class Formation, Capital Accumulation, and the State*, 165.
87. Cockcroft, *Class Formation, Capital Accumulation, and the State*, 165–66.
88. Ibid., 170–74.
89. Ibid., 152–53.

Chapter Four

1. NARA, Truman Library, Official File 496, Box 1370, Messersmith to Truman, Apr. 17, 1945.

2. NARA, Truman Library, President's Secretary's File, Box 88, Dwight Dickinson's Report for Ambassador of President's visit to Mexico, Mar. 15, 1947.
3. Ibid.
4. Milton Brackers, "21-Gun Roar Hails Truman in Mexico: Alemán and his Official Family Lead City's Welcome—U. S. President Gets Medal," *New York Times*, Mar. 4, 1947.
5. Felix Belair Jr., "Truman Sees America's Fall if World Peace is Insecure," *New York Times*, Mar. 6, 1947. Note that despite Truman's claim, Teotihuacán was not an Aztec city.
6. NARA, Truman Library, Untitled Newsreel, MP 72–35.
7. NARA, Truman Library, President's Secretary's File, Box 88, Dwight Dickinson's Report for Ambassador of President's visit to Mexico, Untitled clippings from Mar. 6, 1947, *New York Times* and *New York Herald Tribune*, Mar. 15, 1947.
8. NARA, Truman Library, John Snyder Papers, Box 21, Antonio Espinosa de los Monteros to William McChesney Martin Jr., Feb. 26, 1947; NARA, Truman Library, President's Secretary's File, Box 88, Dwight Dickinson's Report for Ambassador of President's visit to Mexico, Memorandum, Thurston to Truman, Mar. 6, 1947; NARA, Truman Library, Memorandum, Thurston to Truman, Mar. 5, 1947; NARA, Truman Library, Memorandum to White House from Oswald Ryan, Feb. 13, 1947.
9. NARA, Truman Library, President's Secretary's File, Box 88, Dwight Dickinson's Report for Ambassador of President's visit to Mexico, Thurston to Truman, Mar. 6, 1947.
10. NARA, Truman Library, MP 72–33, El Presidente Alemán Visita a Estados Unidos, Newsreel.
11. Ibid.
12. Ibid.
13. NARA, Truman Library, Clarence R. Decker Papers, Box 1, de la Selva to Decker, Jan. 25, 1947; NARA, Truman Library, Decker to Truman, Dec. 17, 1946.
14. NARA, Truman Library, Official File 146, Box 753, Mexico, Truman to Decker, Dec. 24, 1946.
15. NARA, Truman Library, President's Secretary's File, Box 88, Dwight Dickinson's Report for Ambassador of President's visit to Mexico, Untitled clippings from Mar. 6, 1947, *New York Times* and *New York Herald Tribune*, Mar. 15, 1947.
16. NARA, Truman Library, Personal File, 2766, Box 558, Kemp to Truman, Jan. 29, 1947.
17. NARA, Truman Library, Clarence R. Decker Papers, Box 1, Decker to Alemán, Dec. 26, 1946.
18. NARA, Truman Library, Decker to de la Selva, Jan. 18, 1946.
19. NARA, Truman Library, de la Selva to Decker, Jan. 23, 1946.
20. NARA, Truman Library, Decker to de la Selva, Jan. 25, 1947.

21. NARA, Truman Library, de la Selva to Decker, Feb. 6, 1947.
22. NARA, Truman Library, de la Selva to Decker, Mar. 28, 1947.
23. NARA, Truman Library, de la Selva to Decker, Mar. 24, 1947.
24. NARA, Truman Library, Donnelly to Decker, Apr. 11, 1947; NARA, Truman Library, Carlson to Decker, Apr. 4, 1947.
25. Martínez, *Border Boom Town*, 170.
26. NARA, Truman Library, de la Selva to Decker, Mar. 24, 1947; NARA, Truman Library, de la Selva to Decker, Mar. 28, 1947.
27. NARA, Truman Library, Decker to de la Selva, Apr. 19, 1947.
28. NARA, Truman Library, de la Selva to Decker, Mar. 24, 1947; NARA, Truman Library, Decker to de la Selva, Mar. 29, 1947.
29. NARA, Truman Library, Decker to de la Selva, Mar. 27, 1947; NARA, Truman Library, Decker to de la Selva, Mar. 29, 1947.
30. NARA, Truman Library, Decker to de la Selva, Apr. 30, 1947.
31. NARA, Truman Library, Decker to Alemán, May 8, 1947; NARA, Truman Library, Alemán to Decker, May 14, 1947.
32. NARA, Truman Library, President's Secretary's File, Box 88, Mar. 15, 1947, Dwight Dickinson's Report for Ambassador of President's visit to Mexico, Untitled Clipping from *El Popular.*
33. NARA, Truman Library, Political Cartoon Collection, Museum Collection, File 63-970.
34. NARA, Truman Library, Political Cartoon Collection, Museum Collection, File 63-958.
35. NARA, Truman Library, Political Cartoon Collection, Museum Collection, File 63-953.
36. NARA, Truman Library, Political Cartoon Collection, Museum Collection, File 3039.
37. NARA, Truman Library, Political Cartoon Collection, Museum Collection, File 63-954.
38. Milton Brackers, "Truman, Alemán Find some Discord," *New York Times*, Mar. 4, 1947.
39. NARA, Truman Library, Political Cartoon Collection, Museum Collection, File 63-959.
40. NARA, Truman Library, Political Cartoon Collection, Museum Collection, File 63-956.
41. Philip, *Oil and Politics*, 335.
42. Ibid., 330–36.
43. NARA, Truman Library, Official File 146, Box 754, "Petroleum News for the Week Ending August 3, 1951," Latin American News Institute Associates.
44. NARA, Truman Library, John Snyder Papers, Box 48, Address to Mexican Bankers Association, Guadalajara, Apr. 28, 1951.

45. NARA, Truman Library, Official File 146, Box 754, Acheson to Steelman, Aug. 26, 1949; and NARA, Truman Library, President's Secretary's File, Box 112, State Department Aide Memoire, July 6, 1949.
46. NARA, Truman Library, Official File 146, Box 754, Acheson to Steelman, Aug. 26, 1949.
47. NARA, Truman Library, Official File 146, Box 754, Acheson to Steelman, Aug. 26, 1949.
48. NARA, Truman Library, President's Secretary's File, Memorandum, Marshall to Truman, Feb. 27, 1947.
49. NARA, Truman Library, Official File 146, Box 754, Eugene Black to Steelman, Jan. 22, 1952; NARA, Truman Library, Press Release from International Bank for Reconstruction and Development, Jan. 11, 1952.
50. NARA, Truman Library, Official File 146, Box 754, Acheson to Steelman, Aug. 26, 1949.
51. NARA, Truman Library, President's Secretary's File, Box 159, Thurston to Truman, Dec. 10, 1946.
52. NARA, Truman Library, Memorandum by Elsey, Aug. 9, 1950.
53. NARA, Truman Library, Official File 146, Box 754, MJC, "Mexican Oil Loan," Aug. 17, 1949.
54. NARA, Truman Library, "Petroleum News for the Week Ending August 3, 1951," Latin American News Institute Associates.
55. Ibid.
56. NARA, Truman Library, Official File 146, Box 754, Acheson to Steelman, Aug. 26, 1949.
57. NARA, Truman Library, Charles Sawyer Papers, Box 125, Charles R. Burrows to State Department, Oct. 26, 1949, Decimal File 033.1100/10-2649.
58. NARA, Truman Library, President's Secretary's File, Box 159, Memorandum by Elsey, Aug. 9, 1950.
59. NARA, Truman Library, Official File 146, Box 754, MJC, "Mexican Oil Loan," Aug. 17, 1949.
60. Niblo, *Mexico in the 1940s*, 296.
61. Archive.org, Acheson to Kee, Sept. 16, 1949, accessed June 20, 2011, http://www.archive.org/stream/departmentofstatx2149unit/departmentofstatx2149unit_djvu.txt.
62. NARA, Truman Library, President's Secretary's File, Box 159, Memorandum by Elsey, Aug. 9, 1950.
63. NARA, Truman Library, Confidential File, Box 41, Press Release, Export-Import Bank, Sept. 1, 1950.
64. NARA, Truman Library, Truman to Alemán, Sept. 8, 1950; NARA, Truman Library, Alemán to Truman, Oct. 4, 1950.

65. NARA, Truman Library, Memorandum, Webb to Murphy, Aug. 31, 1950.
66. The leading proponents of this position among historians are William Appleman Williams, in his seminal work, first published in 1959, *Tragedy of American Diplomacy*, and Walter LaFeber, a leading voice of the New Left school of diplomacy history; see LaFeber, *American Age*.
67. Snodgrass, "Patronage and Progress," 249–50.
68. Ibid., 254–55.
69. Ibid., 246.
70. Hundreds of letters to Truman and other administration officials representing both positions are interspersed through the following files: NARA, Truman Library, Official File 407D, Boxes 1232 and 1233.
71. Snodgrass, "Patronage and Progress," 248.
72. NARA, Truman Library, Confidential File, Box 39, Thurston to State, Sept. 22, 1948; NARA, Truman Library, Official File 407D, Box 1232, Anderson to Truman, May 26, 1949.
73. NARA, Truman Library, David H. Stowe Papers, Box 6.
74. NARA, Truman Library, David H. Stowe Papers, Box 6, news clipping, "Shivers Hits 40-Cent Decision: Believes Authority Belongs to State," in *Valley Evening Monitor*, Oct. 19, 1949.
75. NARA, Truman Library, David H. Stowe Papers, Box 6, news clipping, "What! Forty Cents an Hour!" *Brownsville Herald*, Oct. 21, 1949.
76. NARA, Truman Library, Official File 407e, Box 1234, Memorandum, James L. Sundquist to Roger W. Jones, Mar. 30, 1950.
77. Ibid.
78. NARA, Truman Library, Official File 407D, Box 1232.
79. NARA, Truman Library, Official File 407e, Box 1234, Committee Recommendations, Mar. 1, 1951; NARA, Truman Library, Official File 407e, Box 1234, Report of the Committee, Apr. 7, 1951.
80. NARA, Truman Library, Official File 407e, Box 1234, Green to Truman, Apr. 16, 1951; NARA, Truman Library, Official File 407e, Box 1234, Patton to Truman, Apr. 11, 1951.
81. NARA, Truman Library, Official File 407d, Box 1233, Truman to Alemán, July 14, 1951; NARA, Truman Library, Official File 407d, Box 1234, Alemán to Truman, July 27, 1951.
82. NARA, Truman Library, Official File 407d, Box 1234, Truman to Alemán, July 25, 1952; NARA, Truman Library, Official File 407d, Box 1234, Alemán to Truman, Aug. 8, 1952.
83. NARA, Truman Library, Michael J. Galvin Papers, Box 8, news clipping, "Contratarán mas de 60 mil Braceros en 1952," *El Porvenir*, Oct. 3, 1951.
84. NARA, Truman Library, Michael J. Galvin Papers, Box 8, news clipping, "Cordial visita del sub-secretario del trabajo de los EE.UU. al gobernador,"

El Porvenir, Oct. 4, 1951; NARA, Truman Library, Michael J. Galvin Papers, Box 8, news clipping, *Excelsior*, Unnamed article, Sept. 13, 1951.

85. NARA, Truman Library, Michael J. Galvin Papers, Box 8, news clippings, "Inmediata Ayuda a los Braceros fué Ordenada," *ABC*, Oct. 24, 1951.
86. NARA, Truman Library, Motion Picture Archives, Newsreel, MP 72–33; El Presidente Alemán Visita a Estados Unidos.
87. NARA, Truman Library, President's Secretary's File, Box 112, Memorandum, Beteta to Messersmith, Dec. 14, 1946; *Libro de Oro conmemorativo.*
88. NARA, Truman Library, Charles Sawyer Papers, Box 125, "Progress in the Americas," US Dept. of Commerce, Oct. 20, 1949.
89. NARA, Truman Library, Charles Sawyer Papers, Box 125, Charles R. Burrows to State Department, Oct. 26, 1949, Decimal File 033.1100/10-2649.
90. Gilderhus, *Second Century*, 113.
91. NARA, Truman Library, Charles Sawyer Papers, Box 125, Burrows to State, Oct. 26, 1949; NARA, Truman Library, Charles Sawyer Papers, Box 125, Sawyer to Alemán, Oct. 24, 1949; NARA, Truman Library, Charles Sawyer Papers, Box 125, Narrative Account of Sec. Sawyer's Trip to Mexico, Dept. of Commerce, Nov. 7, 1949.
92. NARA, Truman Library, Charles Sawyer Papers, Box 125, Narrative Account of Sec. Sawyer's Trip to Mexico, Dept. of Commerce, Nov. 7, 1949.
93. NARA, Truman Library, Charles Sawyer Papers, Box 125, Memorandum, Dept. of Commerce, Sept. 21, 1949.
94. NARA, Truman Library, Charles Sawyer Papers, Box 125, Memorandum, Dept. of Commerce, Sept. 8, 1949.
95. NARA, Truman Library, Charles Sawyer Papers, Box 125, Narrative Account of Sec. Sawyer's Trip to Mexico, Dept. of Commerce, Nov. 7, 1949.
96. NARA, Truman Library, Charles Sawyer Papers, Box 125, Burrows to State, Oct. 26, 1949
97. NARA, Truman Library, Charles Sawyer Papers, Box 125, "Progress in the Americas," US Dept. of Commerce, Oct. 20, 1949.
98. Armando Rivas Torres, "Washington Espera un Saludable Efecto de las Devaluaciones: Una Entrevista con el Srio. de Comercio," *Excelsior*, Oct. 22, 1949.
99. FMA, Testimonio de Antonio Carrillo Flores, Box 7, Exp. 182, June 10, 1985.
100. Leopoldo Ramírez Cárdenas, "No Será Devaluado el Dólar, por Ahora," *La Prensa*, Oct. 22, 1949; "Estados Unidos hallará los medios para que los países escasos de dólares puedan obtenerlos," *Novedades*, Oct. 21, 1949.
101. NARA, Truman Library, Official File 146, Box 754, Ray to Ross, n.d.
102. NARA, Truman Library, Merwin L. Bohan Papers, Box 16, Bohan, Speech to Mexico City Rotary Club, Feb. 12, 1946.
103. NARA, Truman Library, John Snyder Papers, Box 110, Foreign Service Report of the Bankers Association Meeting, May 3, 1951.

104. Ibid.
105. NARA, Truman Library, John Snyder Papers, Box 21, Beteta to Snyder, Aug. 4, 1948; NARA, Truman Library, John Snyder Papers, Box 21, Beteta to Snyder, Aug. 12, 1948.
106. NARA, Truman Library, John Snyder Papers, Box 21, Snyder to Antonio Espinosa de los Monteros, Dec. 22, 1947.
107. NARA, Truman Library, John Snyder Papers, Box 51, Broadcast Transcript, ABC, Sept. 14, 1952.
108. Dusenberry, "Foot and Mouth Disease in Mexico," 82–90; NARA, Truman Library, Official File 395a, Box 1075, Mexican-US Commission for the Eradication of Foot and Mouth Disease.
109. NARA, Truman Library, President's Secretary's File, Box 88, Dwight Dickinson's Report for Ambassador of President's visit to Mexico, Memorandum, Mar. 5, 1947.
110. NARA, Truman Library, George A. Brownell Papers, Box 1, Report on Mission to Mexico, 1948.

Chapter Five

1. NARA, RG 59, Series 712.00, Charles R. Burrows, first secretary of embassy, to State Department, July 19, 1950, 712.00/7-1950.
2. FMA, Testimonio del Lic. Miguel Alemán Velasco, Box 9, Exp. 243, Mar. 29, 1985.
3. NARA, RG 59, Series 712.00, "Further Discussion of Re-election and Futuristic Activities, 712.00/7-2850.
4. Vicente Lombardo Toledano, Interview, Jan. 22, 1965, in Wilkie and Monzón de Wilkie, *México visto en el siglo XX*, 368.
5. FMA, Testimonio de Ernesto Uruchurtu, Box 10, Exp. 267, Apr. 25, 1985.
6. FMA, Testimonio de Roberto Barrios, Box 9, Exp. 241, July 7, 1986.
7. FMA, Testimonio de Fernando Román Lugo, Box 8, Exp. 209, May 29, 1985.
8. FMA, Testimonio de Antonio Carrillo Flores, Box 7, Exp. 182, June 10, 1985.
9. Niblo, *Mexico in the 1940s*, 238.
10. Krauze, *Biography of Power*, 559.
11. Niblo, *Mexico in the 1940s*, 238.
12. The best sketch of Ruiz Cortines's appearance, persona, and health can be found in Agustín, *Tragicomedia mexicana*, 119–21.
13. FMA, Testimonio de Beatriz Alemán de Girón, Box 9, Exp. 242, Mar. 10, 1986.
14. NARA, RG 59, Series 812.00, Political and Economic Report for Aug., 1949, 812.00/9-849; NARA, RG 59, Series 812.00, Report of Political Activity, July 16–Aug., 15, 1949, 812.00/8-1849.

15. AGN, Dirección Federal de Seguridad (hereafter DFS) Exp. 327, Leg. 1, (Expediente Vicente Lombardo Toledano, hereafter VLT), Comité Mexicano por la Paz, June 10, 1950.
16. NARA, RG 59, Series 712.00, Burrows to State, Apr. 1950, 712.00/5-1050.
17. Navarro, *Political Intelligence*, 11.
18. NARA, RG 59, Series 812.00, Memorandum of Conversation between Germán Parra and Harry Turkel, 812.00/11-3048.
19. AGN, DFS, LCR, Report to DFS from Schick, Aug. 6, 1948.
20. AGN, DFS, LCR, Memorandum, Feb. 28, 1951.
21. AGN, DFS, LCR, Tomás Fabregas V. to DFS, May 3, 1948; AGN, DFS, LCR, DFS Memorandum, Aug. 9, 1948; AGN, DFS, LCR, DFS Memorandum, Aug. 4, 1948; NARA, RG 59, Series 712.00, Guy Ray to State Department, Apr. 25, 1950, 712.00/4-1850.
22. AGN, DFS, LCR, DFS Memorandum, Aug. 15, 1950; NARA, RG 59, Series 712.00, William R. Laidlaw, second secretary of embassy, to State Department, Apr. 18, 1950, 712.00/4-2550.
23. AGN, DFS, LCR, Memorandum, July 15, 1950; AGN, DFS, LCR, DFS Memorandum, Aug. 15, 1950
24. AGN, DFS, LCR, Memorandum, Feb. 28, 1951; AGN, DFS, LCR, Memorandum, May 30, 1952.
25. Navarro, *Political Intelligence*, 200–206.
26. NARA, RG 59, Series 812.00, Horace Braun, attaché, to State, July 24, 1950.
27. AGN, DFS, Exp. 489, Leg. 1 (Expediente Adolfo Ruiz Cortines, hereafter ARC), Memorandum, Nov. 23, 1951; AGN, DFS, ARC, Memorandum, Nov. 29, 1951.
28. AGN, DFS, ARC, Memorandum from Puebla to Pablo de la Fuente, Oct. 31, 1951.
29. AGN, DFS, LCR, DFS Memorandum, Oct. 31, 1951.
30. Lombardo Toledano, Interview, Jan. 22, 1965, in Wilkie and Monzón de Wilkie, *México visto en el siglo XX*, 365.
31. Ibid., 366–67.
32. Krauze, *Biography of Power*, 574–75.
33. Lombardo Toledano, Interview, Jan. 22, 1965, in Wilkie and Monzón de Wilkie, *México visto en el siglo XX*, 364.
34. Krauze, *Biography of Power*, 539.
35. Lombardo Toledano, Interview, Jan. 22, 1965, in Wilkie and Monzón de Wilkie, *México visto en el siglo XX*, 366.
36. NARA, State Department Record Group 59, Decimal File 812.00 (hereafter RG 59, Series 812.00), Political Conditions, Nov. 16–Dec. 15, 1948, 812.00/12-2748; AGN, DFS, VLT, Speech by Lombardo Toledano, June 23, 1950.
37. NARA, RG 59, Series 812.00, Political Conditions, Nov. 16–Dec. 15, 1948, 812.00/12-2748; AGN, DFS, VLT, Speech by Lombardo Toledano, June 23, 1950.

38. NARA, RG 59, Series 812.00, Political Conditions, Nov. 16–Dec. 15, 1948, 812.00/12-2748; AGN, DFS, VLT, Speech by Lombardo Toledano, June 23, 1950.
39. Lombardo Toledano, Interview, Jan. 22, 1965, in Wilkie and Monzón de Wilkie, *México visto en el siglo XX*, 367.
40. Ibid., 381; Bernal Tavares, *Vicente Lombardo Toledano y Miguel Alemán*, 171–78.
41. Henestrosa and Gómez Arias had been schoolmates, while Bassols had served as one of his professors; Novo, the famed chronicler of Mexico City and consummate man about town, served as the first director of the *Instituto Nacional de Bellas Artes*, created by the Alemán administration. AGN, DFS, VLT, Leadership of Partido Popular, Apr. 29, 1948.
42. The government in exile of Republican Spain existed first in Mexico City until 1946, before moving to Paris. The government of Lázaro Cárdenas extended it recognition, and numerous exiles permanently established themselves in Mexico.
43. AGN, DFS, VLT, "Personas que se sabe militan y hacen propaganda en favor del Partido Comunista," Mar. 26, 1947; AGN, DFS, VLT, Report on foreign agents to DFS, Sept. 20, 1947; AGN, DFS, VLT, Report on "Amigos de la U.R.S.S." to DFS, Nov. 13, 1947; AGN, DFS, VLT, Memorandum on CROM, Dec. 29, 1949.
44. Lombardo Toledano, Interview, Jan. 29, 1965, in Wilkie and Monzón de Wilkie, *México visto en el siglo XX*, 382.
45. Krauze, *Biography of Power*, 593.
46. Lombardo Toledano, Interview, Jan. 27, 1965, in Wilkie and Monzón de Wilkie, *México visto en el siglo XX*, 369.
47. Ibid., 370.
48. Ibid., 371–73.
49. NARA, RG 59, Series 812.00, Political Conditions, Nov. 16–Dec. 15, 1948, 812.00/12-2748; AGN, DFS, VLT, Speech by Lombardo Toledano, June 23, 1950.
50. NARA, RG 59, Series 812.00, Memorandum, Aug. 2, 1949, 812.00/8-1249.
51. Loaeza, "National Action Party (PAN),", 204–5; Loaeza, *Partido Acción Nacional*, 117, 119–24.
52. Loaeza, *Partido Acción Nacional*, 139–40.
53. Ibid., 109–10, 117–18, 168; Manuel Gómez Morín, Interview, Dec. 11, 1964, in Wilkie and Monzón de Wilkie, *México visto en el siglo XX*, 222–23; MGM, Vol. 2, Exp. 338, Speech to H. Cámara de Diputados, Dec. 23, 1946; MGM, Vol. 2, Exp. 338, Speech to H. Cámara de Diputados, Nov. 12, 1948.
54. Gómez Morín, Interview, Dec. 11, 1964, in Wilkie and Monzón de Wilkie, *México visto en el siglo XX*, 223; Loaeza, *El Partido Acción Nacional*, 217.
55. Gómez Morín, Interview, Dec. 11, 1964, in Wilkie and Monzón de Wilkie, *México visto en el siglo XX*, 222; Loaeza, *Partido Acción Nacional*, 117–18.

56. Gómez Morín, Interview, Dec. 11, 1964, in Wilkie and Monzón de Wilkie, *México visto en el siglo XX*, 163–64, 224; Loaeza, "National Action Party (PAN)," 210.
57. Loaeza, *Partido Acción Nacional*, 209, 219.
58. Ibid., 200–201, 209, 226; Loaeza, "National Action Party (PAN)," 211–12.
59. Loaeza, *Partido Acción Nacional*, 231–32.
60. Gómez Morín, Interview, Dec. 11, 1964, in Wilkie and Monzón de Wilkie, *México visto en el siglo XX*, 193–94.
61. Ibid., 219; MGM, Exp. 172, F26, Manuel Gómez Morín, Acción Nacional Memorandum, Aug. 6, 1948.
62. Navarro, *Political Intelligence*, 225.
63. AGN, Dirección General de Investigaciones Políticas y Sociales, Memorandum, Nov. 1, 1950.
64. Navarro, *Political Intelligence*, 247–48.
65. NARA, RG 59, Series 812.00, Memorandum, Aug. 2, 1949, 812.00/8-1249.
66. Morris, *Corruption and Politics*, 77.
67. Agustín, *Tragicomedia mexicana*, 119–21.
68. Morris, *Corruption and Politics*, 83–101; FMA, Testimonio de Roberto Barrios.
69. I derive most of this discussion from the analysis of anthropologist Claudio Lomnitz, who regards corruption not as a fixed set of behaviors, but rather as a historical construct dependent on contextual forces and containing important discursive elements. Lomnitz, "Prefacio" and "Introducción," in *Vicios públicos, virtudes privadas*, 7–32.
70. FMA, Testimonio de Roberto Barrios.
71. FMA, Testimonio de Antonio Carrillo Flores.
72. FMA, Testimonio de Fernando Román Lugo.
73. FMA, Testimonio de Andrés Serra Rojas, Box 8, Exp. 222, May 28, 1985.
74. Ramón Beteta, Interview, Aug. 11, 1964, in Wilkie and Monzón de Wilkie, *México visto en el siglo XX*, 48.
75. FMA, Testimonio de David Romero Castañeda, Box 6, Exp. 175, Apr. 3, 1985.
76. FMA, Testimonio de Silvestre Aguilar, Box 9, Exp. 248, Apr. 23, 1985.
77. Martínez, *Border Boom Town*, 170.
78. FMA, Testimonio de Antonio Carrillo Flores; Luis Reyna, "Redefining the Authoritarian Regime," 163.
79. Ramón Beteta, Interview, Aug. 11, 1964, in Wilkie and Monzón de Wilkie, *México visto en el siglo XX*, 49.
80. Kaufman, "Mexico and Latin American Authoritarianism," 216; Reyna, "Redefining the Authoritarian Regime," 163.
81. Wilkie, *Mexican Revolution*.
82. FMA, Testimonio de David Romero Castañeda.
83. FMA, Testimonio de Lic. Braulio Maldonado, Box 9, Exp. 231, May 7, 1985.

84. FMA, Testimonio de Lugo; FMA, Testimonio de Alfonso Noriega, Box 6, Exp. 179, Apr. 8, 1985.
85. FMA, Testimonio de Gilberto Limón, Box 7, Exp. 199, Mar. 12, 1985.
86. FMA, Testimonio de Antonio Carrillo Flores.
87. Ramón Beteta, Interview, Aug. 11, 1964, in Wilkie and Monzón de Wilkie, *México visto en el siglo XX*, 65–66.
88. Ibid., 52.
89. Ibid., 66–68.
90. Knight, "Weight of the State in Modern Mexico," 212–53.

Conclusion

1. FMA, Testimonio de Arturo García Formenti, Box 9, Exp. 232, May 20, 1985).
2. Bethell and Roxborough, "Introduction," *Latin America*, 1–32.

Epilogue

1. Alemán was one of the few national political leaders to have occupied a prominent position in the highest echelons of the business community; in most cases, the business elite and the political elite were two distinct groups with little overlap; Smith, *Labyrinths of Power*, 203–14.
2. FMA, Testimonio de Arturo García Formenti, Caja 14, Exp. 346, May 20, 1985.
3. FMA, Testimonio de Carlos Soto Maynez, Caja 8, Exp. 213, May 17, 1985.
4. Ibid.
5. Ibid.
6. Archivo Histórico de El Colegio de México (hereafter AHCM), Archivo Particular de Ramón Beteta, Exp. 18, Alemán to Beteta, Aug. 22, 1963.
7. AHCM, Archivo Particular de Ramón Beteta, Exp. 18, Duveen to Ignacio Beteta Jr., Oct. 10, 1963.
8. AHCM, Archivo Particular de Ramón Beteta, Exp. 18.1, Haynes to Beteta, n.d.
9. AGN, DFS, LCR, Memorandum, May 30, 1952.
10. FMA, Nixon to Alemán, Box 50, Exp. 924, Dec. 7, 1952.
11. AGN, DFS, Exp. 422, Expediente Bruno Pagliai (hereafter BP), Memorandum, Feb. 15, 1970.
12. AGN, DFS, BP, Memorandum, May 3, 1971.
13. AGN, DFS, BP, Memorandum, Dec. 27, 1966; AGN, DFS, BP, Memorandum, Feb. 6, 1971.
14. AGN, DFS, BP, Memorandum, Feb. 23, 1977.
15. FMA, Roosevelt to Alemán, Box 6, Exp. 159, Jan. 7, 1954.

16. Niblo, *Mexico in the 1940s*, 189–90.
17. FMA, Hilton to Alemán, Box 50, Exp. 945, Feb. 17, 1953.
18. FMA, Testimonio de Oscar Soto Maynez.
19. Martínez, *Border Boom Town*, 170.
20. AGN, DFS, BP, Biographical sketch of Bruno Pagliai, n.d.
21. AGN, DFS, BP, Memorandum, Feb. 6, 1971.
22. Alemán Valdés, *Remembranzas y testimonios*, 342.
23. González de Bustamante, *'Muy Buenas Noches,'* xxii–xxiii.
24. FMA, Testimonio de Antonio Carrillo Flores.
25. Niblo, *Mexico in the 1940s*, 207–8.
26. FMA, Testimonio de Carlos Soto Maynez.
27. FMA, Testimonio de Alfonso Noriega.
28. Ibid.
29. Alejandro Carrillo Castro, personal interview with author, Feb. 3, 2011. Carrillo Castro's father, Alejandro Carrillo Marcor, a leader in the organized-labor community, was briefly head of the municipal government of the Federal District before a falling-out with Alemán, and he was later governor of Sonora in the 1970s.
30. FMA, Testimonio de Alfonso Noriega; Testimonio Arturo García Formenti; 1985; Testimonio de David Romero Castañeda.
31. FMA, Testimonio de Carlos Soto Maynez.
32. Ibid.
33. Morris, *Corruption and Politics*, 83–101
34. FMA, Testimonio de Miguel Alemán Velasco, Box 9, Exp. 243, Mar. 29, 1985.
35. Miguel Alemán Velasco, interview with author, June 12, 2007.
36. FMA, Testimonio de Beatriz Alemán de Girón; FMA, Testimonio de Juan González Alpuche, Box 7, Exp. 200, Feb. 26, 1985; FMA, Testimonio de Antonio Carrillo Flores; FMA, Testimonio de David Romero Castañeda; FMA, Testimonio de Arturo García Formenti.
37. FMA, Testimonio de Miguel Alemán Velasco.
38. Teichman, "Competing Visions," 79–80.

Bibliography

Archives

Mexico

Archivo de la Biblioteca Mexicana de la Fundación Miguel Alemán, AC
Archivo General de la Nación (AGN)
—Ramo Presidentes, Lázaro Cárdenas del Río
—Ramo Presidentes, Miguel Alemán Valdés
—Ramo Dirección Federal de Seguridad (DFS)
Archivo General del Estado de Veracruz
Archivo Histórico de El Colegio de México
—Archivo Particular de Ramón Beteta
Archivo Histórico del Instituto de Investigaciones sobre la Universidad y la Educación, Universidad Nacional Autónoma de México (UNAM)
Archivo Manuel Gómez Morín, Instituto Tecnológico Autónomo de México (ITAM)
Instituto de Investigaciones Dr. José Maria Luis Mora

United States

Archive.org
Harry S. Truman Presidential Library
—Charles Sawyer Papers
—Clarence R. Decker Papers
—Confidential File
—David H. Stowe Papers
—George A. Brownell Papers
—John Snyder Papers
—Merwin L. Bohan Papers
—Michael J. Galvin Papers
—Motion Picture Archive
—Official File
—Personal File

—Political Cartoon Collection
—President's Secretary's File
National Archives at College Park, Maryland
—RG 59, Series 712.00 and 812.00, Records of Department of State, Internal Affairs of Mexico
Nettie Lee Benson Latin American Collection, University of Texas at Austin

Newspapers and Periodicals

ABC
Brownsville Herald
El Dictamen
Excelsior
El Nacional
New York Herald Tribune
New York Times
Novedades
El Popular
El Porvenir
La Prensa
Proceso
¡Siempre!
Time
Valley Evening Monitor

Personal Interviews

Miguel Alemán Velasco, June 12, 2007
Soledad Loaeza, Jan. 20, 2011
Lorenzo Lazo, Feb. 1, 2011
Alejandro Carrillo Castro, Feb. 3, 2011

Films

La Ley de Herodes. DVD. Directed by Luis Estrada, 1999. Mexico City: 20th Century Fox, 2004.

Los Olvidados—The Young and the Damned. DVD. Directed by Luis Buñuel, 1950. Mexico City: Ultramar Films, 2004.

Mi multi es mi multi: historia oral del Multifamiliar Miguel Alemán (1949–1999). VHS. Directed by Graciela de Garay, 1999. Mexico City: Instituto Mora/CONACYT, 1999.

Dissertations and Papers

Jones, Halbert. "'The War Has Brought Peace to Mexico': The Political Impact of Mexican Participation in World War II." PhD diss., Harvard University, 2006.

Kram Villareal, Rachel. "Gladiolas for the Children of Sánchez: Ernesto P. Uruchurtu's Mexico City, 1950–1968." PhD diss., University of Arizona, 2008.

López, Amanda. "The Cadaverous City: The Everyday Life of the Dead in Mexico City, 1875–1930." PhD diss., University of Arizona, 2010.

Paxman, Andrew. "Espinosa Yglesias Becomes a Philanthropist: A Private-Sector Response to Mexico's Political Turns, 1963–1982." Paper presented at XIII Reunión de Historiadores de México, Estados Unidos, y Canadá, Santiago de Querétaro, Querétaro, Oct. 29, 2010.

Books, Articles, and Chapters

Aguayo Quezada, Sergio. *La charola: una historia de los servicios de inteligencia en México*. Mexico City: Grijalbo, 2011.

Aguilar, Adrián Guillermo, and Guillermo Olvera L. "El control de la expansión urbana en la ciudad de México. Conjeturas de un falso planamiento." *Estudios Demográficos y Urbanos* 6, no. 1 (Jan.–Apr. 1991): 89–115.

Agustín, José. *Tragicomedia mexicana: la vida en México de 1940 a 1970*. Mexico City: Planeta, 1990.

Alegre, Robert. *Railroad Radicals in Cold War Mexico: Gender, Class, and Memory*. Lincoln: University of Nebraska Press, 2014.

Alemán Valdés, Miguel. *Remembranzas y testimonios*. Mexico City: Grijalbo, 1987.

Ankerson, Dudley. *Agrarian Warlord: Saturnino Cedillo and the Mexican Revolution in San Luis Potosí*. DeKalb, IL: Northern Illinois University Press, 1984.

Aviña, Alexander. *Specters of Revolution: Peasant Guerrillas in the Cold War Mexican Countryside*. New York: Oxford University Press, 2014.

Babb, Sarah. *Managing Mexico: Economists from Nationalism to Neoliberalism.* Princeton, NJ: Princeton University Press, 2004.

Bailes, Kendall Eugene. *Technology and Society under Lenin and Stalin, 1917–1941: The Origin of the Soviet Technological Intelligentsia.* Princeton, NJ: Princeton University Press, 1978.

Bantjes, Adrian A. *As If Jesus Walked on Earth: Cardenismo, Sonora, and the Mexican Revolution.* Wilmington, DE: Scholarly Resources, 1998.

Beezley, William H., ed. *A Companion to Mexican History and Culture.* Malden, MA: Wiley-Blackwell, 2011.

———. "The Role of State Governors in the Mexican Revolution." In *State Governors in the Mexican Revolution, 1910–1952: Portraits in Conflict, Courage, and Corruption*, edited by Jürgen Buchenau and Beezley, 1–18. Lanham, MD: Rowman and Littlefield, 2009.

Beezley, William H., and Colin MacLaughlin, *Mexicans in Revolution, 1910–1946.* Lincoln: University of Nebraska Press, 2009.

Beissinger, Mark R. "In Search of Generations in Soviet Politics." *World Politics* 2 (Jan. 1986): 288–314.

Benjamin, Thomas. *La Revolución: Mexico's Great Revolution as Memory, Myth, and History.* Austin: University of Texas Press, 2000.

Bennett, Douglas, and Kenneth Sharpe. "The State as Banker and Entrepreneur: The Last-Resort Character of the Mexican State's Economic Intervention, 1917–76." *Comparative Politics* 12, no. 2 (Jan. 1980): 165–89.

Berger, Dina, and Monica Rankin. "The Peculiarities of Mexican Diplomacy." In Beezley, *Companion to Mexican History and Culture*, 552–60.

Bernal Tavares, Luis. *Vicente Lombardo Toledano y Miguel Alemán: Una bifurcación en la Revolución mexicana.* Mexico City: UNAM, 1994.

Bethell, Leslie. "Latin America Between the Second World War and the Cold War: Some Reflections on the 1944–48 Conjuncture." *Journal of Latin American Studies* 20, no.1 (May 1988): 167–89.

Bethell, Leslie, and Ian Roxborough. "Introduction: The Postwar Conjuncture in Latin America: Democracy, Labor, and the Left." In *Latin America Between the Second World War and the Cold War, 1944–1948*, edited by Bethell and Roxborough, 1–32. Cambridge: Cambridge University Press, 1992.

Blázquez Domínguez, Carmen. *Breve historia de Veracruz.* Mexico City: Fondo de Cultura Económica, 2000.

Brandenburg, Frank R. *The Making of Modern Mexico.* Englewood Cliffs, New Jersey: Prentice-Hall, 1964.

Bunker, Stephen B. *Creating Mexican Consumer Culture in the Age of Porfirio Díaz, 1876–1911.* Albuquerque: University of New Mexico Press, 2012.

Calderón Vega, Luis. *Los siete sabios de México.* 2nd ed. Mexico City: Editorial Jus, 1972.

Camp, Roderic Ai. "Education and Political Recruitment in Mexico: The Alemán Generation." *Journal of Interamerican Studies and World Affairs* 18, no. 3 (Aug. 1976): 295–321.

———. *Entrepreneurs and Politics in Twentieth-Century Mexico.* New York: Oxford University Press, 1989.

———. "La campaña presidencial de 1929 y el liderazgo político en México." *Historia Mexicana* 27, no. 2 (Oct.–Dec. 1977): 231–59.

———. *The Metamorphosis of Leadership in a Democratic Mexico.* New York: Oxford University Press, 2010.

———. *Mexican Political Biographies, 1935–1981.* 2nd ed. Tucson: University of Arizona Press, 1982.

———. "The Revolution's Second Generation: The Miracle, 1946–1982 and Collapse of the PRI, 1982–2000." In Beezley, *Companion to Mexican History and Culture,* 468–79.

Cárdenas, Enrique. "The Great Depression and Industrialization: The Case of Mexico." In *An Economic History of Twentieth-Century Latin America,* vol. 2, edited by Rosemary Thorpe, 195–211. New York: Palgrave, 2000.

———. "The Process of Accelerated Industrialization in Mexico." In Cárdenas, Ocampo, and Thorpe, *Economic History of Twentieth-Century Latin America,* vol. 3, 176–204.

Cárdenas, Enrique, José Antonio Ocampo, and Rosemary Thorpe, eds. *An Economic History of Twentieth-Century Latin America.* Vol. 3. New York: Palgrave, 2000.

———. "Introduction." In Cárdenas, Ocampo, and Thorpe, *Economic History of Twentieth-Century Latin America,* vol. 3, 1–35.

Cedillo, Juan Alberto. *Los Nazis en México.* Mexico City: Debolsillo, 2010.

Ciudad Universitaria. Crisol del México modero. Mexico City: Fundación UNAM, 2010.

Cline, Howard. *Mexico: Revolution to Evolution, 1940–1960.* New York: Oxford University Press, 1962.

Cockcroft, James D. *Mexico: Class Formation, Capital Accumulation, and the State.* New York: Monthly Review Press, 1983.

———. *Mexico's Revolution Then and Now.* New York: Monthly Review Press, 2010.

Conferencias de mesa redonda. Mexico: Fundación Miguel Alemán, 2009.

Conniff, Michael L., ed., *Populism in Latin America.* Tuscaloosa: The University of Alabama Press, 1999.

Cortés Rocha, Xavier. "Ciudad Satélite." In *Las torres de Satélite,* 15–34. Naucalpan: Municipio de Naucalpan de Juárez, 2009.

Cosío Villegas, Daniel. "La Crisis de México." *Cuadernos Americanos* 32 (Mar.–Apr. 1947): n.p.

Cotter, Joseph. "The Origins of the Green Revolution in Mexico: Continuity or Change?" In *Latin America in the 1940s: War and Postwar Transitions,* edited by David Rock, 224–47. Berkeley: University of California Press, 1994.

———. *Troubled Harvest: Agronomy and Revolution in Mexico, 1880–2002*. Westport, CT: Praeger, 2002.

Davids, René. "Mythical Terrain and the Building of Mexico's UNAM." *Working Paper Series, University of California, Berkeley Center for Latin American Studies*, no. 23 (Oct. 2008): 1–15.

Davis, Diane E. "The Social Construction of Mexico City: Political Conflict and Urban Development, 1910–1966." *Journal of Urban History* 24, no. 3 (Mar. 1998): 364–415.

———. *Urban Leviathan: Mexico City in the Twentieth Century*. Philadelphia, PA: Temple University Press, 1994.

Dulles, John W. F. *Yesterday in Mexico: A Chronicle of the Revolution, 1919–1936*. Austin: University of Texas Press, 1961.

Durán Reveles, José Luis. "Presentación." In *Las torres de Satélite*, 7–100. Naucalpan: Municipio de Naucalpan de Juárez, 2009.

Dusenberry, William. "Foot and Mouth Disease in Mexico, 1946–1951." *Agricultural History* 29, no. 2 (Apr. 1955): 82–90.

Eckstein, Susan. "The State and the Urban Poor." In *Authoritarianism in Mexico*, edited by José Luis Reyna and Richard S. Weinert, 23–46. Philadelphia, PA: Institute for the Study of Human Issues, 1977.

Falcón, Romana. *Revolución y caciquismo: San Luis Potosí, 1910–1938*. Mexico City: El Colegio de México, 1984.

Fallaw, Ben. *Cárdenas Compromised: The Failure of Reform in Postrevolutionary Yucatán*. Durham, NC: Duke University Press, 2001.

Fuentes, Carlos. *The Death of Artemio Cruz*. Translated by Alfred MacAdam. New York: Farrar, Straus, and Giroux, 1991.

Gamboa, Federico. *Santa: A Novel of Mexico City*. Edited and translated by John Charles Chasteen. Chapel Hill: University of North Carolina Press, 2010.

Garay, Graciela de, ed. *Mario Pani, Investigación y entrevistas por Graciela de Garay*. Mexico City: Instituto Mora/CONACYT, 2000.

———. "¿Quién pone el orden el la vivienda moderna? El Multifamiliar Miguel Alemán visto por sus habitants y vecinos." In *Modernidad habitada: Multifamiliar Miguel Alemán, ciudad de México, 1949–1999*, edited by Garay, 13–68. Mexico City: Instituto Mora, 2004.

Gauss, Susan. *Made in Mexico: Regions, Nation, and the State in the Rise of Mexican Industrialism, 1920s–1940s*. University Park: Pennsylvania State University Press, 2010.

Gil, Jorge, Samuel Schmidt, and Jorge Castro. "La red del poder mexicana: El caso de Miguel Alemán." *Revista Mexicana de Sociología* 55, no. 3 (July–Sept. 1993): 103–17.

Gillingham, Paul, and Benjamin T. Smith. "Introduction." In *Dictablanda: Politics, Work, and Culture in Mexico, 1938–1969*, edited by Gillingham and Smith. Durham, NC: Duke University Press, 2014.

González de Bustamante, Celeste. *'Muy Buenas Noches': Mexico, Television, and the Cold War.* Lincoln: University of Nebraska Press, 2012.

Guerra, François-Xavier. *Le Mexique: de l'Ancien Régime à la Révolution.* 2 Vols. Paris: l'Harmattan: Publications de la Sorbonne, 1985.

Hale, Charles A. *The Transformation of Liberalism in Late Nineteenth-Century Mexico.* Princeton, NJ: Princeton University Press, 1989.

Hansen, Roger D. *The Politics of Mexican Development.* Baltimore, MD: Johns Hopkins Press, 1971.

Herrera Calderón, Fernando, and Adela Cedillo, eds. *Challenging Authoritarianism in Mexico: Revolutionary Struggles and the Dirty War, 1964–1982.* New York: Routledge, 2012.

Hershfield, Joanne, and David R. Maciel, eds., *Mexico's Cinema: A Century of Film and Filmmakers.* Wilmington, DE: Scholarly Resources, 1999.

Johnson, Lyman L., ed. *Death, Dismemberment, and Memory: Body Politics in Latin America.* Albuquerque: University of New Mexico Press, 2004.

Joseph, Gilbert M., and Timothy J. Henderson, eds. *The Mexico Reader: History, Culture, Politics.* Durham, NC: Duke University Press, 2003.

Kiddle, Amelia M., and María L. O. Muñoz. "Men of the People: Lázaro Cárdenas, Luis Echeverría, and Revolutionary Populism." In *Populism in Twentieth-Century Mexico: The Presidencies of Lázaro Cárdenas and Luis Echeverría,* edited by Kiddle and Muñoz, 1–14. Tucson: University of Arizona Press, 2010.

Kingstone, Peter. *The Political Economy of Latin America: Reflections on Neoliberalism and Development.* New York: Routledge, 2010.

Knight, Alan. "Cardenismo: Juggernaut or Jalopy?" *Journal of Latin American Studies* 26 (Feb. 1994): 73–107.

———. *The Mexican Revolution,* Two Vols. Cambridge: Cambridge University Press, 1986.

———. "Populism and Neo-Populism in Latin America, Especially Mexico." *Journal of Latin American Studies* 30:2 (May 1998): 223–48.

———. "The Weight of the State in Modern Mexico." In *Studies in the Formation of the Nation-State in Latin America,* edited by James Dunkerley, 212–53. London: Institute of Latin American Studies, 2002.

Krauze, Enrique. *Caudillos culturales en la Revolución mexicana.* Mexico City: Siglo Veintiuno Editores, 1976.

———. *Mexico: Biography of Power: A History of Modern Mexico, 1810–1996.* Translated by Hank Heifetz. New York: Harper Collins, 1997.

Krieger, Peter. "Body, Building, City, and Environment: Iconography in the Mexican Megalopolis." In *Pictorial Cultures and Political Iconographies,* edited by Udo J. Hebel and Christoph Wagner, 401–18. Berlin: DeGruyter, 2011.

LaFeber, Walter. *The American Age: United States Foreign Policy at Home and Abroad Since 1750.* New York: Norton, 1989.

Lewis, Oscar. *The Children of Sánchez: Autobiography of a Mexican Family.* New York: Random House, 1961.

———. *Five Families: Mexican Case Studies in the Culture of Poverty.* New York: Basic Books, 1959.

Libro de oro conmemorativo de las visitas de los presidentes Harry S. Truman a México y Miguel Alemán a los Estados Unidos de América. Mexico City: Policía Auxiliar, 1947.

Lieuwen, Edwin. *The Mexican Military: The Political Rise and Fall of the Revolutionary Army, 1910–1940.* Albuquerque: University of New Mexico Press, 1968.

Loaeza, Soledad. *El llamado de las urnas.* Mexico City: Cal y Arena, 1989.

———. *El Partido Acción Nacional. La larga marcha, 1939–1994. Oposición leal y partido de protesta.* Mexico City: Fondo de Cultura Económica, 1999.

———. "The National Action Party (PAN): From the Fringes of the Political System to the Heart of Change." In *Christian Democracy in Latin America: Electoral Competition and Regime Conflicts,* edited by Scott Mainwaring and Timothy R. Scully, 196–246. Stanford, CA: Stanford University Press, 2003.

Lomnitz, Claudio. "Prefacio" and "Introducción." In *Vicios públicos, virtudes privadas: la corrupción en México,* edited by Lomnitz, 7–32. Mexico City: Centro de Investigaciones y Estudios Superiores en Antropología Social (CIESAS), 2000.

López, Rick A. *Crafting Mexico: Intellectuals, Artisans, and the State after the Revolution.* Durham, NC: Duke University Press, 2010.

Machado, Manuel A., Jr. *Aftosa: Historical Survey of Foot-and-Mouth Disease and Inter-American Relations.* Albany: State University of New York Press, 1969.

Martínez, Maria Antonia. "El modelo económico de la presidencia de Miguel Alemán." In *Gobernantes mexicanos II: 1911–2000,* edited by Will Fowler, 227–62. Mexico City: Fondo de Cultura Económica, 2008.

Martínez, Oscar J. *Border Boom Town: Ciudad Juárez since 1848.* Austin: University of Texas Press, 1978.

Medin, Tzvi. *El sexenio alemanista. Ideología y praxis política de Miguel Alemán.* Mexico City: Ediciones Era, 1990.

Medina, Luis. *Historia de la Revolución Mexicana, 1940–1952: Civilismo y modernización del autoritarismo.* Mexico City: El Colegio de México, 1979.

Meyer, Lorenzo. "Historical Roots of the Authoritarian State in Mexico." In Reyna and Weinert, *Authoritarianism in Mexico,* 3–22.

Mijares Sánchez, Mario Raúl. *Mexico: The Genesis of its Political Decomposition.* Bloomington, IN: Palibrio, 2013.

Moncada, Carlos. *¡Cayeron! 67 gobernadores derrocados (1929–79).* Mexico City: C. Moncada, 1979.

Montes de Oca, Rosa Elena. "The State and the Peasants." In Reyna and Weinert, *Authoritarianism in Mexico,* 47–66.

Moreno, Julio. *Yankee Don't go Home!: Mexican Nationalism, American Business Culture, and the Shaping of Modern Mexico, 1920–1950*. Chapel Hill: University of North Carolina Press, 2003.

Morris, Stephen. *Corruption and Politics in Contemporary Mexico*. Tuscaloosa: University of Alabama Press, 1991.

Nasaw, David, et al. "Roundtable: Historians and Biography." *American Historical Review* 114, no. 3 (June 2009): 573–661.

Navarro, Aaron W. *Political Intelligence and the Creation of Modern Mexico, 1938–1954*. University Park: Pennsylvania State University Press, 2010.

Navarro, Marysa. "The Case of Eva Perón." *Signs* 3, no. 1 (Autumn 1977): 229–40.

Niblo, Stephen R. *Mexico in the 1940s: Modernity, Politics, and Corruption*. Wilmington, DE: Scholarly Resources, 1999.

Niblo, Stephen R., and Diane M. Niblo. "Acapulco in Dreams and Reality." *Mexican Studies/Estudios Mexicanos* 24, no.1 (Winter 2008): 31–51.

Olsen, Patrice. *Artifacts of Revolution: Architecture, Society, and Politics in Mexico City, 1920–1940*. Lanham, MD: Rowman and Littlefield, 2008.

O'Malley, Ilene V. *The Myth of the Revolution: Hero Cults and the Institutionalization of the Mexican State, 1920–1940*. Westport, CT: Greenwood Press, 1986.

Ortega y Gasset, José. *El tema de nuestro tiempo*. Buenos Aires: Espasa-Calpe, 1955.

Padilla, Tanalís, and Louise E. Walker, eds. "Spy Reports: Content, Methodology, and Historiography in Mexico's Secret Police Archive." *Journal of Iberian and Latin American Research* 19, no. 1 (2013): 1–175.

Paxman, Andrew, and Claudia Fernández. *El Tigre: Emilio Azcárraga y su imperio Televisa*. 3rd ed. Mexico City: Grijalbo, 2013.

Paz, Maria Elena. *Strategy, Security, and Spies: Mexico and the U. S. as Allies in World War II*. University Park: Pennsylvania State University Press, 1997.

Pensado, Jaime M. *Rebel Mexico: Student Unrest and Authoritarian Political Culture During the Long Sixties*. Stanford, CA: Stanford University Press, 2013.

Pérez Montfort, Ricardo. "La ciudad de Mexico en los noticieros filmicos de 1940 a 1960." In *Estampas de nacionalismo popular mexicano: Diez ensayos sobre cultura popular y nacionalismo*, 2nd ed, edited by Pérez Montfort, 219–37. Mexico City: Centro de Investigaciones y Estudios Superiores en Antropología Social (CIESAS), 2003.

Perkins, John H. "The Rockefeller Foundation in Mexico: The New International Politics of Plant Breeding, 1941–1945." In *Geopolitics and Green Revolution: Wheat, Genes, and the Cold War*, edited by Perkins, 102–17. New York: Oxford University Press, 1997.

Philip, George. *Oil and Politics in Latin America: Nationalist Movements and State Companies*. Cambridge: Cambridge University Press, 1982.

Pilcher, Jeffrey M. *¡Que Vivan Tamales! Food and the Making of Mexican Identity*. Albuquerque: University of New Mexico Press, 1998.

Porter, Susie. "The Apogee of the Revolution, 1934–1946." In Beezley, *Companion to Mexican History and Culture*, 453–67.

Ramírez, Miguel D. "Mexico's Development Experience: Lessons and Future Prospects." *Journal of Interamerican Studies and World Affairs* 28, no. 2 (Summer 1986): 39–65.

Rath, Thomas. *Myths of Demilitarization in Post-Revolutionary Mexico, 1920–1960*. Chapel Hill: University of North Carolina Press, 2013.

Reyna, José Luis. "Redefining the Authoritarian Regime." In Reyna and Weinert, *Authoriarianism in Mexico*, 155–71.

Reyna, José Luis, and Richard S. Weinert, eds. *Authoritarianism in Mexico*. Philadephia, PA: Institute for the Study of Human Issues, 1977.

Rochfort, Desmond. "The Sickle, the Serpent, and the Soil: History, Revolution, Nationhood, and Modernity in the Murals of Diego Rivera, José Clemente Orozco, and David Alfaro Siqueiros." In Vaughan and Lewis, *Eagle and the Virgin*, 43–57.

Roxborough, Ian. "Mexico," In *Latin America Between World War II and the Cold War, 1944–1948*. Edited by Roxborough and Leslie Bethell, 190–216. Cambridge: Cambridge University Press, 1992.

Rulfo, Juan. *Pedro Páramo*. Translated by Margaret Sayers Peden. Austin: University of Texas Press, 2002.

Sackett, Andrew. "Fun in Acapulco? The Politics of Development on the Mexican Riviera." In *Holiday in Mexico: Critical Reflections on Tourism and Tourist Encounters*, edited by Dina Berger and Andrew Grant Wood, 161–82. Durham, NC: Duke University Press, 2004.

Samuels, Richard J. "Introduction: Political Generations and Political Development." In *Political Generations and Political Development*, edited by Samuels, 1–8. Lexington, MA: Lexington Books, 1977.

Santoyo, Antonio. *La mano negra: Poder regional y Estado en México (Veracruz, 1928–1943)*. Mexico City: Conaculta, 1995.

Scott, James C. *Seeing Like a State: How Certain Schemes to Improve the Human Condition have Failed*. New Haven, CT: Yale University Press, 1998.

Searing, Donald. "The Comparative Study of Elite Socialization." *Comparative Political Studies* 1 (Jan. 1986): 471–500.

Sherman, John W. "The Mexican 'Miracle' and its Collapse." In *The Oxford History of Mexico*, edited by Michael C. Meyer and William H. Beezley, 575–620. New York: Oxford University Press, 2000.

Smith, Ben. "Building a State on the Cheap: Taxation, Social Movements, and Politics." In *Dictablanda: Politics, Work, and Culture in Mexico, 1938–1968*, edited by Paul Gillingham and Smith, 255–76. Durham, NC: Duke University Press, 2014.

Smith, Peter H. *Labyrinths of Power: Political Recruitment in Twentieth-Century Mexico*. Princeton, NJ: Princeton University Press, 1979.

Snodgrass, Michael. "Patronage and Progress: The Bracero Program from the Perspective of Mexico." In *Workers Across the Americas: The Transnational Turn in Labor History*, edited by Leon Fink, 245–66. New York: Oxford University Press, 2011.

Taracena, Alfonso. *La vida en México bajo Miguel Alemán*. Mexico City: Editorial Jus, 1979.

Tatum, Charles. "La Familia Burrón: Inside a Lower Middle-Class Family." *Studies in Latin American Popular Culture* 4 (1985): n.p.

Teichman, Judith A. "Competing Visions of Democracy and Development in the Era of Neoliberalism in Mexico and Chile." *International Political Science Review* 30, no. 67 (2009): 67–87.

Torres, Blanca. *Historia de la Revolución Mexicana, 1940–1952: Hacia la utopia industrial*. Mexico City: El Colegio de México, 1979.

Vaughan, Mary Kay. *Cultural Politics in Revolution: Teachers, Peasants, and Schools in Mexico, 1930–1940*. Tucson: University of Arizona Press, 1997.

Vaughan, Mary Kay, and Stephen E. Lewis, eds. *The Eagle and the Virgin: Nation and Cultural Revolution in Mexico, 1920–1940*. Durham, NC: Duke University Press, 2006.

Villareal, René. "The Policy of Import-Substituting Industrialization, 1929–1975." In Reyna and Weinert, *Authoritarianism in Mexico*, 67–108.

Walker, Louise E. *Waking from the Dream: Mexico's Middle Classes After 1968*. Stanford, CA: Stanford University Press, 2013.

Waters, Wendy. "Remapping Identities: Road Construction and Nation Building in Postrevolutionary Mexico." In Vaughan and Lewis, *Eagle and the Virgin*, 221–42.

Weldon, Jeffrey A. "El presidente como legislador, 1917–1934." In *El poder legislativo en las décadas revolucionarias, 1908–1934*, edited by Pablo Picato, 117–45. Mexico City: Instituto de Investigaciones Legislativas, 1997.

Wicke, Charles R. "The Burrón Family: Class Warfare and the Culture of Poverty." *Studies in Latin American Popular Culture* 2 (1983): n.p.

Wilkie, James W. *The Mexican Revolution: Federal Expenditure and Social Change Since 1910*. Berkeley: University of California Press, 1967.

Wilkie, James W., and Edna Monzón de Wilkie. *México visto en el siglo XX: Entrevistas de historia oral*. Mexico City: Instituto de Investigaciones Económicas, 1969.

Williams, William Appleman. *The Tragedy of American Diplomacy*. New York: W. W. Norton, 1988.

Yahuda, Michael. "Political Generations in China." *China Quarterly* 80 (Dec. 1979): 793–805.

Zolov, Eric. *Refried Elvis: The Rise of the Mexican Counterculture*. Berkeley: University of California Press, 1999.

Index

Page numbers in italic text indicate illustrations.